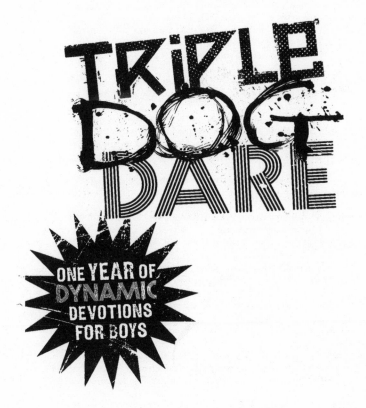

TRIPLE DOG DARE

ONE YEAR OF DYNAMIC DEVOTIONS FOR BOYS

JEREMY V. JONES

David C Cook®

transforming lives together

TRIPLE DOG DARE
Published by David C Cook
4050 Lee Vance View
Colorado Springs, CO 80918 U.S.A.

David C Cook Distribution Canada
55 Woodslee Avenue, Paris, Ontario, Canada N3L 3E5

David C Cook U.K., Kingsway Communications
Eastbourne, East Sussex BN23 6NT, England

The graphic circle C logo is a registered trademark of David C Cook.

The website addresses recommended throughout this book are offered as a
resource to you. These websites are not intended in any way to be or imply an
endorsement on the part of David C Cook, nor do we vouch for their content.

Unless otherwise noted, all Scripture quotations are taken from the Holy Bible, New
International Version®, NIV®. Copyright © 1973, 1978, 1984 by Biblica, Inc™. Used by
permission of Zondervan. All rights reserved worldwide. www.zondervan.com. Scripture
quotations marked NLT are taken from the New Living Translation of the Holy Bible. New
Living Translation copyright © 1996, 2004 by Tyndale Charitable Trust. Used by permission of
Tyndale House Publishers. Scripture quotations marked NIrV are taken from the HOLY BIBLE,
NEW INTERNATIONAL READER'S VERSION®. Copyright © 1996, 1998 International
Bible Society. All rights reserved throughout the world. Used by permission of International
Bible Society. Scripture quotations marked AB are taken from *The Amplified Bible*. Copyright
© 1954, 1958, 1962, 1964, 1965, 1987 by The Lockman Foundation. Used by permission.

The author has added italics to Scripture quotations for emphasis.

LCCN 2011934832
ISBN 978-0-7814-0457-0
eISBN 978-1-4347-0388-0

© 2011 Jeremy V. Jones
The Team: Susan Tjaden, Amy Konyndyk, Nick Lee, Renada Arens, and Karen Athen
Cover and interior design: Luke Flowers

Printed in the United States of America
First Edition 2011

4 5 6 7 8 9 10
041014

For Pax, who is always ready to go for it.
May you always take on God's Triple Dog Dares.

INTRODUCTION

Are You Up for the Triple Dog Dare? Absolutely!

The Triple Dog Dare is the ace in the deck of cards and the Fire Flower in Super Mario Bros. You know what I'm talking about. You're goofing around with your friends when a dare gets laid down, then another and another. Then suddenly one guy lays down a Triple Dog Dare. It's the king of dares. The mac daddy. And there's no backing down from a Triple Dog Dare! Now you've got to man up and do the dare.

Let me put it in an equation for you math lovers:

$$\text{Triple Dog Dare} > \text{all other dares in the world}$$

Why Is the Triple Dog Dare Such a Powerful Force?

Because most of us guys are all about a challenge. We want action. We don't want to sit around and talk. That's for grown-ups and girls. We want to *do* something: skate, ride, throw a ball, play a game, pound each other and evil aliens into oblivion, recreate favorite movie chase scenes and explosions. Lots of us don't even like to read that much because it's too quiet—so I'll keep this short.

This is a book about …

- *doing* faith.
- putting your relationship with God into action.
- making God's love real in you and in the world around you.

We need our faith in our hearts, but the Bible says it's also got to be in our hands. Action shows we really believe what we say and helps us experience God. Jesus wants followers who are willing to roll up their sleeves to launch adventures and take risks living with Him. And our God is the most powerful force in the universe—what have we got to lose?

So How Do You Use This Book?

Easy. Every weekday of the year you get …

- one Bible verse or passage.
- some short thoughts about a real-life situation or connection to God.
- three *Triple Dog Dares*—ideas to put the theme into action.
- two *Mission Accomplished* questions so you can write down your results from yesterday's dares.

Each weekend you get something a little different.

- *Make Triple Dog Tracks* sections give ideas to make something cool, like a movie, comic strip, life list, or Noah's ark out of Legos.
- *From the Triple Dog Pound* sections deliver short stories about guys in the Bible who accomplished God's Triple Dog Dares—plus ideas of how you can do the same.

Your mission is to do something with it all. Read it. Think about it. Open your Bible and see what it says. Talk to God about each day's dares, and go on a great adventure with Him.

Are you up to the Triple Dog Dare? Absolutely! Now it's go time …

YOUR PAGE

It's a new year! It's a fresh start! Write down
some dreams you have for the next 365 days ...

TRUTH
Living for God is all about action.

AND ... ACTION!

Are you bored with the Bible? Does church put you to sleep? Do you think Christians are wimps? Do you feel like following Jesus is only about following rules? Then it's time to wake up.

The truth is that living for God is all about action. God wants more from us than sitting on our pews. He wants us to live out His kingdom. And His kingdom goes against the ways of the world—that can make for some risky and adventurous situations. Take John the Baptist: a first-class wild man who was afraid of no one, not even the emperor. And the Bible is filled with examples of God's warriors, kings, and radical followers putting their lives on the line. Some of their lives would make good action-adventure movie scripts.

It's time to shake off the boredom and wake up from your daze. Get going. Put your faith in action. Ask God to open your eyes, and start living His adventure. Be His man of action.

TRIPLE DOG DARE

- Take a spiritual risk. Talk with someone about Jesus or stand up for something you believe in.

- Read a book about a Christian hero, such as Eric Liddell, Kurt Warner, or Kaká.

- Get involved. What are you passionate about? Put your faith into it and bring God's love to the world.

What did you do? What did you learn?

MISSION ACCOMPLISHED!

TRUTH

We need each other. Close friends help us follow God better.

STRENGTH IN NUMBERS

We think it's cool when our superheroes save the world all by themselves, but where would Batman be without Robin? What would happen to Wolverine without the rest of the X-Men? What good could Albert Pujols, Peyton Manning, or LeBron James do without the rest of the team?

The truth is, in real life, none of us can do everything alone. It's much easier to make the right choice when others are choosing the same thing with you. It helps to face a problem or struggle when we know other people have gone through the same thing. We can reach a goal much easier when someone helps us. It's a relief to have someone we can trust our secrets with.

God gives us other people like our family and close friends to help us learn and grow and live like He wants us to. Those people aren't afraid of telling us when we're wrong, and they make us stronger through their encouragement and support.

TRIPLE DOG DARE

- Is there a secret eating you up inside? Tell a parent or close friend.

- Read this book with a friend or two and talk about what you learn.

- Pick a goal—improve your free-throw shooting, climb a mountain, help poor kids, whatever you want to accomplish—and ask a friend to help you practice and work toward it.

MISSION ACCOMPLISHED!

What did you do? What did you learn?

MATTHEW 7:12

TRUTH

God wants us to treat others the way we want to be treated.

IT'S GOLDEN

Would you rather be laughed at or complimented? Would you prefer a punch in the face or a high-five? Would you rather be offered an ice-cream cone or have one grabbed out of your hand? Picked for a team or left out of a game? Stolen from or given a gift? Invited to a party or uninvited? Included or excluded? Beat up or stood up for?

The truth is God wants us to treat other people the way we want them to treat us. It's so important we call it the Golden Rule. Jesus said it's what the whole Old Testament is about. It doesn't mean we treat others well only if they treat us well. It means we treat them well no matter how they treat us. Think generous, kind, loving, compassionate, forgiving, and welcoming. And if there's any doubt about what to do, think of how you'd want to be treated on the other side of the situation.

TRIPLE DOG DARE

- O Who really bugs you? Do a kind deed toward them.

- O Share with your brothers or sisters today.

- O Tell your friends the guy who always gets picked on isn't so bad and that you're inviting him along so they can get to know him better.

What did you do? What did you learn?

MISSION ACCOMPLISHED!

TRUTH Real men cry.

REAL MEN

Don't believe the lies. They've gone on too long in society. Don't believe it when you hear that boys don't cry or that real men don't show their feelings. Don't buy it when they say showing or feeling emotions makes you weak. Don't take it if they call you a sissy for showing pain.

The truth is that real men cry. They feel and share their emotions. Jesus did it. He cried when He saw His friends so upset that their friend and brother Lazarus had died. Jesus already knew His pal Laz was coming back to life, but He felt for the people He cared about. He joined their pain, and He showed it.

You can too. Dealing with your pain makes you stronger. Feeling it, expressing it, and getting help with it heals you like a cast on a broken bone. Stuffing your tears and denying your hurt builds a dam inside you. It may hold for years or decades, but sooner or later it'll break. Until then it fills you with concrete and walls you off from connecting with other people. Choose to be a man like Jesus.

TRIPLE DOG DARE

- Cry when you need to.
- Talk about bad things that happen to you with your parents and best friends.
- Let it out. Write songs or poems, journal, and pray about your feelings.

MISSION ACCOMPLISHED!

What did you do? What did you learn?

FRIDAY

TRUTH
You always have a helper.

ALWAYS ON

Personal navigation systems are amazing. So is wireless Internet on your parents' phone. Believe it or not, before they existed you actually had to look on a map or ask someone for directions. Now you have an almost constant guide. What info do you need? It's only a few clicks away.

The truth is the Holy Spirit is like that but better. He's part of God living inside of you. How's that for mind-blowing amazing? And He gives more than info. Feeling afraid or worried? He brings comfort. Unsure what choice to make? He gives guidance. Need God? He helps you connect to the Father.

The Holy Spirit never runs out of batteries; His power is unlimited. He never gets confused or steers you wrong. A navigation system can bring peace of mind to you on the road. But the Holy Spirit brings peace that's deeper than any problem in your entire life. Turn to Him for the ultimate help.

TRIPLE DOG DARE

- Look around for ways gadgets and other things in your life remind you of God.

- Draw a display screen and write your problems and needs to God on it.

- What's troubling your heart? Write a letter to God telling Him about it and asking for help.

What did you do? What did you learn?

MISSION ACCOMPLISHED!

Go for Goals

A new year is a fresh start. It's a clean slate and an unfolding adventure. That's exciting, whether it's New Year's Day or the first day of school. The old year is over. The new one is full of possibilities. That's probably why so many people make New Year's resolutions. It's a good chance to look back and learn from the past, then decide to make some changes and go for new opportunities.

TRIPLE DOG DARE!

Make a list of goals for the coming year. Consider these categories: physical, spiritual, mental/academic, friends, family, habits. And here are some samples to get you started:

- Stop picking my nose (at least in public).
- Floss my teeth every day.
- Improve my free-throw shooting accuracy to 80 percent.
- Spend fifteen minutes each day reading and writing in *Triple Dog Dare* and my Bible. (See the Introduction for tips.)

MY GOALS FOR THE NEW YEAR

TRIPLE DOG BONUS

O Add one action step for each goal that
explains *how* you plan to accomplish it.

Draw a self-portrait.

TRUTH *Do good.*

JUST DO IT

If the apostle James were around today, he would wear Nikes. He probably wouldn't even care if they matched his robe. He'd be styling them simply because they helped him Just Do It. The guy could've written the slogan. He did write that part of the Bible.

The truth is God wants us to do the good He tells us to and the good we see a chance to do. No excuses. No "I'll do it later." No "when I have time." No "I've got better things to do." To *just don't do it* is sin.

So don't walk past that lonely person in the hall. Don't ignore the old lady on your block whose yard is always unmowed. Don't ignore the homeless person on the corner. Don't pick on your brother. Do turn off the Xbox at the time your mom tells you. Do treat your teacher with respect. Do speak encouraging, positive words. In a slogan, *Just Do It.*

TRIPLE DOG DARE

O What good deeds have you been ignoring? Do them.

O Look around your home, school, and neighborhood. Make a list of ways you can serve others.

O Do one anonymous good deed every day this week.

What did you do? What did you learn?

MISSION ACCOMPLISHED!

TRUTH

God wants guys to treat girls with respect and purity.

HOW TO TREAT GIRLS

Mama jokes are funny till they're about *your* mother. That's when the laughing and joking take a nosedive from good times to beat downs. If you've been on the wrong side, you know the change takes a sharper turn than a MotoGP rider.

The same is true when it comes to your sister. You can make an art form out of insulting her, but the other dude who goes dissing your sis better batten down the hatches before tropical storm *you* unleashes its fury.

The truth is that God wants us to treat all girls and older women as if they were our sisters and mothers. That means with respect and purity. It means we talk kindly to them, not put them down. It means we use our strength to stick up for them, not hit or pick on them. It means we remember they're real people, not objects of our selfish lusts— that goes for the ones in pictures as much as in real life. Start practicing how to treat other girls and older women as your own sister or mom.

TRIPLE DOG DARE

- Buy or make your sister or mom a small, thoughtful gift.

- If you are ever tempted by lust, ask yourself how you'd feel about another guy thinking that way about your sister or mom.

- Go three days straight without picking on your sister.

MISSION ACCOMPLISHED!

What did you do? What did you learn?

TRUTH It's easier to learn from your mistakes.

DON'T BE THAT GUY

Don't be that guy. You know the one. He's in your class, and he's always getting in trouble. He's earned himself a frequent-flyer ticket to the principal's office—they're on a first-name basis and not for good reasons. He's a world champion of detention, and he's lost enough privileges to reward a whole school district. The thing about it, you can see it coming from miles away. When the teacher says don't, you know he's gonna do. When she says do, you know he won't. It's same song, second verse. Won't that guy ever learn?

The truth is that we make life harder on ourselves when we don't learn from discipline. A smart guy gets a clue really quickly that if breaking a rule means bad results, like punishment, then it's not worth breaking the rule. The guy who's, shall we say, dense doesn't catch on that repeating the same mistakes over and over again is a recipe for frustration and disaster. Don't be the poster child for bad examples. Be the guy who learns from his mistakes.

TRIPLE DOG DARE

- What do you get in trouble for most? Make a learning-action plan. What trips you up? How can you avoid it? Ask for help from a parent.

- Learn from others. Watch the kids who always and never get in trouble. List tips to do and not to do.

- Don't beat yourself up over mistakes. Learn and do it differently next time.

What did you do? What did you learn?

MISSION ACCOMPLISHED!

TRUTH

God will satisfy us way more than our money ever will.

MORE THAN MONEY

How much money do you have? When's the last time you counted it? How often do you buy stuff? How often do you beg your parents for new things? Do you just *have to have* the latest technology? How much time to do you spend thinking about things to buy and how much money you can get? How much have you given away?

There's no escaping that money is important in our world. We need it to buy basic necessities like food, clothes, and homes. It's how we're rewarded for the work we do. But it can throw our priorities out of whack and eat us up on the inside.

The truth is that God wants us to be content because He's taking care of us, not because of how much money we have. It's easy to feel safe and powerful because we can afford nice, cool stuff—but none of that stuff will last. It could be lost or burned tomorrow. God will always, always be there for us. He gives us all that we have, and He will satisfy us more than cash. Love God, not money.

TRIPLE DOG DARE

O Stop shopping. Stay away from malls and stores for a week, and you'll avoid being blasted by stuff "you've just got to have."

O Clean your closet. Got some old toys or clothes you don't use? Donate them to a local charity.

O Next time you're longing to buy a new gadget, stop and thank God for all the gadgets and other things you already have.

MISSION ACCOMPLISHED!

What did you do? What did you learn?

TRUTH

We can be brave and courageous because God is always with us.

GOD'S GOT YOUR BACK

Life can get scary sometimes, and we can feel pretty intimidated, small, afraid, and weak. What is it that makes your knees knock together? Moving to a new school? A bully? Talking in front of the class? A big test that you need to do well on? Talking to someone about Jesus? Making the team? Maybe there's something you know you *should* do, something you *want* to do, something you know you *can* do—but you're avoiding it like moldy broccoli.

Fear can come in many different packages and situations. It can freeze us like an arctic icicle and keep us from ever even trying.

The truth is that no matter what our hugest, biggest, meanest fear is, God is bigger. He has promised that He's always with us and always helping us. That doesn't mean we'll always be successful. And there's usually a part of things that is up to us—we've got to study for the test or practice the jump shot. But no matter the results, we can trust that we're not alone. God is with us, and that's what truly makes everything okay.

TRIPLE DOG DARE

- Stare down your fear. Ask God to help you. Then take the first step toward reaching your goal.

- Practice talking to God when you first start to feel afraid.

- Memorize Joshua 1:9 and say it out loud often.

What did you do? What did you learn?

MISSION ACCOMPLISHED!

Paint Your Life

Mural artists weave together lots of different images, colors, symbols, words, and designs to tell a story or capture many feelings in one picture. You've probably seen murals that take up whole sides of buildings.

So how's your week been? How about your month? What's been good? What's been bad? How are you feeling? What have you seen God do?

TRIPLE DOG DARE!

Draw, paint, or color your own mural that answers the questions above. Use the space here if you want!

YOUR PAGE

If I could have a superpower, it would be ...

GALATIANS 3:26–29

TRUTH

God loves people of all colors, and He wants us to do the same.

RED AND YELLOW, BLACK AND WHITE

Red and yellow, black and white, they are precious in His sight. Jesus loves the little children of the world.

You remember the song from when you were little. But it's more than a kids' song, and its truth is about more than children.

The truth is God loves people of all colors, and He wants us to do the same. God created every race of people in His image. He gave us some different characteristics, but we're all part of His creativity. And He's not happy when we put other people down or mistrust each other because our skin colors are different. Through Jesus we're all brothers and sisters in God's family.

Reach out to people of different colors and cultures. Look for similarities and learn to appreciate the differences. It makes God a happy Father to see all His kids treating each other with His love.

TRIPLE DOG DARE

O Make a friend of another race. Start by introducing yourself.

O Be honest with friends of other races. Ask questions about their culture or heritage and be willing to take part in different traditions they might have.

O When a guy tells mean jokes about another race, tell him it's not funny and walk away.

What did you do? What did you learn?

MISSION ACCOMPLISHED!

TRUTH

Seeing the big picture helps set the right priorities.

YOUR LAST DAY

What would you do today if you knew it was your last day on earth? Anything different from what you're doing now? Looking at the end makes each part seem more valuable. It's kind of like a bag of M&M's. You gobble up the first few handfuls without thinking, but then start appreciating each individual one as you get to the bottom of the bag.

The truth is that every day counts in the big picture of our whole lives. Remembering that there's more to come later helps us realize what's really important now. That's wisdom, and it helps us make good choices and set smart priorities. Studying for a test isn't as fun as PlayStation, but its benefits will last you much longer. Practicing an instrument is harder than watching TV, but it gives you a skill you can use. Exercising makes you sweat more than eating junk food, but it causes you to feel much stronger and healthier—it can even add days and years to your life.

Your days are still at the top of the M&M's bag, but the candy-coated yummies will run out. Remember there's a bottom. Choose what's most important. Make the most of today!

TRIPLE DOG DARE

- Retitle a calendar so that each month represents one year: "sixth grade," "seventh grade," "eighth grade." Write things you want to do or accomplish that year, like "Win science fair" or "Make the school team."

- Put a dollar a day (or even a quarter) into a savings account and don't spend it. By the time you're old, you'll have *a lot* of money.

- Live each day like you'll be seeing Jesus in heaven tomorrow.

MISSION ACCOMPLISHED!

What did you do? What did you learn?

MATTHEW 18:21-35

TRUTH Forgive—because you've been forgiven.

WHAT GOES AROUND

You stole from your brother. He'd been saving his money for three years to buy a new computer. He worked hard. He did odd jobs to earn extra cash. He didn't buy anything else, just saved every penny possible. Finally, he had enough … and you stole it. You snuck right in, cleaned out his bank account, and spent every cent. He caught you and was furious. But you begged and he forgave you.

The next week it happened to you. Your best friend ripped off your entire savings—all you'd been working for. You caught him and were furious. He begged and you … called the police and had him thrown in jail. What's wrong with this picture?

The truth is God wants us to forgive—like we've been forgiven. We should be in jail. We deserve the death penalty. We are all guilty of murder. We put Jesus on the cross, but He forgave us. And He expects us to do the same. It doesn't mean we won't get hurt by others. It doesn't mean forgiving will be easy. But it does mean we start by realizing what we've been given and offering the same to others. It's the least we can do.

TRIPLE DOG DARE

- O Forgive the person who has hurt you the most.

- O Apologize to someone you have hurt or wronged.

- O Get a small cross to hold as a reminder when it's hard to forgive someone.

What did you do? What did you learn?

MISSION ACCOMPLISHED!

1 CORINTHIANS 10:12–13

TRUTH

No matter how big or strong temptation feels, there's always a way out. Get up and get out of there!

BEAT TEMPTATION

Don't think about a pink elephant. Don't do it!

Okay, now you're thinking about pink elephants. Don't worry; it's normal. It's the way your brain works. And it's the way temptation works.

The longer you stare at the DVD case of the movie you know you're not supposed to watch, the more it fills your brain. It's all you can think about. You try to make yourself obey your parents and not watch it, but the longer you stare at the disc, the more you want to watch. Next thing you know, you're pressing the play button. It feels like you never had a chance.

The truth is we always have a chance to beat temptation. God will help us and give us the strength when we ask. Our part of the action plan is to get ourselves—our actual bodies—out of the tempting situation. You'll lose a stare down with temptation, so get out while you can. Walk, skip, or run if you have to. You, and God, will be glad you did.

TRIPLE DOG DARE

- Stop hanging out with a friend who is always encouraging you to do things you know are wrong.

- What's your biggest downfall? Write an action plan for how you can get away from the temptation before it becomes too strong.

- Throw away anything you're hiding from your parents.

MISSION ACCOMPLISHED!

What did you do? What did you learn?

TRUTH You have an opportunity to help.

TOTALLY UNFAIR

Life isn't fair. We're all tempted to feel like we've gotten the short end of the stick. But look around you. You probably live in a nice house … with heat and air-conditioning and running water. You might even have your own room, or maybe you share it with one brother. You can walk to the pantry and refrigerator any time and pull out a snack. You can wear different clothes every day for … how long—weeks? Months? No, there's nothing fair about the fact that you just happened to have been born in one of the richest nations on earth.

The truth is you are rich—in possessions and opportunities—compared to most kids in the rest of the world, and God wants you to use what you've been given to help the poor. That doesn't mean you have to give all your money to a lazy person who refuses to work. But it means to look around the world, see where unfair systems keep people in poverty, and do something about it. Millions of kids your age live on less than two dollars a day—for their whole family! Don't feel guilty about it. Do something about it. Your small steps can help make a difference.

TRIPLE DOG DARE

○ Set a giving goal. Ask God and your parents to help you choose a ministry; then give money and volunteer to help them in their work.

○ Help your parents buy fair-trade products that make sure growers and producers get a fair price.

○ Volunteer to help the poor in your area at a food pantry or homeless shelter. Take your whole family.

What did you do? What did you learn?

MISSION ACCOMPLISHED!

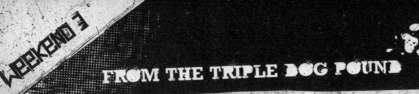

FROM THE TRIPLE DOG POUND

Peter Learned from His Mistakes

Peter was a Triple Dog Dare kind of guy. He never met a dare he didn't like, and he was always ready to jump in with both feet. Peter was all about action—often without thinking. He frequently got himself into trouble, but with God's help, Peter learned from his mistakes.

Sometimes Peter was the only disciple willing to take a Triple Dog Dare. He sunk when he took his eyes off Jesus, but Peter was the only guy willing to get out of the boat to even try walking on water to Jesus. Sometimes he took action even when there wasn't a dare—like when he started swinging his sword when the religious leaders came to arrest Jesus. And sometimes Peter failed miserably when a dare showed up. His biggest failure was when he denied Jesus three times in a row—even though he had just sworn he would never do that.

But Peter is a great example of how we can learn from our mistakes. Jesus forgave and restored Peter for his denials. God used and blessed Peter's go-for-it attitude. Peter went from denying Jesus to boldly preaching about Him in the streets, and God used Peter as one of the leaders to build the new church after Jesus' resurrection. Peter shows us that it's sometimes better to go for it and fail than to be too afraid to ever try.

TRIPLE DOG DARE!

- Read about Peter in Matthew 14:22–36, Matthew 16:13–20, Matthew 26:31–35, 69–75, John 21, and Acts 2.

- Write yourself into one of Peter's stories. What do you think you would have done?

- Fill in these lists:

THINGS I NEED TO JUST GO FOR

THINGS I NEED TO THINK FIRST BEFORE DOING

YOUR PAGE

My favorite things are ...

TRUTH You have a choice of paths: life or destruction.

I'LL HAVE THE SALMON

You've heard of lemmings. Small, mouse-like arctic rodents with a reputation for being pretty dumb. They've gotten a bit of a bad rap—they don't really commit mass suicide, like some people think they do. But when their food gets scarce, they all take off and migrate across the tundra. The problem comes when they reach a cliff or riverbank. The lemmings often keep marching right over each other, and many are killed. By following the raging pack, many lemmings stampede to their deaths.

Salmon migrate together too, but they follow a more intense call. A salmon is on an upstream mission. Nothing can stop it, except death. No matter where other fish swim, each salmon somehow knows the way back to the specific river or stream where it was born. It has focus and won't let any other fish confuse it.

The truth is we have a choice between the salmon path and the lemming path—and Jesus gave us directions. He told us to take the narrow road, not the wide one. The lemming superhighway is crowded with many people you probably know, and it can look like fun. But it ultimately runs off a cliff. Jesus' way is narrower and less populated, but it leads to true life and satisfaction. Make your choice. Don't just follow the crowd.

TRIPLE DOG DARE

- O Choose your road today. Be a salmon and not a lemming.

- O Say no to the crowd today when your conscience tells you something's wrong.

- O Bring a friend. Encourage another guy to say no with you.

What did you do? What did you learn?

MISSION ACCOMPLISHED!

HATE

TRUTH

With God's amazing love, you can conquer anything!

CONQUER

In the bottom of the ninth, with no one on base, keep swinging. When the scoreboard is lopsided in the other team's favor, dig deep. When you hear the guy behind you breathing down your neck, keep running. When you take another wave on the head, keep paddling. When your lungs are screaming, breathe deep and press on. When you play the wrong notes again, keep practicing. When the test is harder than you expected, keep thinking. When life hurts too much, keep praying.

The truth is we are more than conquerors in any situation because we have God's incredible love. It doesn't mean we'll win every game or pass every test, but we can do even better. We can experience God. We can feel His love and strength like never before. We can learn and grow into who He wants to make us. We can get a taste of God's love—the love that satisfies more deeply than winning ever will.

When the challenge looks too big, when everything inside you wants to quit, keep going. Turn to God, rely on His love, and give it all you've got!

TRIPLE DOG DARE

- Where are you tempted to give up? Dig deep, practice hard, and keep going.

- Make a reminder bracelet, necklace, or card to carry that says "More than a conqueror."

- Write down your biggest challenges or problems. Then stomp all over the paper and throw it in the trash.

MISSION ACCOMPLISHED!

What did you do? What did you learn?

TRUTH God wants us to talk to Him.

TALK TO YOUR BEST FRIEND

Imagine a friend who never talked to you. You might hang out sometimes or play some fun games, but how would you know anything about him? You wouldn't know what he was thinking, and you couldn't get to know him. Not much of a friendship.

We get to know people by talking with them, asking questions, listening to their responses, giving our answers back, sharing laughs and even sometimes tears. Friendship is a two-way street, and communication and conversation are important lanes on its superhighway.

The truth is that prayer is our way of talking with God. He is much more than a Santa Claus whom we give a list of demands. He's the ultimate living Being, and having discussions with Him like we do with our human friends is a key way of getting to know Him. He wants to hear from us. He wants us to ask Him questions and tell Him what we need. He usually doesn't answer out loud, but His Spirit changes our hearts and attitudes.

TRIPLE DOG DARE

O Start a prayer notebook where you list people, requests, or questions you're talking with God about. Write down His answers, too.

O Ask friends and family how you can pray for them. Then do it!

O Start a prayer group with a few friends and invite others to join you.

What did you do? What did you learn?

MISSION ACCOMPLISHED!

PROVERBS 12:18

TRUTH

Our words tear down or build up. God wants our speech to lift people up.

PUT AWAY PUT-DOWNS

Words are powerful. Think about it. Encouragement, compliments, and positive feedback pump us up with confidence and make us feel good inside. But put-downs, criticism, and harsh words deflate us like a popped balloon.

Sticks and stones can break my bones, but words can never hurt me. Whoever made up that lie? No matter how much we try to hide it, the sting of a put-down cuts deep. We guys get into power battles with words. You know the game: Find a guy's weakness, make a cutting comment that sounds funny, get everyone laughing, and get one up on him. What starts good-natured quickly gets nasty—and hurts when the laughs are against you. You know because you've been on the receiving end, too.

The truth is God wants us to use our words to build others up. Giving out positive words of encouragement shows true strength, the kind that earns people's respect.

TRIPLE DOG DARE

O Count to ten before you talk about another person. If you wouldn't want it said about you, then turn your cut-down into a compliment.

O When your friends make fun of another guy, remind them that if you're really better, you can prove it by being friendly and speaking kindly to him.

O Who gets picked on the most? Find ways to compliment him.

MISSION ACCOMPLISHED!

What did you do? What did you learn?

TRUTH

God has every detail of our lives under control. He doesn't want us to worry about a thing.

DON'T WORRY ABOUT IT

What's bugging you? What's got your stomach flipping like an army of butterflies on a triple-loop roller coaster?

There will always be situations in our lives that make us nervous, like … oh say, making a speech in front of an all-girls beauty academy or wearing an all-meat suit to the International Convention of Guard Dogs. Okay, really, a big test or a sick relative can make us feel uncertain, agitated, and worried. That's normal.

The truth is that God wants to change our view of what's normal. He has everything under control—every situation, every day, every detail. We can trust Him that He's always looking out for us and working to take care of us.

TRIPLE DOG DARE

- Write out what's bothering you. Tell it to God; then write GOD in big letters over the top to remind you that He's bigger.

- Tackle worry head-on. If you're stressing about a test, study now so you're ready. If you're concerned about a person, talk to a parent or that person face-to-face.

- Draw a picture of God stomping on whatever it is that's got you worried.

What did you do? What did you learn?

MISSION ACCOMPLISHED!

MAKE TRIPLE DOG TRACKS

Make a Movie: Old Testament

Movies are a powerful way to tell a story. Film connects with our eyes, ears, and emotions, and it can take us right into the middle of the action. But there's a lot that goes into making a movie. A good producer knows his story. He looks at every detail and thinks about every angle. Making a movie is an awesome way to go deeper into a story and bring it into multidimensional life. So …

TRIPLE DOG DARE!

Make a movie. It doesn't have to be feature length. Aim for ten minutes. Ask your friends and family to act in it. Use costumes. Shoot close-ups and wide shots. Edit scenes and add special effects and a soundtrack using software such as iMovie or Windows Live Movie Maker. Oh, and be sure to yell "Action!" and "Cut!"

Here are some starter ideas. Look through the Bible for more.

- The Israelites crossing the Red Sea (Exodus 12–14)
- The fall of humanity (Genesis 3)
- Elijah on Mount Carmel (1 Kings 18)
- Daniel and the lion's den (Daniel 6)

Add your own ideas.

TRIPLE DOG BONUS

Produce a trilogy. Use the space below to brainstorm!

My ultimate accomplishment looks something like this ...
⟨draw a picture⟩.

TRUTH
You can avoid electronic gossip even when everyone else is doing it.

DON'T FORWARD THIS TO ALL YOUR FRIENDS

It's easy to spread rumors, lies, gossip, and just plain mean stuff through our phones and computers—too easy. You know how it goes. Someone sends you something about someone else. It's mean but funny. You've got to show somebody else, so you click Forward. That's all it takes: one button, one click. What started as a spark spreads like a wildfire. What's easy to forget is that fire torches somebody else's feelings and can burn him to the ground.

The truth is you have the power to stop electronic gossip in its tracks. Resist the urge to forward. Use Delete instead. Send it to the trash. If a friend shows you on his phone, ask him to delete it. Post a comment in defense of the kid being ridiculed. Use the "just because you can doesn't mean you should" rule of thumb. Follow John's direction from the Bible: Don't imitate what is evil but what is good.

Don't have your own email account or phone? Someday you will. Plant this message in your brain now to avoid trouble later. In the meantime, you can practice this by not passing on gossip or mean stuff about other people.

TRIPLE DOG DARE

○ Delete any malicious messages or posts on your phone, computer, or other devices.

○ Get rid of anything on your computer or phone that you wouldn't want to show to Jesus.

○ Don't write, post, or send anything electronically that you wouldn't say to a person's face.

What did you do? What did you learn?

MISSION ACCOMPLISHED!

TRUTH

God's Word guides our path one step at a time.

TURN ON YOUR HEADLAMP

I like a good headlamp. Have you ever used one? It's a simple but amazing invention: a little light that straps around your head so you can see where you're going in the dark. The LED bulbs make them super bright, and your hands are free. It beats a flashlight any day. I use mine whenever I'm out walking or running in the dark, and it's perfect for camping.

The truth is God has given us a spiritual headlamp to light our path: His Word. We can turn to it whenever the way of our life is dark and we don't know which way to go. Sometimes the Bible clearly spells out things to do or not to do. Sometimes it gives us principles we can use to make our decisions. Often we find stories of how God worked in other people's lives.

Just remember: The Bible works like a headlamp, not stadium lights. God doesn't show us our entire trail from beginning to end. He usually shows us just the next step or two. He helps us keep moving, but we have to keep trusting Him and looking to Him to light our path as we go.

TRIPLE DOG DARE

- O Got a decision to make? Pray and seek in the Bible for principles to guide you.

- O Read one chapter from the Bible first thing every morning this week.

- O Memorize Psalm 119:105 to remind you where to turn for guidance.

MISSION ACCOMPLISHED!

What did you do? What did you learn?

TRUTH You can glorify God in everything you do.

EVERY LITTLE THING

You don't have to be a preacher to praise God in what you do. You can honor Him telling jokes, eating ice cream, and riding your skateboard. You can glorify Him in the classroom, playground, locker room, and ice rink—even the bathroom! You can worship Him surfing, hunting, painting, and going to sleep. He can be pleased by the way you do your homework, hang out with friends, and even brush your teeth.

The truth is you can glorify God in any and every thing you do. Some activities might look like more natural ways to honor God, like going to church or reading our Bibles. But that's only the beginning. Living for God isn't about marking off "spiritual" checklists and then living the rest of our lives—it's about learning to see and experience God in *everything* we do. It's about *how* we do everything.

Fill every action with thankfulness, love, compassion, and joy—that's letting God's life flow through you. Put Him in the middle of everything.

TRIPLE DOG DARE

○ Write *God* on your hand. Think of Him and thank Him every time you see it.

○ Look for God everywhere today: in nature, good friends, and strangers who might need Him.

○ Memorize Colossians 3:17. Set your watch to chime on the hour and say the verse every time it dings.

What did you do? What did you learn?

MISSION ACCOMPLISHED!

SHAME

TRUTH

God says no cheating, or if you do, pay up.

PLAY FAIR

It's not *really* cheating. That's the number one excuse we make when it comes to bending the rules. Using a friend's homework answers—it's just homework. Glancing at a neighbor's test—it's just one answer to remind me of the rest. Copying a paragraph from the Internet or a book for a paper—it's only a little bit. Intentionally fouling an opponent in a game—it's just part of the game and the ref didn't see it. Sorry. It's all still cheating.

The truth is God doesn't like cheating one bit. He gave the ancient Israelites rules from the start to keep them from cheating. If they did, they had to make things right by paying back what they gained, plus a penalty.

What's the big deal? God wants His followers to be honest and truthful all the way. Cheating is cutting corners and trying to hide the truth. It's selfishly trying to gain something at somebody else's expense. Honor God by playing fair and following the rules. If you haven't been, confess and make things right.

TRIPLE DOG DARE

- Tell your parents and teachers if you've been cheating on schoolwork and be ready to make up the credit.

- Set an internal alarm. Whenever you hear *It's just ...* in your head, stop and don't do it.

- Play by the rules at school and at play.

MISSION ACCOMPLISHED!

What did you do? What did you learn?

TRUTH *Get confidence from God.*

UNDERDOG'S SECRET

It's fun to root for an underdog. He's the little guy. They're the lesser-known team. She's from a less-powerful school or club. And while we might be surprised when an underdog wins, the underdog usually isn't. The underdog knows a secret. He knows how hard he's practiced and how good his team can be. She believes she can win. He knows the power no one has seen—yet.

The truth is we can have confidence in God's unseen power. It's the secret our foes can't see. We can face a huge army and rely on God's promises to always help us. We can shake off our fear and find confidence by looking away from the size of our enemy and focusing on the size of our God. He is always bigger and greater. He will give us strength and courage. Turn to Him; then go show 'em what an underdog can do.

TRIPLE DOG DARE

O Get your eyes off the size of your challenge and onto God's power.

O Make a list of your struggles and challenges. Before each, write *God is greater than …*

O Look through the Bible and make a list of underdogs who won because they relied on God.

What did you do? What did you learn?

MISSION ACCOMPLISHED!

MAKE TRIPLE DOG TRACKS

Be These Attitudes

One of Jesus' most famous talks was called the Sermon on the Mount—yes, He was on a mountainside. And it included a list of what people will be blessed for and with. The list is officially called the Beatitudes, which basically means blessings, but maybe you've heard them called the Be Attitudes. They're great attitudes, traits, and actions to live out—and they come with blessings in return.

Draw lines to match the action with the right blessing. Hint: You can find all the answers in Matthew 5. (Answers are also in the back of this book.)

ATTITUDE / ACTION

1. poor in spirit (humble, realize need for God)

2. hungry and thirsty to do right

3. insulted and put down

4. pure hearted

5. mourn

6. merciful

7. persecuted for living for God

8. meek (not weak, gentle and keeping control of your strength)

9. peacemakers

REWARD

a. comfort

b. mercy

c. earth

d. kingdom of heaven

e. satisfaction and filling

f. called children of God

g. great reward in heaven

h. kingdom of heaven

i. see God

TRIPLE DOG DARE!

Read Matthew 5:1–12. Pick one beatitude each day and find a way to live it out. Make a list of ideas here.

SHAME

YOUR PAGE

If I were king of the world, I would ...

TRUTH Deal with your anger before it turns to bitterness.

MAKE THINGS RIGHT BEFORE TONIGHT

Mad. Angry. Steamed. Seeing red. Losing your cool. Enraged. Furious. Irate. Livid. Infuriated. Fuming. Up in arms. Ticked off. Beside yourself. Incensed. Annoyed. Peeved. Tweaked. Miffed. Put out. Cheesed. Feathers ruffled. Irked. In a fury. Perturbed. Exasperated. Spittin' nails. Overheated. Blew your top. Flipped your lid. Flew off the handle. Riled up. Berserk.

Add your favorite. We've got a million words and phrases for anger, probably because we all get mad. And mad people often do stupid things. Maybe that's why the Bible tells us not to sin *in our anger*.

The truth is it's okay to get angry, but we must still honor God. How? Don't lose control. Don't sling harsh words and insults you'll later regret. And don't let your anger fester inside and turn to bitterness. Forgive instead. Make things right the same day they happen. That might mean forgiving someone. It might mean apologizing. Just make sure to make things right before tonight.

TRIPLE DOG DARE

- ○ Talk to a friend or family member you've been fighting with. Apologize and forgive.

- ○ Count to ten before doing or saying anything when you're angry.

- ○ Watch and learn from someone else losing his cool. Pay attention to ways he looks or sounds foolish. Then stop and remember so you don't repeat his mistakes.

What did you do? What did you learn?

MISSION ACCOMPLISHED!

TRUTH

What you look like inside is worth more and lasts longer than outward appearance.

LOOKING GOOD

Big muscles, little muscles, skinny legs, chubby legs, short, tall, curly hair, straight hair, red hair, black hair, clear skin, freckles … *Ahhhhh!* We might not be as bad about it as girls, but we guys can still get obsessed when we look in the mirror.

It's easy to get caught wishing we looked like a famous star or the most popular kid in class. It's easy to feel like people might like us better if we had cooler hair or didn't need glasses.

The truth is it's what's inside you that draws people to you and keeps them sticking around as friends. Call it your inner appearance—your positive attitude, honesty, and kindness are just a few of the attractive traits that shine through no matter what your outside looks like. Those are the qualities people look for in friends. Sure, there are lots of grooming products that promise guys fame, strength, and girl magnetism—but really they just want your money. (Don't get me wrong. Clean teeth and deodorant are a good idea.) But God's love inside of us is free, and that's what really makes a guy appealing where it counts.

TRIPLE DOG DARE

- Instead of telling a friend you like his clothes—or how awful they look—tell him you like his sense of humor or honesty.

- Get rid of whatever makes you think too much about your appearance, such as a movie or muscle magazine or poster.

- Instead of buying yourself a smell-good product, use the money to buy your mom or dad a small gift.

MISSION ACCOMPLISHED!

What did you do? What did you learn?

PROVERBS 15:27

TRUTH Greed will ruin you and your family.

DO YOUR FAMILY A FAVOR

Billionaires don't lie on their deathbeds and say, "I wish I had more money." But there are countless articles and biographies of billionaires reaching the end of life and saying, "I wish I would have spent more time with my kids, or wife, or friends." As they realize their time is up, they wish they could have do-overs in their relationships. They've had more money than they could possibly spend, and they realize people are much more valuable.

Greed can make you blind to that reality. It eats you up inside. It gnaws and drives you to get more, more, more. It doesn't care about other people, even the people closest to you. It causes you to push them aside or walk over them on the way to more. But greed is never satisfied.

The truth is unselfishness will make you and your family stronger. Sharing with your brothers and sisters brings peace. Obeying and helping your parents brings trust and happiness. And when you're older and married, spending time with your wife and kids instead of obsessing over more money and possessions brings love. Those will bring you satisfaction—now and at the end of your life.

TRIPLE DOG DARE

○ Let your brother or sister use something you have never wanted to share.

○ Do an unselfish deed for each member of your family this week.

○ Ask each family member what they want to be remembered for most after they die.

What did you do? What did you learn?

MISSION ACCOMPLISHED!

SHAME

TRUTH

God is working for our good even in bad times.

GOOD IN ALL THINGS

Nobody wants to watch a movie where nothing bad ever happens to the main character. No dragons or enemies to fight. No princesses to rescue. No races or games to win. No challenges to figure out. No lessons to learn. Borrrrr-ing! Why should we expect our lives to be any different?

The truth is God uses even our bad times to work for our good. And we will have bad times. It's the reality of life. The good thing is that God uses them to teach us and help us grow, no matter how terrible our problems are. That's hard to see in the middle of a crisis. But don't give up. Turn to God for strength. Trust that He's with you, and look for what He's doing. He will bring some good out of your bad eventually. Count on it.

TRIPLE DOG DARE

- O Memorize Romans 8:28 and say it out loud when your problems seem big.

- O Interview people you respect and ask them what they learned from a big obstacle or problem.

- O Write a story with you as the hero, facing and overcoming your real problems with God's help.

MISSION ACCOMPLISHED!

What did you do? What did you learn?

TRUTH

God wants us to "eat" a healthy media diet.

YOU ARE WHAT YOU EAT

We're surrounded by media. We can't go to the gas station without a screen blasting a video at us. Of course, we've got video screens in our houses and cars and we carry devices that will play games, videos, music—not to mention allow us to communicate with friends, surf the Internet, and more. We live with a constant all-you-can-eat media buffet.

The problem is that too often it's a buffet overflowing with junk food and poison—but many people don't realize it. They think it smells and looks and tastes and sounds awesomely delicious! Sometimes it does taste good. But the poison will destroy us. And you know what would happen if all you ate all day was empty, unhealthy, bloated junk calories. Bye-bye health. Hello obesity and heart disease.

The truth is God wants us to eat a healthy media diet. He wants us to choose music and games and movies that measure up to His ways in the Bible. He wants us to reject media that glorifies sin. Because you are what you eat.

TRIPLE DOG DARE

- List your five favorite TV shows, movies, songs, and video games and what each is about. Is it stuff that makes God happy?

- Delete a song or trash a game that you know doesn't honor God. Ask your parents to help you replace it with one that does.

- Take a media fast. Go a day, weekend, or whole week without your favorite type of media. Can you do it?

What did you do? What did you learn?

MISSION ACCOMPLISHED!

MAKE TRIPLE DOG TRACKS

Note to Self

"I will make every effort to see that after my departure you will always be able to remember these things" (2 Peter 1:15).

Remembering is an important theme of the Bible. It's one of the main reasons it was written—to remind people of what God did and taught them. In the days of the early church, the disciples and apostles wrote letters to teach and remind the people of God's truths.

What do you need to remember? What do you want to remember? Here's your chance to jog your memory.

TRIPLE DOG DARE!

Write a letter to yourself. What do you want to remember about this time in your life? What are you learning about God? What are you feeling? What are your life wins and losses? Write whatever you want. Then address and stamp an envelope to yourself. Write today's date on the back and give it to your mom or dad. Ask one of them to write a reminder on the calendar to mail it for you in a year.

TRIPLE DOG BONUS

Write more letters to yourself at different life stages: when you're a teenager, when you're going to college, when you're getting married, or even having kids of your own. Put them in a safe place and only open them when it's time. In this space, make a list of letters you want to write.

SHAMe

YOUR PAGE

My heroes are _____ because _____ .
⟨Write down as many as you want.⟩

TRUTH *Love is the greatest of all.*

LOVE RULES

You could move Mount Everest with your telepathic mind. You could speak every language in the world, plus talk with angels. You could understand all the mysteries of the universe. You could survive the world's worst torture. And you could cure the world of poverty and end all wars. None of it would matter without love in your heart.

The truth is love is the greatest power in the universe. Everything else will eventually fade away or be destroyed. Even good things like faith and hope will be done; we won't need them anymore once we are with God. But love is eternal.

Love is way more than gooey romance or physical attraction. Love always puts other people first. It forgives and serves and waits and keeps going when times are tough. There's a great list in 1 Corinthians 13:4–8. Fill yourself with God's love and let it flow through you to others. Experience the world's greatest superpower.

TRIPLE DOG DARE

- ○ Put your heart into your actions. Make sure your greatest accomplishments come with an unselfish attitude.

- ○ List all of love's characteristics from 1 Corinthians 13. Write ways you see them in your loved ones' actions. Thank each person for showing you love.

- ○ Add to your list specific ways you can express each trait.

What did you do? What did you learn?

MISSION ACCOMPLISHED!

TRUTH
Don't rush falling in love.

NO GIRLFRIEND, NO PROBLEM

Romantic love is like fire. Sometimes it rages, and sometimes it glows. Fire is warm in a fireplace and helpful when you're exploring a mysterious cave. But fire destroys if it's in your bedroom and melts any action figures it gets its flames on. Fire on your stove cooks food, but fire on your body cooks you to burns or death. Romantic love is kind of the same. It brings closeness and commitment in marriage, but it can bring emotional scars and inappropriate physical involvement in immature relationships.

The truth is there's no need to rush romantic love. There's a right time and place for romantic relationships—just like for fire—and that time will come with maturity. For now, don't worry if you've never had a girlfriend. Enjoy your freedom to have fun with your friends, have plenty of time for your hobbies, and get to know lots of girls as friends.

Being friends with girls can teach you a lot. You can see personality traits you like in girls and learn how different females think and act. That's good knowledge for later in life when you're ready to commit to one girl or think about getting married. Until then, don't play with romantic matches.

TRIPLE DOG DARE

- If you're wanting a girl-friend, write down why. Then list the benefits of not being tied to any one girl at this point in your life.

- Make a list of personality traits you hope to see in your future wife.

- Practice being nice to all the girls in your class.

MISSION ACCOMPLISHED!

What did you do? What did you learn?

TRUTH God is always with us.

NEVER ALONE

No one likes to feel left out. No one enjoys rejection. Nobody begs to be the last one picked. But everybody feels lonely sometimes.

The truth is you're never alone. God is always with you. And He knows how you feel.

There's just no escape from Him—and that's a good thing. Feel like you've fallen off the face of the earth? He's there in the heavens. Feel like you've sunk to the bottom of the sea? He's got it covered. Cross the widest ocean? Climb the highest mountain? Dig the darkest cave? There, there, and there, too, ready to shine His light on you, wrap you in His biggest bear hug, and fill you with His hope. We all need other people, but they'll all let us down sometime. God will always be there for you.

TRIPLE DOG DARE

O What are you trying to hide from God? Give it up. He already knows.

O Who else needs a reminder that God is with him? Reach out today to someone who looks like he's bummed out.

O Hang out with God. Invite Him to do one of your favorite activities with you. Think about Him as you do. Listen to some praise music to help keep your mind on Him.

What did you do? What did you learn?

MISSION ACCOMPLISHED!

GREED

TRUTH

God wants you to keep your mouth and heart pure.

GOD'S GUARDS

Those guards at Buckingham Palace in England are famous for a reason. Well, a few reasons, actually. A lot of it's got to be the bright red coats and big bushy cone-hats. I mean, what's up with those hats? You could hide an attack dog or another small guard in there—hey, maybe that's their secret! Just when you think you've got 'em, out pops miniguard to take you out. Or maybe the hat's stashed with secret weapons and spy gadgets: remote-control ballistic boomerangs, truth serum, atomic grenades, and heat-seeking ninja stars. Cool! And just think, people stand right next to those guards for snapshots without realizing they could detonate World War III with the guard's hat. No wonder the guards never smile.

The truth is you want a guard like that protecting your lips and heart. The Household Division has been guarding British royalty since the 1400s. They don't let up, and they've got the history to prove it. Nothing's getting in or out of the palace that shouldn't be there. Ask God for that kind of consistent guard to catch any rogue speech from coming out and any sneaky evil from getting in.

TRIPLE DOG DARE

O Having trouble with your language? Cut off whatever source you're hearing it from.

O Draw a picture of the guard at your mouth—and his weapons, of course.

O Use mouthwash each morning while you ask God to give you positive speech.

MISSION ACCOMPLISHED!

What did you do? What did you learn?

TRUTH Sin is never secret.

YOUR REALITY TV

Every robber thinks he'll get away with it. He thinks he's got a foolproof plan. He thinks no one must have ever thought of this one. He's convinced he can beat the system. Most robbers end up in jail.

The truth is that our sins are never secret. God sees everything we do much clearer than a security camera. And He knows what's in our hearts even if we don't put it into action. Don't let Satan's subtle temptations fool you when he tells you no one will ever know. Don't let your sinful flesh trick you when you think you can get away with it just this once. Live like spiritual reality TV cameras are always following you. Live your life out in the open. And if you feel like you've got to hide to do something, don't do it. You'll never get away with it.

TRIPLE DOG DARE

- ⭕ When you're tempted to sin in secret, leave where you are to go be around other people.

- ⭕ When you're questioning an activity, ask how you'd feel if your entire family were watching live or on replay.

- ⭕ Live without secrets. Don't do it if you have to hide it.

What did you do? What did you learn?

MISSION ACCOMPLISHED!

GREED

FROM THE TRIPLE DOG POUND

Joseph the Triple Dog Dreamer (from Genesis 37-50)

It all started with that coat, the fancy multicolored one from his dad. As if it weren't already obvious enough, now there was no denying that Joseph was Dad's favorite. That part wasn't Joseph's fault, but it didn't go over well with his eleven brothers. And Joe didn't help his cause when he bragged about his dreams, in which he ruled over them. Your older brother would probably give you a good beat-down if you told him to bow down to you, too. Hopefully he wouldn't sell you into slavery like Joseph's brothers did to him.

You probably know the rest of Joseph's story: Egypt, resisting Potiphar's wife, false accusations, prison, interpreting dreams, Pharaoh calling, vice president of Egypt, and a reunion with his family. Talk about a roller-coaster life.

Joseph faced a long list of Triple Dog Dares, and he rose to each challenge.

- Learn humility the hard way as a slave.

- Stay true to God in a foreign culture that didn't worship Him.

- Stay pure instead of justifying easy temptation.

- Keep hope while being unfairly imprisoned.

- Be bold and speak truth even to the Pharaoh.

- Lead with fairness and wisdom.

- Stay faithful to God even with power and every material thing he wanted.

- Choose forgiveness over revenge.

In every situation, Joseph took the dare to learn this overarching lesson: "You intended to harm me, but God intended it all for good. He brought me to this position so I could save the lives of many people" (Genesis 50:20 NLT).

TRIPLE DOG BONUS

○ Read Joseph's story in Genesis 37, 39—50.

○ What bad things in your life can God turn into good?

○ Fill in these lists:

Times Joseph could've given up hope:	Good that came out of it:	Times I'm tempted to give up hope:	Good that can come out of it:

I'm going to invent ...

TRUTH

You may not like it, but it'll make your life better: Obey your parents.

IT PAYS TO OBEY

You think you know better. Come on, you've lived about a decade, plenty of time to figure out your own life. And *they* haven't been kids in, like, forever. Everything is way different now.

The truth is your parents know a lot more than you realize. Maybe not all the coolest words and latest trends you and your friends know, but they have a bigger, broader perspective. And they're looking out for your best, even if it doesn't seem like it.

God has given your mom and dad a not-so-easy job: to raise you. You know, give you food and clothes, teach you right and wrong, love you—basically get you ready to take responsibility for the life God has for you. Your job is to obey your parents, as long as it matches God's instructions in the Bible.

Want the good news? Obeying will make your life better. It'll make home more peaceful and fun, protect you from problems you don't even realize, teach you stuff you're going to need, and help your parents trust you more. And that gives you more future freedom.

TRIPLE DOG DARE

○ Obey the rule you hate the most—all week.

○ Talk to your parents when everybody's calm about a rule you don't like. Ask to find a compromise, but obey even if they say no (make sure you do).

○ Use a reminder—drawing on your hand, wearing a wrist band, tying a string around your finger—to obey the first time all day. Try all week.

What did you do? What did you learn?

MISSION ACCOMPLISHED!

GREED

TRUTH

God likes to give us good things. Ask Him.

GOD LIKES TO GIVE

What do you do when you want something really, really badly? You don't talk about it or tell anyone and keep forgetting about it, right? Wrong! You tell your friends and your cousins and your neighbor's great-aunt's cat. You talk it about it so much that your friends roll their eyes and tell you to be quiet. And you ask your parents 947 times in a row until they tell you that there's no way in the world you're going to get it unless you stop driving them crazy.

The truth is that God wants us to be that way about Him. He likes taking care of our needs. He likes giving us good gifts. But He wants us to pursue Him like He's the newest, coolest game on Christmas morning. Why? Because He wants us to remember that we need Him more than anything.

Keep in mind that God's not a vending machine that just lets you make your selection and get whatever you want. He's much smarter than that. He knows what we really need. He won't give us bad things; He'll give us the best!

TRIPLE DOG DARE

- What do you need? Ask God.

- Count how many times you ask your parents for things this week. Seek God just as much—or more.

- Ask God for important things for three other people.

MISSION ACCOMPLISHED!

What did you do? What did you learn?

TRUTH
God wants us to pray for our enemies.

A DIFFERENT WAY TO FIGHT

We're supposed to *what?!* That's crazy! Enemies are people against us. They don't like us. They attack and persecute us. Maybe you're thinking of a bully at school or a kid who just doesn't like you. Those people feel like enemies. So do foreign armies or terrorists who attack our country.

The truth is that God's ways are totally different from our human ways. Sometimes they seem downright crazy. That's why we have to seek God and allow Him to change the ways we think and feel. When it comes to enemies, the Bible is clear: We're supposed to pray for them.

That doesn't mean we let a bully beat us up. There's a time to defend ourselves, get help, and make sure a person is held accountable for what he does—especially when it hurts someone else. But it does mean we forgive a bully, pray for him, and try to treat him with God's love. So what do we pray? Ask God to help your enemy know God. Ask God to stop his hurtful actions and bring justice. Ask God to work in his life and to help you love and forgive.

TRIPLE DOG DARE

- Pray for your enemy every day this week.

- Talk nicely or write a note of forgiveness to someone you've fought or argued with.

- Pray for terrorists and countries who oppose our nation.

What did you do? What did you learn?

MISSION ACCOMPLISHED!

MATTHEW 25:14-30

TRUTH
God wants you to use what you've been given.

MAKE THE MOST OF IT

Don't just sit there—do something with what you've got! Don't try to claim you don't have anything to work with. God has given each of us abilities, resources, money, ideas, and opportunities. You may not have as much of those as the guy next door, or you may have more. The amount doesn't matter.

The truth is what matters is what you do with what you're given. God has given something to everyone, you included. He didn't give you unique talents so you can keep them a secret; He gave you abilities to use to help and serve other people and to glorify Him.

What's more, God gave us spiritual, eternal life through Jesus—not so we can lie around waiting for heaven. God wants us to live out the love and forgiveness He's given us by sharing it with other people. He wants us to tell others about Him and point others to Him with our actions. Don't waste God's gifts. Make the most of them.

TRIPLE DOG DARE

O Plan and do one action each day that looks like something Jesus would do.

O Invest your time by volunteering at church or school.

O Give some money this week to a ministry helping others.

MISSION ACCOMPLISHED!

What did you do? What did you learn?

TRUTH
It's better to listen more than you speak.

LISTEN QUICK

Everybody knows that guy who jumps in with the answer, a long and expert answer, before the teacher can even finish the question. Too bad, because he's not even answering the right question. Oops. Everybody laughs—again. You'd think he'd learn. But that's the thing about know-it-alls. They're convinced they know it all. They just can't seem to quit showing their ignorance.

The truth is we should listen first and then speak. Listening is learning. It's taking in the info you need to consider or know. Listening also keeps you out of trouble. You can hear the instructions you need to follow. You can get the brain tools you need to use. And you can think before you say something angry, rude, mean, or stupid.

It might take practice, but start by closing your mouth and picturing your ears opening instead. Remember that hearing is only the first part. Take the words and sounds and engage your brain. Think about what you hear. Mentally search for the main points. Repeat them to yourself. Ask questions when you can to make sure you understand. Practice, and you can listen fast, speak slow.

TRIPLE DOG DARE

- Count to five before saying anything today.

- Count to ten before saying anything when you're feeling mad.

- Practice listening. Start with music. What is the rhythm like? What are the words? What do they mean?

What did you do? What did you learn?

MISSION ACCOMPLISHED!

MAKE TRIPLE DOG TRACKS

Pray It Out

"Give all your worries and cares to God, for he cares about you" (1 Peter 5:7 NLT).

God cares about every detail of your life. He knows everything in your heart and mind, but He wants you to talk to Him about it all. He knows you need to get it out. He wants you to give it to Him so He can help you. And He wants you to help others by praying for them, too.

TRIPLE DOG DARE!

Start a list of your prayers or requests and their answers. Include dates for both prayers and answers. Start with these sample categories and add your own.

ME
example: *5/16 science test—5/18 God helped me study 30 mins. and get an 88.*

FAMILY
example: *7/16 Dad's doctor appt.—7/21 no cancer! Thank you, God!!!*

FRIENDS

CHURCH

MY COUNTRY

THE WORLD

TRIPLE DOG BONUS

Use this page. Then get a notebook or journal especially for writing your prayers and answers.

YOUR PAGE

The best ways I can help someone are ...

TRUTH

To be ready, you've got to get ready.

GET READY

You know the biggest problem with pop quizzes? You don't have any time to get ready. Sure, you're supposed to know the info from listening in class or doing your homework. But you get no chance to study. What you've got in your brain is what you get to tackle the quiz. But have you ever taken a test that you'd studied for—and knew all the answers? That feels good.

The truth is that most real-life tests are the unexpected pop-quiz type. But you know they're going to come sometime. That's why the Bible tells us to be ready, especially when it comes to explaining why we follow Jesus. Living for God means you will make different choices from many people. Treating others with God's love will probably seem strange to some, and sometime they're going to ask you what's up with your "weird" actions. Be ready to answer by studying the Bible and getting to know Jesus better. You'll ace the chance to tell them what He means to you.

TRIPLE DOG DARE

- Eat lunch with a kid who always eats alone.

- Practice telling your parents why you love Jesus and how He helps you.

- Read the book of 1 Peter in a Bible version easy to understand, such as the New Living Translation or *The Message*.

What did you do? What did you learn?

MISSION ACCOMPLISHED!

GREED

TRUTH Your God is crazy strong!

THE FURY OF THE HEAVENS

You might have felt an earthquake if you live in California. You've seen violent lightning if you live in Colorado or Florida. You understand the ocean's depth if you live on a coast. You've rumbled with crashing thunder. You've probably felt the heat from a raging bonfire. Can you imagine God raging with all those forces at once? How about coming to your rescue with the power of all the natural disasters rolled into one?

The truth is there's nothing God can't do, and He gives you His strength. He rescues you and protects you. He gives you courage and ability. He trains you and guides you. Even when it looks like you're done for, He will come when you call and give you what you need. Call for His help even when you're not in trouble. Trust in His care. There's nothing He can't save you from.

TRIPLE DOG DARE

○ List all the things 2 Samuel 22 says God is. Make another list of what the chapter says He helps you do.

○ Draw or paint a picture based on 2 Samuel 22.

○ Sing a praise song to God and really mean it.

MISSION ACCOMPLISHED!

What did you do? What did you learn?

TRUTH *God brings value to our work.*

THE WAY YOU WORK

Some people love their jobs. Some people hate what they do. Some guys are excited about the possibilities each day's work will bring them. Others dread going to the office. Some people would keep doing what they do even if you didn't pay them. You couldn't pay others not to quit.

The truth is God brings value to our work no matter what we do. But we have to keep our attitudes positive by looking to Him and remembering that. Every job has its bad days where nothing goes right and it all seems like the same old boring routine—that's true even for guys who love what they do. No job is a be-all, end-all happiness factory. Every job is an opportunity and a platform to use your abilities and to live for God.

School is your job right now. There are parts you hate and parts you might even like. Keep your attitude focused on God. Do your best, look for good, and view it as your platform to live for God. Satisfaction will follow.

TRIPLE DOG DARE

O List all your school subjects and one positive thing about each.

O Talk to God about your problems with school. Whenever you're tempted to complain, stop and pray instead.

O Ask for help if you're having trouble with a school subject. Talk to your parents about seeing a tutor.

What did you do? What did you learn?

MISSION ACCOMPLISHED!

TRUTH

Having money without wisdom is a waste.

DON'T GIVE DIAMONDS TO YOUR DOG

It's like giving your Wii to your dog. It's like buying an iPod for a deaf person. It's like me giving you a Ferrari today. It's building a fire with dollar bills. It's a car dealership after the world's oil has run out. It's a hunting license for Dodo birds. It's a diamond necklace for your cat. It's a werewolf detector. It's having money and not knowing how to use it. It's a waste.

The truth is wisdom is more valuable than money. And wisdom will help you earn and use your money. The Bible talks a lot about money. That shows us that God cares about how and what we do with it. After all, it all belongs to Him. He's the one who allows us to use it. Learn how to use money wisely. Ask your parents for help. Work diligently. Give generously. Save faithfully. Spend smartly. Invest insightfully. Chances are it will end up earning you more money. And you'll know how to use it.

TRIPLE DOG DARE

- ○ Open a savings account (if you don't have one) and put money in it every time you earn cash.

- ○ Get a job. It doesn't have to be big. Mow grass or wash cars or shovel sidewalks. Learn the value of hard work.

- ○ Make a budget. It's a plan of how to use your money. Include how much you will give, save, and invest.

MISSION ACCOMPLISHED!

What did you do? What did you learn?

TRUTH

Our love for people should reveal our love for Jesus.

LIVE BY LOVE

It won't be because of our rules, worship songs, buildings, political power, schools, denominations, or fish bumper decals. It's not that there's not some good in those things; it's that there's some bad, too. Those are often things that get Christians fighting—with each other and with non-Christians. And that's when love goes out the window.

The truth is our love for each other should define us as Christians. Jesus said so. Even when we disagree with other Christians or those who don't believe in God, love should still show through.

There was a time in ancient Rome when the church was new. A terrible plague was killing people left and right, and Romans were fleeing the cities to escape. The Christians stayed to take care of the dying and to minister to them. The Christians weren't afraid of death; they knew the sick needed care and God. Their love defeated fear. That's amazing love! That's the kind of love we need!

TRIPLE DOG DARE

○ Who's the "them" in your school or church's "us versus them"? Find three ways to do something kind and loving for "them."

○ Do a kind deed for the most unlovable person in your class.

○ Live in ways that make people ask, "Are you a Christian?" because of your actions.

What did you do? What did you learn?

MISSION ACCOMPLISHED!

Shamgar, the One-Verse Wonder

"After Ehud came Shamgar son of Anath, who struck down six hundred Philistines with an oxgoad. He too saved Israel" (Judges 3:31).

One verse. That's all he got. *Boom.* One judge. Six hundred enemies. One herder's stick. Six hundred dead Philistines. Peace in Israel again. End of story.

So I'll keep this short too. Shamgar did what he could, where he was, with what he had.

All you have to do is the same thing. Do something, whatever you can, no matter how small it seems. Do it here, now, wherever you are. Use what you've got. God uses willingness and multiplies efforts. Don't hold back, and don't let the size of your challenge hold you back.

Read it again out loud. Shamgar did what he could … where he was … with what he had. Now fill in your name. _____ did what he could … where he was … with what he had.

TRIPLE DOG DARE!

- ○ Read Judges 3:31 again.
- ○ How do you want people to remember your story? Write yourself a one-verse wonder.
- ○ What can you do with what you have to work with? List some skills, talents, abilities, and desires.

ANGER:

YOUR PAGE

If Jesus were a human on earth today, He would ...

PSALM 34:4–5

TRUTH You're not alone. Don't let Satan bury you in shame.

BEAT THE PREDATOR

You've seen those nature shows where the predator always tries to isolate the weak member of the herd. The wildebeests or gazelles are stronger together. They can fight and cover for each other, and the predator knows it. So he stalks and watches and tries to cut off the weak or young away from the pack. Your enemy, Satan, tries to do the same.

The truth is you can be free from shame because you're not alone. One of the Devil's favorite tricks is to bury a guy under shame, to cut him off from family and friends and convince him he's the only one that bad.

Guys entering their teenage years can be especially snagged that way. Once your body hits puberty, your hormones kick in and send you racing toward manhood. If you haven't reached that stage yet, it probably isn't too far away. Sometimes the changes are exciting; sometimes they're confusing. Emotions and feelings about girls can feel overwhelming and overpowering. But you're not alone—don't let Satan convince you otherwise. Stay close to your pack: your family, friends, and wise Christians. Talk to them about your questions and ask for their help to beat temptations. And remember that Jesus takes away shame.

TRIPLE DOG DARE

- Get your sin out in the open. Confess it to God and ask for help from your parents or best friend.

- Ask your dad or another man you trust for some time to hang out and ask questions about puberty.

- Where do you feel weak or confused? Ask for help.

What did you do? What did you learn?

MISSION ACCOMPLISHED!

ANGER

TRUTH

We can be confident that God is always listening.

COME ON IN

Have you ever known you were going to ace a test? You'd studied. You'd practiced. And what you expected was there on the test because you knew and understood the material.

Being sure of something is being confident. Often we build up confidence by doing something so many times we know what to expect. We're sure instead of worried.

The truth is we can be confident that God is always listening to us. He hears us. We can test it and prove it time and again. He wants to give things to us—not any old trinket or gadget, but good things that are part of His will. That means we can ask Him whatever's on our minds. We don't have to be afraid of offending God. We don't have to worry that He's too busy. He's given us an open invitation to talk any time. Because of that, we can be sure and secure. We can know what to expect. We can be confident that we matter—to God and to this world.

TRIPLE DOG DARE

- Talk to God right now, out loud if no one else is around.
- Ask God to replace any fears with confidence in Him.
- Build confidence by remembering all the answers to prayer God has given you. Make a list.

MISSION ACCOMPLISHED!

What did you do? What did you learn?

TRUTH It's a tough task, but tame your tongue.

TAME YOUR TONGUE

Your tongue is like a wolverine: small, not too harmful-looking from a distance, fuzzy (if you haven't brushed your teeth). But back it into a corner and the slobbering, snarling fierceness comes out. It packs a huge punch for such a little guy.

The truth is the tongue is tough to tame, but we can turn it toward God. Why does it matter? Because our tongues and our speech reflect who we are. They point toward God or away from Him. In the Bible, James compares our tongues to a horse's bit, a ship's rudder, and a spark that starts a forest fire—all small but powerful things.

We'll all mess up with our mouths. We'll say things we regret. We'll let words slip that we wish we could grab back. We'll complain or curse or insult with the same mouth we'll use to praise God. It's part of being human. But we also have the power to use our tongue for healing. Apologize. Admit your wrongs. Ask forgiveness. Build others up. Learn to turn your tongue toward God and ask for His help to tame that little beast.

TRIPLE DOG DARE

○ Apologize to your mom for talking back or saying something mean.

○ Admit it when you're wrong.

○ Sing a praise song to start every day this week.

What did you do? What did you learn?

MISSION ACCOMPLISHED!

1 TIMOTHY 6:11–12

TRUTH Faith is a fight. Keep battling!

KEEP FIGHTING

Ah, the good life: PlayStation all day, all-you-can-eat pizza, your own private roller coaster, and a butler to clean up after you. God? Yeah, sure, you go to church once a week. You believe in Him. He fits in your fantasy.

Uh, time to wake up, dreamer.

The truth is that faith is a fight. You might enjoy some good perks along the way. But let down your guard and you'll get knocked in the kisser or KO'd into unconsciousness—when you don't realize there's a battle raging around you. Sometimes you'll have to fight doubt to believe in God or that He's really in control. Sometimes you'll have to fight temptation. Sometimes you'll have to fight distraction to hear God's voice. Always you'll have to fight Satan's sneaky lies and obstacles and instead go after righteousness, godliness, faith, love, endurance, and gentleness. Keep fighting like your life depends on it. It does.

TRIPLE DOG DARE

- Train for the battle. Read a chapter of your battle plan, the Bible, every day this week.

- Don't give up. What's your biggest war? Focus only on today's battles, or this hour's. Ask for God's strength and win.

- Practice random acts of faith, love, and gentleness today.

MISSION ACCOMPLISHED! What did you do? What did you learn?

TRUTH
God is your Daddy. You are His son.

HE'S YOUR DADDY

How do you picture God? Jolly Santa Claus giving you whatever you want? Harsh prison warden waiting to smack you when you step out of line? Maybe you see Him as distracted—tuned into a giant TV set showing everything in the world and too busy for you. Or is your idea a God who's cheering you on from the sidelines of your game? There's a good chance that the way you view God is a lot like the way you view your dad.

The truth is that God is your loving, caring Father. He wants us to call Him "Daddy." He wants to guide us and nurture us and give us good gifts. We can hug and wrestle with Him. Yes, He's powerful and fierce toward evil, and He could squash us like bugs without twitching a muscle. But we don't have to be afraid of Him. He uses His strength to protect us. He calls us close and gives us the rights of His kingdom. He's proud of His sons, and He loves us like a perfect dad.

TRIPLE DOG DARE

- Practice calling God "Daddy" or "heavenly Daddy" when you pray.

- Make lists describing your earthly dad and your heavenly Dad.

- Invite your dad to do something fun together this week and ask him to tell you stories about your grandfather. (If you don't live near your dad, call or video chat with him. If you don't have a dad, invite a close male family member, friend, or teacher.)

What did you do? What did you learn?

MISSION ACCOMPLISHED!

MAKE TRIPLE DOG TRACKS

What You Want, What You Need

Contentment comes from being thankful no matter what's going on around you. It comes from being satisfied with what you have.

Psalm 37:4 says, "Take delight in the LORD, and he will give you the desires of your heart." *Cool! Like a free pass to getting whatever I want?* Not so fast. The process starts with delighting—taking great pleasure or really getting into—God. You can't do that without Him changing your heart and becoming more like Him. As that happens, some of the desires of your heart will change; they'll be shaped by what God wants. You'll still want some of the same things, but you'll also start to learn how to be content. You'll start to learn the difference between what you want and what you need.

TRIPLE DOG DARE!

Practice now by adding to this list.

What I Want...	*What I Need...*
a Porsche	a reliable vehicle to get around
the latest hot brand of jeans	some jeans to wear to school
the coolest pro-model shoes	some decent shoes that fit
an all-you-can-eat ice-cream buffet	a nutritious meal
my own gigantic room	a comfy bed and some space to store stuff

TRIPLE DOG BONUS

Use this space to add more!

YOUR PAGE

Create your own cartoon character here.

TRUTH We all need good friends.

BFF

What is it about your best friend? Does he make you laugh? Is he always there ready to help when you need it? Are you totally alike or polar opposites? Maybe you've never even thought about why he's your best friend—he's just the guy you'd rather hang with more than anybody.

The truth is that we need good friends. Being a good friend is treating another person with God's traits: love, unselfishness, sacrifice, kindness, honesty, faithfulness, forgiveness, and generosity. It means standing by someone else in good and bad times, sticking up for him, expecting the best of him, and helping him when he's in trouble.

David and Jonathan are great examples of friendship. They stuck together even in danger. Jonathan was willing to give his life to protect David even when it cost him his own position and power as future king. Jonathan trusted God and knew what was right, and he was willing to put his friend's well-being ahead of even his own. Be a friend like that and you'll never be short of friends.

TRIPLE DOG DARE

- Read about David and Jonathan in 1 Samuel 19—20.

- Do something nice for your best friend today, just because.

- Make a new friend this week by introducing yourself to someone.

What did you do? What did you learn?

MISSION ACCOMPLISHED!

TRUTH

What you let into your heart is what comes out in your life.

LEAVE GARBAGE IN THE DUMP

Garbage in. Garbage out. You've probably heard the saying. It means if you fill yourself with trash, then trash will come out. It can't help it. It's all you've got to work and overflow with. It's true of your physical body. If all you eat is fatty junk food, all your body has to work with is fat, and it will begin to show. You won't have enough complex carbohydrates to burn for energy. You won't have enough protein to build strong muscles. And you probably won't feel too good either. Our spirits work the same way.

The truth is that what you fill your heart and mind with begins to show in your thoughts and actions. It's all your spirit has to work with. Overdose on violence from movies or video games and you'll probably start to get mad easier or lash out aggressively when you're bugged. Fill your ears with music about sex, drugs, violence, or other trash, you can bet your heart isn't being filled with any kind of positive messages. Pay attention to what you let into your life. Guard your heart. Keep it from becoming a stinking garbage dump.

TRIPLE DOG DARE

- O Eat some fruit and veggies every day this week.

- O Had trouble with temptations lately? Check the source and cut off any garbage trails you find.

- O Take out the trash. Is anything polluting your heart? Dump or delete it.

MISSION ACCOMPLISHED!

What did you do? What did you learn?

TRUTH A good reputation is priceless.

BETTER THAN GOLD

People notice what you do. Every action you take is a brick, stacking together to form your reputation. We all have one. Think about who comes to mind when you read these words: *hard worker, smart, lazy, funny, whiner, friendly.* Faces and names probably popped into your mind immediately. Your face would pop up in someone else's list.

The truth is having a good reputation is priceless. Your character shows through and lasts like precious metals. It lets people know they can trust you. Your rep also acts like a protective coating. When someone says something untrue, a good reputation lets it slide right off. Others know when accusations don't match your character.

We all make mistakes. A good reputation doesn't mean we're perfect, but it shows the consistency we've built up over time. It also takes time to build a bad rep, and a long time to turn one around. Don't get stuck playing catch-up with your reputation. Start building a good one now.

TRIPLE DOG DARE

- O Ask parents, teachers, and friends what you're known for.

- O Start changing a bad rep by apologizing to parents, teachers, and friends for ways you've hurt them. Tell them you're working on changing.

- O Build up others. Make a list of friends' good traits; then compliment them for the good things you see.

What did you do? What did you learn?

MISSION ACCOMPLISHED!

TRUTH

God wants our hearts and words to be filled with gratitude and thankfulness—not complaining and discontentment.

QUIT COMPLAINING

"I don't like this. I don't like that. You should treat me more _____. You should give me more _____. Teacher did _____. Coach didn't do _____ … not fair … too big … too hard … too much … not enough." *Blah. Blah. Blah.*

It's easy to let complaints flow out of our mouths. Sometimes the reasons seem legitimate, but usually they're really trivial. Sure, bad things happen, circumstances don't go our way, and people mistreat us. But while you grumble because your mom didn't cook your favorite dinner, millions of people around the world aren't eating anything at all that night.

Complaining comes from a self-centered outlook and pollutes our own attitudes and the atmosphere around us.

The truth is God has given us incredible blessings and way more than we can imagine—even when things just don't seem to be going our way. He wants us to remember His goodness and let thankfulness guide our attitudes and speech. When we're busy thanking God and the people around us, there's no room for complaining.

TRIPLE DOG DARE

- Do twenty-five push-ups every time you complain.

- Write a thank-you note to your parents. Tell them ten things you appreciate.

- Tell your least-favorite teacher thank you for something he or she has helped you learn.

MISSION ACCOMPLISHED!

What did you do? What did you learn?

TRUTH You can worship God anywhere.

ANYTIME, ANYWHERE

You don't have to be at an amusement park to have fun. You don't have to be at a funeral to be sad. You don't have to go to a haunted house to feel scared, and you don't have to be at the X Games to feel excited.

The truth is you don't have to be at church to worship God; you can worship Him anywhere. And you can worship Him doing just about anything—not just singing praise songs. What matters to God is the attitude and expression of your heart.

What brings your soul alive? Art? Draw or paint as an expression of God's gift of creativity to you. Physical activity? Run or snowboard as an offering of thanks. Nature? Get out in it as an appreciation of God's creativity. Turn to God whenever, wherever, and let your spirit say thanks.

TRIPLE DOG DARE

- Do what you do, and praise God all along the way.

- Take a walk or run. Pray along the way.

- Create something while you think about and appreciate God's creativity.

What did you do? What did you learn?

MISSION ACCOMPLISHED!

FROM THE TRIPLE DOG POUND

James, the Triple Dog Brother

Do you get sick of living in your older brother's shadow? Do you ever feel like he never gets in trouble, but you get punished all the time? Imagine what it must have felt like growing up with Jesus as a brother. He never did anything wrong. Then when you're grown up He starts preaching and doing miracles and claiming He's the Son of God. Can you blame Jesus' brothers for not believing Him at first? (Check out John 7:5.)

James was one of them. Jesus was the oldest brother, and James was probably next in order. And James and the others didn't get what Jesus was doing when He started His ministry. It was a big Triple Dog Dare for James and his bros: Be able to believe that Jesus was God's Son, not just the normal human big brother they grew up with. And somewhere along the line James took that dare. Eventually he even became a leader in the early church and probably wrote the book of the Bible that has his name.

It's that book of the Bible that shows us James was a real Triple Dog kind of guy. He was all about action, and the letter he wrote to early Jewish Christians is full of encouragement to put their faith into action. Just hearing about truth or believing in Jesus isn't good enough, according to James. We've got to do it to prove we really believe it. Maybe that's what turned the tide for James to believe—seeing his big bro die and then rise again. What we know for sure is that James gives us a good Triple Dog Dare to live what we say we believe.

TRIPLE DOG DARE!

- Read the book of James.

- Put yourself in James' position. What would you do if your brother starting performing miracles and claiming to be the Son of God? What would make you believe or disbelieve?

- Fill in these lists:

I SAY I BELIEVE: HOW MY ACTIONS SHOW IT:

PRIDE

YOUR PAGE

Now it's time to ...

TRUTH
You can obey God by fighting slavery.

SLAVERY STILL HAPPENS

You thought slavery ended with the Civil War, right? Wrong. Slavery still exists today. Not just here and there. It's a big problem. There are an estimated twenty-seven million slaves today all around the world. Many of them are kids forced to do work and beaten or wounded if they don't work fast enough. Many of them make products you probably own, such as clothes or foods. Most countries have laws against slavery, but slave owners aren't exactly law-abiding folk.

The truth is you can obey God by fighting slavery. It's seeking justice and trying to right the wrongs of human mistreatment. It's showing mercy and compassion to slavery's victims. It's joining God in the work of His kingdom by fighting for people who can't fight for themselves.

Learn more about the problem. Find ways you can help by raising awareness and raising money for groups working on the front lines of the fight against slavery.

TRIPLE DOG DARE

- Raise money and awareness to stop slavery through organizations like Loose Change to Loosen Chains or the International Justice Mission.

- Watch *Amazing Grace,* a movie about William Wilberforce's battle to end slavery in England, with your parents.

- With your parents' help, look into the clothing stores and brands you buy most, and stop buying if they're known for problems with slave labor. Start with chocolates and clothes.

What did you do? What did you learn?

MISSION ACCOMPLISHED!

PRIDE

TRUTH

God's joy carries us through hard times.

JUMP FOR JOY

Nobody's laughing in a car crash. Nobody's celebrating when they lose the championship. Nobody's jumping up and down when a loved one dies. Those aren't situations for happiness, but they're places joy can live.

The truth is God gives us joy that carries us through hard times. Happiness is an emotion that's based on good times and events. You probably know it well. But joy runs much deeper. Joy doesn't depend on the circumstances around us. It comes from seeing the big picture. It often mixes with contentment and shows up in painful places where it doesn't belong if it weren't for God bringing it there.

God's joy can carry us through our hardest times. He fills us up and gives us nimble feet to climb the hard mountains, like a mountain goat dancing up steep, rocky cliffs. Look at God instead of your problems, and feel His joy fill you up.

TRIPLE DOG DARE

- When you're sad, read Psalms and ask for God's joy.

- Find a reason to celebrate in hard times.

- Talk to your mom or dad about a problem you're facing.

MISSION ACCOMPLISHED!

What did you do? What did you learn?

MATTHEW 10:7-8

TRUTH

God wants us to give freely just like we've received.

YOU GOT A BARGAIN

Let's say your friend has a never-ending supply of milkshakes—a machine that constantly churns ice cream and milk into any flavor he wants. He doesn't have to load it. He doesn't have to clean it. He doesn't have to pay a cent—never has—for each milkshake or for the whole glorious invention. (Let's say he has a mad scientist uncle who gave it to him.) But he's trying to charge you five bucks a shake. Fair? No way!

The truth is God has given you the most incredible, superawesome gift in the world for absolutely nothing, and He wants you to give it the same way. Jesus gave His love and His life, no strings attached. If there was a price tag, you couldn't afford it. You couldn't deserve it. You couldn't earn it. It came free to you. He wants you to give it free to others. Share His love. Be generous with His life. Don't hold back.

TRIPLE DOG DARE

- ○ Compliment ten different people today. Bonus: Compliment ten strangers.

- ○ Smile all day at people who are frowning.

- ○ Offer to let your brother use the coolest Christmas present you got last year.

What did you do? What did you learn?

MISSION ACCOMPLISHED!

TRUTH
Obedience matters more to God than sacrifice.

WHAT GOD WANTS MORE

You've probably done it yourself lots of times: obeying about 80 percent. You know, like cleaning your room, feeding the dog, and turning off the Xbox after *two* hours instead of *one* hour like your mom told you. You came pretty close, right? You should get some credit for that.

King Saul thought the same thing in 1 Samuel 15, but he made God angry by not following God's instructions all the way. Saul even seemed to have a good excuse: He was going to offer all the best stuff as sacrifices to God.

The truth is that God cares much more about our obedience than our excuses and sacrifices. He doesn't want us to cut corners; He wants us to go all the way. He doesn't want our excuses. He wants our actions, because those show our love and devotion. Don't try to see how much you can get away with. Go all out to obey God.

TRIPLE DOG DARE

- Quit cutting corners. Go all out to obey God's commands.

- No excuses. When you're caught misbehaving, confess and accept your punishment without complaining.

- Make yourself a reminder to obey the first time you're told.

MISSION ACCOMPLISHED!

What did you do? What did you learn?

TRUTH God will give you the strength to do what He wants you to do.

NO EXCUSES

What's your excuse? Too shy? Too small? Too young? Not smart enough? Not strong enough? Not ready? Can't concentrate? Can't wait? Can't see how? Scared? Confused? Nervous? Don't care? Don't want to?

Doesn't matter.

The truth is God will help you do whatever He wants you to do. He wants us to use the natural gifts He's given us—the things we're good at automatically. But sometimes He calls us to do things we're not so comfortable with. Those tasks take us out of our comfort zone, and that's the point. We *have* to rely on God. We realize how much we need Him. Compared to God, we're all tiny weaklings. But He uses us anyway. He gives us strength we don't have. He gives us His words and fills us with courage. He brings other people to help us. He gives us the chance to be part of His big works. No excuses.

TRIPLE DOG DARE

- What's been nagging at you inside that you haven't wanted to do? Talk to God about it. Trust Him and do it.

- Write down all your excuses. Tear the paper up or throw it into the fireplace.

- Ask a helper. Who can help and support you?

What did you do? What did you learn?

MISSION ACCOMPLISHED!

MAKE TRIPLE DOG TRACKS

Star in Your Own Action Flick

When movie producers are creating their films, they use storyboards. Storyboards are rough drawings that show key scenes, changes, and actions in the story. Producers can talk them through one at a time or post them on the wall all at once. And they can use them to talk about what they'll need to film or how to move characters from one event to another.

So what do you want to be the adventure of your life in the next year? How would you write the action movie about you? Here's your chance.

TRIPLE DOG DARE!

Storyboard the adventures of your life—what you expect and hope will happen in the next year and how you will overcome any obstacles to reach those actions. Go for twelve drawings or panels, one for each month.

YOUR PAGE

The people at my school who could use a
friendly word the most are ...

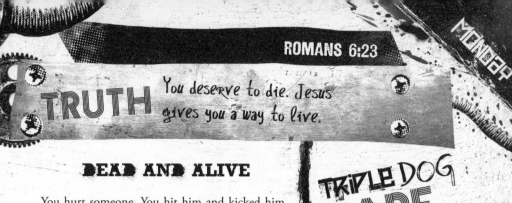

TRUTH

You deserve to die. Jesus gives you a way to live.

DEAD AND ALIVE

You hurt someone. You hit him and kicked him and spit on him and called him names. He was bleeding and you stabbed him. He was your best friend. But you tortured him and laughed. In fact, you killed him. We all did.

He was Jesus. It was His choice to give His life, but our sin was the reason He needed to die. Let's face it: We all do wrong. We all sin. Because of that, we're the ones who deserve to die and have our spirits separated from God forever.

The truth is that we can have life, real spiritual life with God forever, even after our earthly lives are done—not because we deserve it, but because God offers grace (something we don't deserve). It comes from choosing to believe that Jesus is God's Son and from living in agreement with what He said and did. It comes from accepting the gift of His life and giving Him ours.

TRIPLE DOG DARE

- O Read The Ultimate Triple Dog Dare at the back of this book. Give your life to Jesus if you never have.

- O Tell a friend about how you've received the best gift in the entire world.

- O Read the Bible book of Romans, which explains faith and salvation.

What did you do? What did you learn?

MISSION ACCOMPLISHED!

PRIDE

TRUTH

God can change our hearts and attitudes.

HEART SURGERY

Have you ever felt like you just don't care? You don't want to do what you're supposed to. You don't feel like it. You don't feel like much of anything—except maybe kicking your dog, complaining, and slamming doors. You don't even care that you don't care. You kind of enjoy snarling at people.

The truth is God can change our hearts and attitudes. He wants to. Sometimes we get so mad, spiritually grouchy, or ashamed of the way we've acted that it's hard to know what to say to God. We might feel embarrassed or foolish. Don't worry about it. Just call out for God. He wants to replace your stone-cold, rebellious heart with a feeling, caring, soft, and loving heart. He wants to trade out your rebellious, deathlike attitude for a willing, life-giving attitude. Let God do His heart surgery on you.

TRIPLE DOG DARE

- Do a heart-check. Is it cold and uncaring or soft and loving?

- Raise your heart rate by working out your spirit each day in whatever way gets your blood pumping for God.

- Track your attitude on a calendar. Add a quarter to a jar for every good-attitude day. Subtract a quarter for every bad-attitude day. Reward yourself every week or month with the money you've earned.

MISSION ACCOMPLISHED!

What did you do? What did you learn?

TRUTH
Just because you can doesn't mean you should.

JUST BECAUSE YOU CAN

You *can* drink soda with a straw through your nose. You *can* eat McDonald's and Taco Bell for every meal of every day of your life. You *can* watch every channel on your satellite dish network non-stop for a year straight. You *can* lick honey out of a beehive. You *can* starve your dog for a month and then wear a meat suit.

The truth is just because you *can* doesn't mean you *should*. God gives us a lot of freedom to make choices in life. But He wants us to remember that our lives are not all about us. He wants them to be about Him and other people. He wants us to consider how our actions affect others around us.

How can we tell? Try answering these questions: *Will I be sorry? Is this going to hurt me? Will my choice hurt anyone's feelings? Will my action encourage a friend to go against his conscience? Does this look bad? Is there a way to give or share with someone else? Is there a way to glorify God in this decision?*

TRIPLE DOG DARE

- Offer the last helping to someone else.

- Draw a reminder on your hand to stop and think how a hard decision will affect others around you.

- List how you spend your time this week. Are your choices good for you? For others?

What did you do? What did you learn?

MISSION ACCOMPLISHED!

TRUTH

God hates lies, but He loves trustworthiness.

AVOID ALIEN INVASION

Lies are like mutating aliens. You can never get just one. As soon as one pops out, it starts to multiply. It has to in order to cover for itself. Before you know it you're over-run with a full-galaxy invasion, and you're going down—unless you come clean. Truth is the only smart bomb that can wipe out the lies.

The truth is God hates lies, but He loves trustworthiness. He delights in people who tell the truth. He celebrates them. You can trust someone who tells the truth; he can be counted on. He's like a defender of the galaxy fighting off the evil aliens for all time. Be smart: Choose what God delights in, not what He detests.

TRIPLE DOG DARE

- O Don't fall for little white lies (you know, the ones we justify as just *stretching* the truth). Stop *any* lies before they can mutate.

- O Tell the truth even when it's hard.

- O Draw a picture of a web or map showing how one lie you've told led to others.

MISSION ACCOMPLISHED!

What did you do? What did you learn?

TRUTH

Fix your own weaknesses before you blame others for theirs.

LOOK AT YOURSELF

When you point the finger, there are four fingers pointing back at you. It's a silly statement, but it makes the point (pun intended). Nobody likes a hypocrite, a person who tells others not to do something then turns around and does it himself. It's even worse when a hypocrite tries to make others change without changing himself.

Would you take math tutoring from a student who flunked math? Would you buy skin medicine from a salesperson with an oozy rash? How about eating meat from a farmer with food poisoning?

The truth is God wants us to deal with our own problems before we go blaming others for their problems. We all make mistakes. We all have weaknesses. We all come up short—often in the same areas. Don't blame and accuse others. Instead look at your own life. Avoid doing the thing that annoys you in others. Let the changes start with you.

TRIPLE DOG DARE

- What are you blaming other people for? Stop. How are you doing the same thing?

- What bugs you most about your parents? Think about how you do the same thing.

- List your three biggest weaknesses. Don't complain about those actions in others for a week.

What did you do? What did you learn?

MISSION ACCOMPLISHED!

MAKE TRIPLE DOG TRACKS

Triple Dog Quiz

Pop quiz! By now you're getting the idea that being a Triple Dog Daredevil is about learning what the Bible says and then putting it into action in real, everyday ways. So test yourself in these situations:

1. There's a new guy at school. You …

   a. don't really care. You've got friends.
   b. say hi but figure he'll find some guys to hang with.
   c. invite him to sit with you and your friends at lunch and to join your team at break or PE.

2. The guys are laughing at something when you walk up. One sticks his phone in your face with a picture of a naked woman. You …

   a. grab the phone and stare.
   b. try not to look but laugh along with the other guys.
   c. tell your friends you don't want to look at that kind of stuff because it disrespects women and God.

3. Words gets around fast that somebody swiped the answer key for the history test, and anybody can use it. You …

   a. seize the chance for a good grade.
   b. don't use it but keep quiet.
   c. let your teacher know, maybe even anonymously, that the answers are spreading so the test won't be fair.

4. Your neighbor's yard is covered in leaves and broken limbs because she's too old to pick them up. You …

   a. don't care. It's just a few leaves and sticks.
   b. throw the sticks from the sidewalk into her grass so you can skateboard past.
   c. grab a friend and a rake and go clean up her yard.

5. You're playing the team you're tied with for first place. It's a back-and-forth game filled with great plays, but they win by one. You …

   a. stomp off the field and bolt as soon as it's over.
   b. complain about the refs all weekend.
   c. congratulate the other team and practice a new move that same afternoon.

How'd You Do?

If you scored …

O Mostly *As*—You're not quite getting it. Keep reading the Bible and *Triple Dog Dare* each day, but ask your parents or teachers questions about what the verses mean. Then focus on putting them into practice!

O Mostly *Bs*—You've got some basic understanding of how God wants you to live, but you're acting scared to live it out. Ask God for strength. Ask a friend to help you. Then take a Triple Dog Dare and stand up for God and others.

O Mostly *Cs*—You're understanding and making wise choices about living out God's Word. Keep it up, and give some help and encouragement to other guys to do the same.

YOUR PAGE

My favorite story about one of my grandparents is ...

TRUTH

God has chosen you to be part of His crazy, amazing plans.

UPSIDE DOWN

You've got one reason to brag: God. He gave you every skill and ability you have. Not so you can be cool but so you can reflect God's glory and power.

The truth is that God likes to turn the ways of our world upside down. He chooses unimportant people for important tasks. He makes smart human thoughts and plans seem foolish. He makes weak people strong. He likes to make the impossible possible. Why? So we can see that it *had* to be God.

Think about it. God can use the young to teach the old. He can use the ordinary to accomplish the extraordinary. And God has chosen you. He's called you His son and has gifted you with talents and abilities. Fill yourself up with Him and unleash His love and power around you. Turn your world upside down for God.

TRIPLE DOG DARE

○ What do you keep saying you can't do? Ask for God's strength and do it one step at a time.

○ Choose one way you want to change the world. Start with one action to do it.

○ Look closely at your challenges from God's perspective.

What did you do? What did you learn?

MISSION ACCOMPLISHED!

TRUTH
God's character in our lives makes us strong.

BUILD YOUR PYRAMID

The Egyptian pyramids are architectural marvels even though they were built thousands of years ago. They still inspire us today. Their stones are ginormous, and their triangular shapes are intriguing.

The truth is we build character in our lives like a pyramid, adding traits and godly qualities one on top of another. We can picture Peter's list as a pyramid. Each of the stones is important, but none of them is separate. Faith, goodness, knowledge, self-control, perseverance, godliness, mutual affection, and love all work together.

Our faith in God is the foundation. We put it into action with good actions, and we learn more about God and following Him in our world. We control ourselves to avoid temptations, and we keep going even when life is hard. That helps us grow stronger and godlier like Jesus. Jesus gives us care and compassion for others that grows into love. The more we practice all these character traits, the stronger our spiritual pyramid grows.

TRIPLE DOG DARE

- Draw a pyramid and write in these character traits on the stones.

- Where does your character need maintenance? Choose one way to improve your weakest trait from Peter's list.

- Build knowledge. Do your homework without complaining all week. Read about the Egyptian pyramids, and read about Moses and the Egyptians in the Bible.

MISSION ACCOMPLISHED!

What did you do? What did you learn?

WEDNESDAY

TRUTH

Jesus suffered and died—for you.

DEATH BY CHOICE

You can't imagine a worse torture. Go ahead and try. Being thrown into a swimming pool filled with poisonous snakes instead of water? Being eaten alive by maggots from the inside out while you're totally conscious? Watching your family be cut into pieces before it's your turn? All truly awful, but none of them comes close to the suffering Jesus endured.

The truth is Jesus suffered the entire pain of the whole world for all of human history, and He chose to die because He loves you. He experienced the atrocity and punishment for every single sin, from the worst unthinkable crimes to the most common wrongs that we dismiss every day. The physical pain was excruciating, but the spiritual pain was even worse. And He chose to take it all.

Love held Jesus on the cross, not nails. Love for you and me and everyone around us. The best thank you is to love Him back.

TRIPLE DOG DARE

○ Ask your parents to take you to a Maundy Thursday or Holy Thursday service to recognize the Last Supper and Jesus' crucifixion and prepare for Easter.

○ Make a small cross out of sticks or cardboard. Write down your sins as you confess them to God. Attach them to the cross and bury it under a pile of rocks in your yard.

○ Ask your parents if you're ready to watch *The Passion of the Christ* movie with them.

What did you do? What did you learn?

MISSION ACCOMPLISHED!

TRUTH

Jesus gives the purest, strongest love.

THE STRONGEST LOVE

Jesus didn't have to die. He could've gotten off the cross at any second. He could've called a million angels to obliterate the Roman army and Jewish leaders who had accused and were crucifying Him. He could have taken Satan up on his offer to rule the world and skipped the suffering altogether. He could have told God the Father, "Sorry, not gonna do it." But love kept Jesus on the cross.

The truth is Jesus gave us the purest, strongest love by giving up His life for us. He did it for His friends. And we can do it for Him. That doesn't mean you will have to throw yourself in front of a speeding train to save a friend. It means you should give your life every day to follow God. You can live out your friendship with Jesus by obeying His commands even when they feel unpopular or inconvenient. You can show your love for God by loving other people like He wants, even when you don't like the other people. Follow Jesus' perfect example by choosing what He wants even when it's not what you want.

TRIPLE DOG DARE

O Draw, write, or sing about Jesus' love that kept Him on the cross.

O Make a list of actions you can take to love each of your friends this week.

O Give someone else a great opportunity or reward you get this week.

MISSION ACCOMPLISHED!

What did you do? What did you learn?

TRUTH

Jesus came back to life to beat sin and give you life forever.

ALIVE—AGAIN!

It's the single most important, most incredible event in all time. It was the key play that turned human existence around. It was the victorious battle that ensured the war would be won. It was the ransom that paid for the release of all the prisoners. It changed absolutely everything.

The truth is Jesus came back to life. He beat sin so you can have life forever. Love triumphed, and now nothing can keep you separated from God. It was an almost impossibly steep price to pay, but it was worth it.

Now He welcomes you to Himself with open arms. It's time to celebrate and dance for joy. Sing with all your might. Shout at the top of your lungs. Give high fives, fist bumps, and hugs. He is risen!

TRIPLE DOG DARE

- Go to an Easter sunrise service. Celebrate the Son as you meet the first rays of the sun.

- Dig up the cross and confessions you made two days ago. Destroy the list of sins and be relieved that you are forgiven.

- Make your own short film called *The Resurrection of the Christ*. Capture the disciples' and women's surprise at seeing Jesus alive again. Consider what must have gone on in hell—not a happy day there.

What did you do? What did you learn?

MISSION ACCOMPLISHED!

MAKE TRIPLE DOG TRACKS

Express Easter

Artists think, see, and connect in pictures. Here's your chance …

TRIPLE DOG DARE!

Draw what Easter means to you. Show what it looks, feels, smells, tastes, and sounds like, from the first Easter to this year. Use the space on this page and the next one.

YOUR PAGE

My favorite Bible characters are ...

TRUTH Imitate God instead of the crowd.

INNER COOL

Fashion is funny—and fickle. One year skinny jeans are in; the next year it's bell-bottoms. One month Nike shoes are the coolest; the next month Adidas rules. You wouldn't be caught dead with short hair last year; next year you'll be embarrassed by shaggy hair. Cool changes fast, and we follow like a dog on a leash.

The truth is we should imitate God more than each other. That can be hard to remember when you're young, and it gets even harder when you're a teen. Nobody likes to be labeled uncool, and not fitting in can make you feel nervous, scared, and insecure.

Choose now to look at Jesus as your example. Act like Him, not the people around you. He'll never reject you. He'll fill you with His love, strength, confidence, and security. The more you have of those, the more people will respect you. The more you'll set the standards. The more cool you'll be— inner cool that lasts.

TRIPLE DOG DARE

- ○ Act like Jesus. Picture what He would do in a situation and follow His lead.

- ○ Get a couple friends to join you in wearing old, thrift-store, unstylish clothes to school. Write "Redefine cool" on plain white T-shirts.

- ○ Offer to help pay for those new shoes or clothes you want.

What did you do? What did you learn?

MISSION ACCOMPLISHED!

TRUTH Confessing to others sets us free.

LET IT OUT

Letting out a big secret feels like an eighteen-wheeler lifting off your shoulders. Do you know that feeling? I'm not talking about telling a friend's secret that he's trusted you with. I'm talking about something we've been hiding that's eating us up inside like a dog in a kibble factory. Often it's something we've done wrong, something we're trying to hide. The fear that we're going to be found out spreads inside like cancer; sometimes it even feels like the disease.

The truth is confessing our sins to other people brings healing and freedom. It releases the weight. It opens the dam to let the guilt and fear flow out. It brings us help from other people who can support and pray for us. It brings us power over the lie that we're the only one bad enough to do something like that, and it brings us strength and encouragement from other people who have struggled with and overcome the same sin. No matter how bad your secret seems, let it out to your mom, dad, or a close friend you trust.

TRIPLE DOG DARE

- Talk to your mom, dad, or trusted friend today.

- Confess your sin to God; then ask forgiveness from the person you've hurt.

- Deal with sin quickly. The longer you try to hide it, the more it eats you up.

MISSION ACCOMPLISHED!

What did you do? What did you learn?

TRUTH
You can learn a lot from your family tree.

CLIMB A TREE

Admit it: You think some parts of the Bible are just plain boring. The names are hard to pronounce, the language sounds funny, or the rules don't seem to make much sense. You'd choose the action of David and Goliath or Jesus raising people from the dead any day.

Genealogies are often the parts that make our eyes glaze over. They're the family trees of the Bible, and they're filled with funky names. It's easy to wonder why they're even there. But look a little closer at Jesus' family line and it shows God's faithfulness to His people for all those generations. It shows us how God fulfilled His covenant promises to Abraham way, way back in the day. And it shows how even the people we never heard of played their small parts.

The truth is God uses our families to shape us. We can learn a lot from looking at our own family trees. The heritage and characteristics of your ancestors have helped to shape who you are. Whether they followed God faithfully or not, He has been at work in your family. Take a closer look at your past relatives. You'll be surprised what you can learn.

TRIPLE DOG DARE

O Trace your family tree.

O Find your oldest living relative and record him or her telling family stories.

O Make a list of what you want your great-great-grandchildren to know about you.

What did you do? What did you learn?

MISSION ACCOMPLISHED!

TRUTH

You have a real enemy, but victory lies ahead.

YOUR ENEMY

It's like a spy story. It's all about subtlety and deceit. The best way to defeat an enemy is to convince him that you're not an enemy. Then when he least suspects it, you stab him in the back. That's the way the Devil plays.

The truth is that you have a real enemy, but he will one day be defeated. Satan likes to whisper lies. He's been doing it all of history: "It's not that bad. … God didn't really mean it.…It won't hurt to try.… I'm not such a bad guy." Don't let him fool you.

The Devil is a murderous dragon and a serpent who's been waging war against God and His children for all time. He accuses us and attacks us. His future is defeat, but he'll cause as much destruction as he can before the end. See him in all his ugly dishonor and fight back. Your victory comes by following God's commands and sticking close to Jesus.

TRIPLE DOG DARE

- Act out this Scripture passage with your favorite action figures.

- When you face temptation, picture Satan as a terrible creature and defeat him by choosing God's path.

- Live your life today like you know you win in the end.

MISSION ACCOMPLISHED!

What did you do? What did you learn?

TRUTH

God celebrates His children with singing

GOD SINGS ABOUT YOU

It feels great to have someone sing your praises. Not just say "good job," but celebrate you and your accomplishments. And keep going on and on and on …

The truth is that God wants to celebrate over His people with singing. Can you imagine that? God, the Creator of everything, singing about you, celebrating His victory in your life? He delights in His children, including you. That means He finds satisfaction in and enjoys you, and He's not afraid to show it.

Oh, and did you notice that this verse also describes God as a mighty warrior? That's like the top five-star general of the whole world praising and singing songs to celebrate the lowest-ranking military porta-outhouse transporter. Talk about feeling humble and undeserving and filled with encouragement. Remember that the next time you're discouraged.

TRIPLE DOG DARE

O Make up a song about you delighting in and celebrating God.

O Draw a picture of what you think it looks like for God to "rejoice over you with singing."

O Sing the praises of a friend, especially one who's down.

What did you do? What did you learn?

MISSION ACCOMPLISHED!

Daniel Didn't Doubt

You know Daniel's story of the lion's den. It's awesome! Daniel keeps getting promoted because of his honesty and wisdom. The other leaders are jealous and can't come up with a way to bribe or corrupt Daniel. So they get the king to pass a law: Everybody must pray only to the king for the next month. Triple Dog Dare time for Daniel! Does he keep praying to God even though it risks his life, or does he save his skin and check back in with God next month?

It's a no-brainer for Daniel, and you know what happens. He keeps praying to God. The leaders say "Gotcha!" The king can't change the law. Daniel gets dumped in with the lions. God's angel shows up. The angel, Daniel, and the lions spend a peaceful night together. The king rejoices, throws the other leaders to the now-hungry-again lions, and tells everyone to worship God.

Daniel's decision to keep praying was so easy because he had been taking on tough Triple Dog Dares since he was young. He had already been studying God's laws when he was boy, and he stayed true to God even when he was taken away to Babylon. Once there he took the Triple Dog Dare not to go with the flow, choosing to stay healthy and pure by not eating the fancy food sacrificed to idols. And every time Daniel stood strong for what he believed, God came through and blessed him.

TRIPLE DOG DARE!

- Read about Daniel's life and prophecies in the book of Daniel.

- What choices are you facing that risk your social status or position? What do you think God wants you to do?

- List the actions you sense God wants you to take.

YOUR PAGE

I feel loved by God when ...

TRUTH Good nutrition honors God.

ALL YOU CAN EAT

Are you a connoisseur of all-you-can-eat buffets? Do you walk out or roll out afterward? Maybe your idea of health food is pickles on your McBurger. Maybe your favorite vegetable is french fries. Maybe you would have loved the spread laid out for Daniel and his friends. Talk about a royal feast! It was straight from the table of the most powerful king in the world, and he was eatin' good.

The truth is that the easiest foods usually aren't the best for you. Daniel and his friends chose to stick to their convictions because the king's food was sacrificed to idols. They chose vegetables and water over the Babylonian equivalent of steak and lobster. They trusted God, chose discipline, took care of their bodies, and ended up the healthiest of all the other young men in the palace.

You don't have to give up steak and lobster, but how's your vegetable intake? You might need to put down the fries (french fries or other fried objects) and pick up more fruit. You live in a time with more knowledge and more dining options than ever. Eating wisely is more than a physical choice; it's a spiritual choice. It's taking care of the body God gave you, and that's a way to worship.

TRIPLE DOG DARE

O Write down everything you eat today. How healthy is it?

O Help grocery shop. Spend more time in the produce aisle than the microwaveable aisle. Better yet, go to a farmer's market.

O Eat a rainbow. Put more colorful foods and less fried browns on your plate.

What did you do? What did you learn?

MISSION ACCOMPLISHED!

TRUTH

You can train your eyes to avoid lust.

ATTACK OF THE EYES

Girls will soon go from gross to *wow* if it hasn't happened already. Once you start to become a teenager, you probably won't be able to get enough of looking at them. It's a normal thing. It's the way God made guys. But sometimes it will feel like your eyes and body ambush you, and all you can think about are girls and their bodies. That's called lust; it's kind of like an intense desire or a selfish greed for another person.

The truth is that you can learn to control your eyes and avoid lust. It starts with a decision ahead of time. Job called it a covenant—a serious commitment. Then it takes practice and discipline to form a good habit.

See, your eyes and brain will naturally say *ka-ching!* when you see a beautiful girl or a woman. That's natural. The trick is to move your eyes away before you're staring, gawking, and feeling selfish and greedy about that girl. "Bouncing the eyes" is what one great book, *Every Young Man's Battle,* calls it. There will be times you fail, but don't give up. Practice like you practice baseball or trumpet. Build a strong visual habit not to look at girls with lust, and you'll be avoiding temptation and keeping your mind and body pure. That's worshipping God with your body.

TRIPLE DOG DARE

- Make a battle plan for your eyes. Write it down.

- Avoid any places that make you lust, from cheerleading practice to websites or friends' houses.

- Thank God for the way He made you. Commit your body to Him.

MISSION ACCOMPLISHED!

What did you do? What did you learn?

JAMES 4:13–16

TRUTH
God knows your future. Seek Him when you make your plans.

INCLUDE THE ULTIMATE PLANNER

Do you know what you want to be when you grow up? Do you know where you want to go to college? Where you want to live? How about next year? Are you going to play on the team or in the band? Be elected a class officer? Grow two feet taller?

The truth is that only God can see what will really happen in the future. He gives us many gifts and abilities and lots of room to make decisions about how to use them. But He also wants us to remember the source of everything—Him. That keeps us humble and thankful. It also reminds us that when things aren't going the way we expected, God is still in control. Talk to Him about your plans and desires. Trust Him to guide you and take care of you even if things don't work out like you thought they would.

TRIPLE DOG DARE

- Have a conversation with God about your plans. Ask what He wants.

- Don't have plans? Make one for this year. Pray as you do. What do you want to accomplish?

- Make a list of your gifts, talents, and abilities. Write ideas how to use them.

What did you do? What did you learn?

MISSION ACCOMPLISHED!

TRUTH Our lives give off a smell—hopefully of God's love and goodness.

MMM, YOU SMELL GOOD

A steak sizzling on a grill. Steaming homemade bread. Popping, smoking kettle corn. Catch a whiff of those and your stomach automatically screams, "*That's* what I want. Now!" Smell is powerful. It can change our moods and make us hungry.

Unfortunately, body-spray companies—you know the ones—spend millions to convince you that their smell-in-a-can will make you irresistible to girls. (If that doesn't sound good to you yet, it will in a few years.) It's smart to avoid body odor, but don't let the marketers fool you—they're paid to make you want to give them your money. However, girls will not flock to you no matter what you spray all over you. And if you spray it on too strong, they might just run the other way.

The truth is that your life gives off a smell, either fresh and appealing or bitter and rotting. Girls will be attracted to your kindness, sincerity, and willingness to stand up for underdogs and for what's right. God wants to put that kind of smell, His kind of smell, inside us—the kind that makes others say, "*That's* what I want. Now!"

TRIPLE DOG DARE

O Go without any body spray or cologne this week. (Keep the deodorant, though.) Pay attention to your spiritual smell.

O Don't buy the body spray. Give the money to church or another group that helps people.

O Take a smell test. What do you reek of? Write down one way to smell good.

MISSION ACCOMPLISHED! What did you do? What did you learn?

TRUTH

We'll take a beating in this life, but Jesus inside us will win in the end.

THE COMEBACK KID

Have you ever seen the old *Rocky* movies, with Sylvester Stallone as a boxer? Talk about sequels—there are six movies altogether. And they're all basically about the same thing: the comeback. At some point in every movie, Rocky Balboa is taking a beating of some sort, usually in the ring by a bigger or stronger foe. Just when you think there's absolutely no way any human could withstand another blow, Rocky somehow fights his way back to victory. Awesome stuff!

The truth is we're more like Rocky than we realize—because we have Jesus inside, we can endure whatever life throws at us and come out on the winning end. There will be times when we feel attacked, crushed, and even defeated, but ultimately we'll experience Jesus' victory. Sometimes we'll taste that victory quickly. Sometimes we won't see the win until we reach heaven. Either way, keep on fighting. With God you're the comeback kid!

TRIPLE DOG DARE

- Today's the day you start your comeback. Decide now to keep fighting!

- Ask your dad to watch *Rocky* with you.

- Take a victory lap. Run a mile and pray.

What did you do? What did you learn?

MISSION ACCOMPLISHED

Josiah, the Good Boy-King

How would you like to be king? No, really, as in supreme ruler of all the land? That dream came true for Josiah when he was eight years old. Talk about a Triple Dog Dare!

Josiah didn't have good examples to follow. His grandfather had been a wicked king who led the nation to worship idols for decades, and Josiah's father did the same—before he was murdered after being king for only two years. But when Josiah was sixteen, he began to follow God and lead his people back to God's ways. He learned as he went, and when King Josiah was twenty-six, the priests rediscovered God's Law during renovation of the temple.

It was a new Triple Dog Dare for Josiah: listen and follow God's Law now that he could finally read and learn it clearly. Josiah wasted no time. He humbled himself and confessed his and his nation's sins to God. He taught the law to the entire population and turned his country back to God's ways. He stayed true to God the rest of his life. He gives us an example that we can learn to follow God no matter what our relatives before us have done.

TRIPLE DOG DARE!

- Read about Josiah in 2 Kings 22—23 and 2 Chronicles 34—35.

- What would you do if you suddenly became the president or leader of your country right now?

- Fill in these lists:

GOOD AND BAD EXAMPLES IN MY LIFE:

WAYS I SHOULD FOLLOW THEM OR NOT:

YOUR PAGE

Draw a picture of a creature created in your imagination.

TRUTH
Be a good sport, even if you dominate.

TAME THE TRASH TALK

You hate it if you've been on the wrong side of an arrogant winner or a trash-talker. It's one thing for a player or team to celebrate and be happy about scoring, making a good play, or winning. But it's flat-out obnoxious for a player or team to point and taunt and rub it in.

The truth is God says no gloating. It honors Him to be a good sport on the field and in life. Be excited when you score or win, but be a good winner. Beat your opponent with your best play, but leave out the trash talk. Be happy when you get a good gift, but don't rub it in your sister's face. Be satisfied with a good grade, but don't brag about how easy it was.

Why? Because it all comes back around. You won't win every game. You won't shut out every team. You won't ace every test, and you won't always get the best gift. Then people will treat you the way you treated them.

TRIPLE DOG DARE

- O Say thanks to God whenever you score, win, or get a good grade.

- O Tell your team you're all going to play and celebrate like good sports.

- O Congratulate other players when they make a good play.

What did you do? What did you learn?

MISSION ACCOMPLISHED!

1 THESSALONIANS 5:16–18

Prayer is an all-the-time attitude.

KEEP PRAYING

It sounds impossible, doesn't it? Pray continually … like, don't stop. Like do it all the time. But how would you ever do your homework or answer your teacher's questions?

Hmmm, it could make a good excuse though. "Sorry, Mom, I can't take out the trash, I'm praying … Clean my room tomorrow? Nope, still praying then, too … Ooh, yeah, piano practice—can't make that one either, all booked up praying." Don't think that's gonna fly with Mom and Dad.

The truth is that prayer is also an attitude, an awareness of God. And that's something we can have all the time.

Think of it like radio waves. They're all around us all the time, but we only hear them when we turn on and tune in the radio. And then we listen in the background while we do all sorts of other activities. God wants us to stay tuned in to Him all the time—remembering Him, looking and listening for Him at home, at school, on the bus, during practice, all the time. He's with us in all those places. Tune in and pay attention.

TRIPLE DOG DARE

- Get a symbol—a ring, wrist band, or drawing on your hand—to remind you of God's presence every time you see it.

- When you hear your watch chime every hour or the school bell ring, say hi and thanks to God.

- Silently ask God to help your friends whenever you think of or see them.

MISSION ACCOMPLISHED!

What did you do? What did you learn?

TRUTH

God says the way to get even is with kindness.

PAYBACK TIME

Some people can make you so mad! A pesky little brother or a mean girl whose comments make you feel stupid in front of the whole class. Your face burns and steam blows out of your ears (at least it *feels* like it). The only thing you can think about is getting them back!

It just seems fair, doesn't it? Somebody does you wrong, you do them wrong right back. After all, revenge is the stuff of legends. Whole movies and books are based on it.

The truth is God says it's up to Him to pay back wrongs, not us. He sees every little thing that happens on earth: every insult, every hit, every time somebody takes the credit for your hard work. Sometimes the perpetrators get caught and get their punishment right away; sometimes it seems like they go free. But one day God will judge all of us and make every wrong right. In the meantime, Jesus said the best revenge is overcoming bad with good.

TRIPLE DOG DARE

- Return an insult with a compliment.

- Forgive the person you most want revenge against. Ask God to take care of him or her.

- Give a small gift to your brother or sister or the kid who gets on your nerves.

What did you do? What did you learn?

MISSION ACCOMPLISHED!

ECCLESIASTES 12:1

TRUTH
Now is the time to seek and walk with God.

NOW!

It doesn't get any easier. Maybe the peer pressure fades a little, but it's still there, just more subtle. You can build up more experience at avoiding temptations over time, but you also gain access to even more temptations. Yes, school and body changes and girls can be distracting now, but they snowball even bigger in the future into work and bills and family relationships.

The truth is now is the time to build a solid relationship with God. He is the only reliable foundation for life. Start getting to know Him while you're young, and keep growing closer to Him. It will save you lots of scars and trouble down the road. And becoming best friends with Jesus now will help you maintain that close friendship with Him when you're an adult. He'll help you walk through the distractions and growing pains, and He'll bring meaning to your life all along the way.

TRIPLE DOG DARE

○ Use your youthful energy for God. Serve Him by serving other people. Pick three ways this week.

○ Ask your mom and dad how they got to know Jesus through their lifetimes.

○ Tell a friend about Jesus this week.

MISSION ACCOMPLISHED!

What did you do? What did you learn?

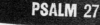

FRIDAY

TRUTH

God helps you overcome any fear.

BIGGER THAN FEAR

What are you afraid of? The dark, bullies, death, embarrassment, speaking in front of a crowd, disease, terrorist attack, losing, your parents getting divorced, enclosed spaces, heights, failing, getting bad grades, letting people down, alien invasion?

The truth is no matter who or what scares you, God is much greater. He can calm your fear and help you overcome any challenge. Psalm 27 reminds us that God gives us confidence. *Attack* comes in verses two and three, a whole army's worth. But the psalmist, King David, focuses our *attention* in verses four through six and leads us to *action:* turning to God, worshipping, and asking for His help. What good does it do? It brings *assurance* that we will see God's goodness. That truth brings comfort and strength—enough to defeat any fear. Walk through Psalm 27 with God the next time you're feeling afraid.

TRIPLE DOG DARE

- Pray through Psalm 27 about anything that's bothering you.

- Rewrite Psalm 27 in your own words.

- Talk to a parent or friend about something you're feeling afraid of.

What did you do? What did you learn?

MISSION ACCOMPLISHED!

Live Life to the Fullest

"The thief comes only to steal and kill and destroy; I have come that they may have life, and have it to the full" (John 10:10).

Other Bible translations call it "rich and satisfying life" (NLT), "[life] to the full" (AB), and "in the fullest possible way" (NIrV). It's all the same idea: Jesus wants us to experience good life in every way. He wants to guide you through awesome adventures. Some of those will surprise you, but many you can choose. And you've got most of your life ahead to accomplish them. So what do you want to do? Play tuba or electric guitar? Visit the moon? Ski across Antarctica? Explore the sea floor? Read the entire Bible? Write a book? Discover a cure for cancer? Dream big and don't hold back—then go for it!

TRIPLE DOG DARE!

Make a life list: things you want to do, be, see, explore, learn, visit, and experience before you die.

TRIPLE DOG BONUS

Draw pictures of yourself accomplishing your goals.

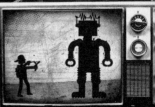

YOUR PAGE

I am ...

TRUTH

God calls us to respect authorities even if we don't agree with them.

FREEDOM OF GOOD SPEECH

You can go off about a teacher or principal you don't like. You can say whatever you want about the president. You can tell jokes about the police. You enjoy freedom of speech in our country, so nobody will arrest or kill you. But that doesn't mean you won't get in trouble for your words, and it doesn't mean you're free to disobey authority figures you don't like.

The truth is that God wants us to respect authorities even if we don't agree with them. That means even our speech to or about them should be respectful—no calling names or making untrue accusations. You can tell someone you don't agree with his opinion without attacking him and calling him a jerk or lunatic.

Remember that rules are put in place to protect you and to look out for the good of everyone, and it's the job of your teacher or mayor or parents to help you learn to follow those rules. Show respect for the people in charge, and you'll find it's much easier to get along with them and the rules.

TRIPLE DOG DARE

○ Tell your buddies to punch you in the arm if you complain about a teacher.

○ Pay your parents five dollars every time you call someone names.

○ Apologize to an authority figure you've had trouble with and tell her you respect the job she's doing.

What did you do? What did you learn?

MISSION ACCOMPLISHED!

TRUTH

God wants us to give our best to the very end.

FINISH STRONG

Hit the walk-off homer in extra innings. Break the tape in a photo finish. Catch the Hail-Mary pass on fourth and ten with no time left on the clock. Head in the golden goal. Work every problem to pass the final exam. Keep going when the odds are stacked against you, and fight till the finish.

The truth is God wants us to give our best to the very end. That goes for life in general and for the responsibilities and contests we face every day. Don't quit. Stay faithful. Give your best. Practice to get better. Study to learn. Get backup when you fail. And enjoy the rewards: the satisfaction of a job well done, good consequences, victory, good grades, the fun of finishing—and God's rewards in heaven someday. Live Paul's words every day and plan to go to your death with them on your lips: "I have fought the good fight, I have finished the race, I have kept the faith."

TRIPLE DOG DARE

- Read and say 2 Timothy 4:7 each night this week. Live each day so it's true.

- Draw comic strips showing the spiritual highlight plays from your day.

- Don't quit. Keep going until you fulfill your commitment.

MISSION ACCOMPLISHED!

What did you do? What did you learn?

TRUTH

Words of blessing are powerful. Share them often.

UNLEASH YOUR WORDS

It must have been one amazing scene! Picture yourself there. You were hanging out watching this crazy prophet guy, John the Baptizer, dunk people in the river when Jesus walks up. He wants to be baptized too, so John agrees. Then it happens. This voice—God's voice!—comes booming out of the sky and says, "You are my Son, whom I love; with you I am well pleased." Unbelievable!

The truth is words of blessing are powerful, so powerful it seems even Jesus needed them. He was just starting the mission He came to earth for, but He'd been here for thirty years. God the Father told Jesus He was proud of Him in a way that let everyone around know, "Hey, that's My boy!" Then immediately after that Jesus went into the wilderness for forty days with no food to confront the Devil face-to-face. He must have been looking to those words from God to encourage Him then.

We can share powerful words of blessing too. The kind that build others up and include them. The kind that say "I'm proud of you" and "What you did was awesome." That kind can blow somebody away.

TRIPLE DOG DARE

- Watch for ways to tell somebody he's awesome every day this week.

- Speak a kind word to someone you don't know every day at school.

- Find three things to praise your brothers or sisters about this week.

What did you do? What did you learn?

MISSION ACCOMPLISHED!

TRUTH

God doesn't want empty praise; He wants action for justice.

NO EMPTY WORDS

We're good at going through the motions. Go to church. Sing praise songs. Pray before meals. Answer the questions in Sunday school. It's all well and good, but if that's all God's getting from you—then He's sick of it.

The truth is that God wants more than empty words; He wants us to obey and to seek justice. *Justice like becoming a cop, lawyer, or judge?* No, anyone can do justice. It's righting a wrong, or at least trying to. Isaiah gives us a couple examples: encourage the oppressed, defend orphans, and stand up for widows—all big-time underdogs in Bible times and even still today. God wants us to look out for people who need help. He wants us to stop people from being used or taken advantage of. He wants us to stand up for what's right. He wants us to get our hands dirty living out His love for other people. Without action, our worship is just empty words.

TRIPLE DOG DARE

- Make a list of people or groups in need. Come up with one idea to help; then do it.

- Have a car wash, bake sale, or lemonade stand to raise money to give to a ministry helping orphans, widows, poor or oppressed people.

- Write a letter to your elected leaders asking them to change unfair laws or create more fair ones.

MISSION ACCOMPLISHED!

What did you do? What did you learn?

TRUTH

God wants us to give to Him so we learn to be unselfish.

TRY A TITHE

What's the first thing you do when you get your allowance? Or get paid? Or get a birthday check? What's your most important possession? Are you willing to share it? Do you spend time helping around the house? Or volunteering at church or in your community to help people in need? Or are you all *mine, mine, mine* with your life?

The truth is giving to God first helps us to remember who owns what (uh, that'd be God who owns everything). And it teaches us to be unselfish, starting with our stuff and spreading to how we treat other people in general. God called it a tithe when He told the Israelites in the Bible to give the first tenth of their crops and herds (their wealth) to Him. He didn't need it. But He knew they did. And so do we. Give first to God, and keep being unselfish with family and friends and complete strangers.

TRIPLE DOG DARE

- Tithe. Set aside 10 percent of whatever money you get and give it to church as soon as you can.

- Give your time and self. Volunteer at church or in your neighborhood. Start with little kids' Sunday school or an older neighbor who needs help around the house.

- Give more than 10 percent. Look around. Find someone who needs something and give it. Don't even tell them it's from you.

What did you do? What did you learn?

MISSION ACCOMPLISHED!

MAKE TRIPLE DOG TRACKS

Favorite Fruit

I love fruit! Talk about a gift from nature—it's sweet and good for you. What's your favorite? Apple or orange? Maybe something more exotic like a star fruit or pomegranate? Whatever kind you like, fruit is the part of a plant or tree that we can use. Without oranges, an orange tree might as well be any other tree. A fruit tree has to grow fruit to reach its potential and be what it was meant to be—just like a Christian has to grow actions to live out what God has made him to be. That's why Paul talked about the fruit of the Spirit. It's a list of qualities that God wants to grow in our lives. They show our potential and are sweet and nutritious to other people around us.

TRIPLE DOG DARE!

Complete the crossword puzzle. You can find all your answer choices in Galatians 5:22–23. But where can you find them in your life? Answers to the puzzle are at the end of the book.

Across
1. moral excellence
3. affection and devotion; God's main quality
5. being able to keep your head
7. calm, quiet, and lack of fighting
8. staying true

Down
1. avoiding hurt or painful aggression
2. friendliness and generosity
4. stronger than happiness; God's shows up when you'd least expect it
6. the ability to wait

YOUR PAGE

When my mom was a kid my age, she liked to ...

TRUTH

We need to take time to be quiet and listen to God.

BE QUIET

You are surrounded by noise. Do you even notice? You've got friends at school, radios in the car, iPod earbuds everywhere, phones ringing, texts bleeping, computers playing, video games exploding, traffic roaring, gas-pump video screens yelling, jets sonic booming, and TVs blaring. We've gotten so used to all the noise that it sounds weird if we're in a truly quiet place. Are you surprised that it's hard to hear God?

The truth is we need to turn off the noise to be quiet and listen to God. There's nothing wrong with sound. It's a vital part of our world. But noise distracts us like static. It keeps us from being able to hear what's important. It's up to us to turn down the volume. Our spirits need silence on a regular, even daily, basis. Quiet stillness lets us listen for God's voice. It reminds us of our place— how small we are before our ginormous Creator. And it lets God's peace calm and flow into us. Try it. Be quiet.

TRIPLE DOG DARE

○ Take a sound fast for a week. Choose quiet every chance you get. Turn off the iPod, radio, TV, and game console.

○ Spend five minutes a day in complete silence. Read a Bible verse first and think about it through that time.

○ Ask your parents to take you to true quiet. Drive into the country. Find a place far away and simply listen.

What did you do? What did you learn?

MISSION ACCOMPLISHED!

TRUTH

We all make mistakes. Be smart enough to learn from yours.

DON'T BE AN ANIMAL

What separates us humans from animals—besides opposable thumbs? Okay, most monkeys have those too. I'm going for our ability to reason. You know, figure things out. Think things through. Learn from our mistakes.

Usually we're much smarter about what we put into our mouths, too. Take dogs for example. If you have one, you've probably seen him eat some extremely nasty stuff—including vomit. (Please tell me you've never hurled into a bowl, then—bottoms up!—chugged it back down!)

The truth is that if you don't learn from your mistakes, you're basically doing the same thing. We all mess up and do things wrong. Stupid things. And then we pay the price. It's part of being human. But God has given us the ability to learn from those errors and sins, and He gives us the strength to make smart decisions. Don't be an animal!

TRIPLE DOG DARE

○ Ask your mom or dad what you need to learn to stay out of trouble and follow their advice.

○ Do you own something that tempts you into trouble every time? Throw it out.

○ Confess a problem to a friend or mentor and ask him to check up on you each week. Pay him a dollar for every time you messed up again.

MISSION ACCOMPLISHED!

What did you do? What did you learn?

JEREMIAH 29:11

TRUTH
God has plans and purpose for your life.

GOD'S GOT PLANS

It's no fun if your family forgets your birthday. Helloooo. It's *only* your special day of the year. The one when people are supposed to celebrate you. Talk about a downer—until you walk into the room with all your family, friends, and favorite people yelling "Surprise!" and singing "Happy Birthday." They knew all along!

The truth is God has plans and a purpose for your life, and He never forgets. Even when life looks bad, He wants to give you hope and good things for the future. That was His message to the Israelites after seventy years of bad days. They were captives in Babylon, but God reminded them He hadn't forgotten them. He was still there for them, and He knew how He wanted to help them. They needed to turn to Him and trust Him and know that He hadn't forgotten.

The same goes for us. You matter to God. He never forgets you. He gives your life purpose. Seek Him and trust His plans.

TRIPLE DOG DARE

- Write down your plans for the next year. Where do you want to go? What do you want to do? Talk to God about them.

- Let a friend know he matters by giving him a small gift this week, even if it isn't his birthday.

- Tell your friends God has plans for their lives. Ask what they hope those plans are.

What did you do? What did you learn?

MISSION ACCOMPLISHED!

TRUTH

Wisdom starts with respecting God.

FEAR THIS

You know that look in your dad's eye? The one that says, "You better shape up. Now." It'll put you back in line—if you're smart. Of course, you're not always smart, and then you know what's coming: punishment, discipline, correction. It's no fun. It hurts. But do you ever doubt your dad's love for you? Do you love him any less? No. You still love him and have a healthy respect for him.

The truth is that kind of respect for God leads to wisdom. Fearing God isn't being scared of Him. Fearing God is admiring and respecting Him. It's being in awe of Him. Those feelings mix with love for Him and remind us of God's greatness and power. They help us obey Him by reminding us that His commands have our best interests at heart. They remind us that His discipline is for our good.

The more we catch on and learn, the wiser we become. And the wiser we become, the more we understand God's ways, shape our hearts like His, and enjoy His blessings. Don't be afraid of just anything. Fear God.

TRIPLE DOG DARE

○ Tell your dad three things you respect about him.

○ Make a list of things you respect God for.

○ The next time you're disciplined, write yourself a story about how you got in trouble. Look for a way to change the ending, and do that next time instead.

MISSION ACCOMPLISHED!

What did you do? What did you learn?

TRUTH
You can learn a lot from the hall of famers.

HALL OF FAMERS

The Hall of Fame is the home of the records and the greatest of the all-stars. Every sport and every music style has its own hall of fame. It's where the exceptional are immortalized. It's not enough to just be good to make the HOF. You've got to be great.

The truth is the Bible has its own hall—the Hall of Faith—and its members are the men and women to learn from. These are the people from the beginning of time who trusted God even when things didn't look good. They held onto God's promises and acted like they believed them. And God rewarded them.

But they had something in common with you and me. They never saw Jesus. They died before Jesus lived. We live after Jesus. All of us must trust that what God says is true. Believe like the Hall of Faithers. Act like you know God's promises are true. Follow the example of the heroes.

TRIPLE DOG DARE

- Learn as many Bible verses as you know sports or music statistics.

- Read more about a Bible hero and look for ways to copy him or her.

- Plan your induction to the HOF. What great things will you do for God?

What did you do? What did you learn?

MISSION ACCOMPLISHED!

MAKE TRIPLE DOG TRACKS

Every Mother's Son

"Children, obey your parents because you belong to the Lord, for this is the right thing to do. 'Honor your father and mother.' This is the first commandment with a promise: If you honor your father and mother, 'things will go well for you, and you will have a long life on the earth'" (Ephesians 6:1–3 NLT).

Your mom probably does good things for you every day that you don't even realize or think about. She probably drives you around a lot, makes good meals, and washes your clothes. She shapes and teaches you with her words and actions. You know she loves you, but have you let her know how much you love her?

Your relationship with your mom is one of the most important in your life. How you treat her is probably how you'll one day treat your wife and kids. Get in the habit now of expressing gratitude and love for your mom every day.

TRIPLE DOG DARE!

Hang out with your mom. Ask her to spend time together, and put it on your schedules.

Things I want to do with Mom:

Ways I want to be like Mom:

Ways I don't want to be like Mom:

Ways I'm already like Mom:

Things I can learn from Mom or ask her about:

TRIPLE DOG BONUS

Show your mom these lists and talk about them.

YOUR PAGE

⟨Do whatever you want with this space. Be creative!⟩

MONDAY

TRUTH
Your enemy will eat you up. Learn self-control to beat him.

WATCH YOURSELF

Have you ever seen a show where a character is about to get eaten by a wild beast or captured by some monster—and he doesn't even have a clue he's in danger? Some people are like that when it comes to the Devil. They have no idea there's any danger nearby. They try whatever other people offer them—maybe cigarettes, alcohol, or drugs—without ever thinking they'll get addicted. They do whatever they feel like whether it's wise, wrong, or even illegal.

The truth is the Devil is like a mean, hungry lion hunting for whomever he can sink his jaws into, and he'll use whatever he can to devour us. The truth is also that you don't have to give him a chance.

Don't be that clueless character. Pay attention and be ready. Ask God to help you learn self-control. Decide now what activities you will say no to; then it will be easier to resist the temptation when it pops up. With God's help, you can beat the hungry lion.

TRIPLE DOG DARE

O End a bad habit. Write down what it is, how you can stop, and whom you will ask for help.

O Make a plan. Write it down. What will you do when someone offers you drugs, cigarettes, or alcohol?

O Avoid your biggest temptation. Where and when do you stumble? How can you avoid it in the first place?

What did you do? What did you learn?

MISSION ACCOMPLISHED!

TRUTH

God uses everyone for His work.

WHAT DO YOU WANT TO BE?

You don't have to be a pastor, youth leader, Sunday school teacher, or missionary. Those are all great things, but there's no such thing as a professional Christian.

The truth is God uses everyone for His work. Sometimes we get confused into thinking some jobs or careers are more spiritual than others. Wrong. For followers of God, every part of life is spiritual, and whatever job we do is a place where God can use us.

Amos was a shepherd, but God sent him with messages to the king. God wants businessmen, builders, mechanics, doctors, lawyers, lifeguards, teachers, soldiers, firefighters, movie producers, musicians, veterinarians, janitors, athletes, you name it—including students. What do you want to be when you grow up? Learn all you can in school now and have fun figuring out what you're good at. Whatever career you choose, use it as a platform to live for God.

TRIPLE DOG DARE

- Make a list of your strengths and weaknesses.

- Make a list of jobs you might like to do someday.

- Ask your mom and dad about their jobs: what they like, don't like, and how God uses them there.

MISSION ACCOMPLISHED!

What did you do? What did you learn?

GENESIS 2:15

TRUTH
God gave us the job of taking care of His creation.

CARE FOR CREATION

Oil spills are more than ugly. They kill and destroy, gluing birds' wings to uselessness and clogging fishes' gills like cement. You've seen the pictures. You've heard how pollution makes people sick. You've learned how trees fill our air with life-giving oxygen—and how clear-cutting them leads to erosion, flooding, and polluted river systems. Destroying our environment is not being good stewards, or caretakers, of the resources God has given us.

The truth is God gave humans the job of caring for His creation. Our world was part of God's original perfect design. Sin scarred nature just like it scarred people—but that doesn't mean people should keep trashing nature. One day God will restore us and our earth to His perfect designs. In the meantime, we should take care of the animals, plants, and ecosystems around us.

There are many small ways you can do that, but they all begin by replacing selfishness and greed with patience and long-term vision. If you only *take* things from your backyard garden, it will eventually die. If you *give* it water and replenish nutrients in the soil, it will give you healthy foods for a long time. The earth is the same. Be God's gardener.

TRIPLE DOG DARE

- ○ Reduce, reuse, recycle. Ask your parents to get recycling pickup at your house.

- ○ Save energy by turning off lights and replacing incandescent light bulbs with compact fluorescent ones.

- ○ Don't let the water run while you brush your teeth.

What did you do? What did you learn?

MISSION ACCOMPLISHED!

MATTHEW 7:12

TRUTH

Treat other people the way you want to be treated.

GET GOLDEN

You've heard it since you were little. It's Rule No. 1 for dealing with other people: friends, enemies, allies, competitors, strangers, and passersby. Sometimes it's easy, like when it's with our friends whom we know and like and trust. Sometimes it's hard, like when it's with somebody who's rude or unknown or just plain mean.

The truth is God calls us to treat other people the way we want to be treated, no matter who they are or what they're like. There's good reason we call it the Golden Rule. It works. Want to have good friends? Be a good friend. Having trouble getting along with someone? Treat him better and see if he doesn't start treating you better too—a little kindness goes a long way. People are drawn to kindness and generosity. Think about it. How do you like to be treated? What makes you feel good? Probably encouragement, praise, sharing, patience, and laughter. Give those things to others.

TRIPLE DOG DARE

- List the ways other people make you feel good. Treat others with those traits.

- Go all day speaking only positive words, not negative, complaining, or insulting ones.

- What would make your day? Do it to make a friend's day.

MISSION ACCOMPLISHED!

What did you do? What did you learn?

TRUTH
God's grace isn't a free pass to sin.

LIFE, NOT LOOPHOLE

Have you ever shared your game console with somebody then gotten bugged because he wouldn't give it back? Or generously loaned your new bike to a friend—who brought it back scuffed and scratched? Nobody likes to be taken advantage of. God included.

The truth is that God's forgiveness doesn't give us a free pass to sin. It might be tempting to view His grace (the eternal life we don't deserve) as a loophole: *You mean I can do whatever I want, then just say I'm sorry and get away with it?* Nope.

God has given us a new life in Him, and He wants us to live like it. Part of the reason He wants us to avoid sin is to save us from pain and hurtful consequences on earth. Those don't go away. Lie and you still have to clean up the mess of broken friendships. Murder and you still go to jail. So live like you're dead to sin. Obey God because you're so thankful for the life He's given you.

TRIPLE DOG DARE

- Confess any ways you've been trying to take advantage of God.

- Get help to beat a sin that's dragging you down. Ask your dad, mom, or best friend to check up on your progress.

- Draw a comic strip of you dying with Jesus, then resurrecting to a new life.

What did you do? What did you learn?

MISSION ACCOMPLISHED!

FROM THE TRIPLE DOG POUND

The Mighty Warriors: David Couldn't Have Done It Without Them

Behind every great leader are a whole lot of people working hard and making things happen. King David was no exception. Everybody knows about David, but have you ever heard of Josheb-Basshebeth, Shammah, Abishai, or Benaiah? They and about thirty others were David's mighty warriors, his trusted companions and soldiers.

The mighty warriors were loyal and brave and willing to risk their lives for their king. If they were afraid, they didn't let it keep them from defeating enemy armies. They fought bravely and stood their ground, even when other soldiers fled and even when they were outnumbered. And they won many great victories for David, Israel, and God.

Are you a leader? Pay attention to the people around you. You won't get far without friends you can count on. Treat them well, and they'll be willing to come through for you when you need it. Are you a doer who would rather work quietly and let somebody point you in the right direction? Give it all you've got, but don't be afraid to speak up with your ideas. You may not ever be king, but you can always be a mighty warrior.

TRIPLE DOG DARE!

O Read about David's warriors in 2 Samuel 23 and 1 Chronicles 11. Then read those books of the Bible and look for their names.

O Who are the authorities and leaders in your life you should follow?

O What battles and challenges are you facing? Make a battle plan. List steps you can take to win.

MY BATTLE PLAN

I wish ...

TRUTH Hypocrisy makes God sick.

NOBODY LIKES A HYPOCRITE

Some graves look like miniature castles on the outside. They're big and polished and fancy. But inside they still hold dead bodies: rotting corpses or skeletons.

The truth is that a hypocrite is like those graves: shiny on the outside, dead and stinky within. Nobody likes hypocrisy, including Jesus. He unleashed harsh words on the Pharisees, the religious leaders when He was on earth, for talking and looking spiritual while their hearts and attitudes were selfish and sinful.

If you're going to talk the talk, walk the walk. People can see if what you say is true by the way you live your life. Back up your words with consistent actions. That doesn't mean you won't make mistakes. Just make sure you don't jump on other people's cases for making mistakes. If you say you love God, love people around you.

TRIPLE DOG DARE

- ○ Where is your attitude stinking? Clean it up.

- ○ Ask for forgiveness if you've accused someone of something but then done the same thing.

- ○ Choose humility. Forgive quickly. Show compassion.

What did you do? What did you learn?

MISSION ACCOMPLISHED!

TRUTH

Witnessing is simply sharing what you know.

NO WRONG ANSWER

"Do you swear to tell the truth, the whole truth, and nothing but the truth, so help you God?" You've seen enough shows to know that's how a witness is sworn in at a legal trial. A witness is someone called to the court to tell what he knows or saw. That's all he has to do.

The truth is witnessing about Jesus is telling what you know about God working in your life, It's not giving a speech or reciting a magic formula guaranteed to make other people believe. It doesn't have to include Bible verses, though sometimes it can. Witnessing is just you talking about your life with God.

The hardest part can be getting started, but just use what comes naturally. Ask about a friend's life. What's going on in your life? Ask how you can pray for someone. Comment on the amazing nature around you that God created. Ask someone what he thinks about the theory of evolution in science class. Tell about a cool answer to prayer. Be yourself and be honest about how you see God working.

TRIPLE DOG DARE

- Be ready. Write a few sentences about how you gave your life to Jesus and what you're learning about God now. Practice telling it to your mom or dad.

- Ask a friend today how you can pray for him.

- Ask a friend what he or she believes about God.

MISSION ACCOMPLISHED!

What did you do? What did you learn?

TRUTH The reward is worth the fight.

PRIZE FIGHTER

The belt would pull you over it's so huge. Have you seen those boxing trophies? They're not trophies. They're belts, ginormous belts, with plaques and lettering. They'd set off a metal detector from a boxing ring away. Even on a mongo-huge heavyweight champion, they take up lots of real estate. Championship boxing belts are serious prizes.

The truth is you have an even better prize waiting for you at the end of your faith fight. It's a priceless treasure. It's perfect life with God that never ends, along with what the Bible calls a "crown of righteousness" (2 Timothy 4:8). That's a serious jewel that blows away a heavyweight belt.

It comes from pressing on toward the goal of winning God's prize. It takes endurance to keep running and keep battling. It takes discipline to train your spirit in the ways of God's warfare. It takes patience to train your ear to hear your Commander's voice. It takes humility to ask for God's strength. It takes courage to stand strong in the face of your ugly enemy. It takes persistence to clean your wounds and get back up after losing a skirmish. But when God hands you that amazing prize, you'll realize it's totally worth it!

TRIPLE DOG DARE

- Write a paragraph about how you picture heaven.
- Draw a picture of your heavenly rewards.
- Read about D-Day, the hard-fought battle that led to the Allies' victory in World War II. Think about how it's like our spiritual battles.

What did you do? What did you learn?

MISSION ACCOMPLISHED!

TRUTH

God wants to trade His peace for your worry.

YOUR BEST TRADE EVER

What's your best trade ever? Half a PB&J for a chocolate pudding Snack Pack? You can do better than that. A Mark Prior baseball card for a rookie Albert Pujols? Now you're getting warmer. Your magic rock collection for your neighbor's go-cart? Um, you need to take that one back before you're arrested for stealing.

The truth is God gives you the best trade ever: He gives you His peace for your problems and worry. Try it. What's eating at your insides? A girl? A bully? A teacher? A test? Fitting in? Looking cool? Your parents' divorce?

Here's how to make the trade. Pray—talk to God about your problem, but start thanking Him for the good things He's done for you. Focus on who God is. Read your Bible for some reminders. Realize how much bigger He is than your problem. And notice your mind and spirit relaxing. That's God's peace replacing your worry and filling you up. And it's a gift, so you won't even be arrested for stealing!

TRIPLE DOG DARE

- Get to the bottom of it. Make a list to figure out what's eating at you.

- Get help. Talk to your parents about your problem too.

- Eat a peace milkshake. Talk to God to get your worry out and picture the shake as His peace flowing into you. Just do this one once or twice for the visual aid; otherwise *you'll* start to look like a gooey, super-sized milkshake.

MISSION ACCOMPLISHED!

What did you do? What did you learn?

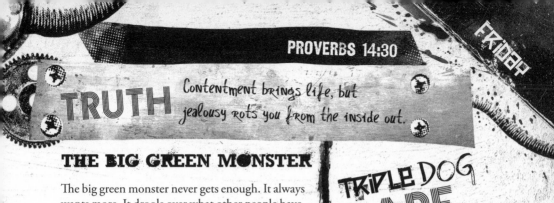

TRUTH Contentment brings life, but jealousy rots you from the inside out.

THE BIG GREEN MONSTER

The big green monster never gets enough. It always wants more. It drools over what other people have. It doesn't care what it has; it's always looking at what it doesn't have. It can roll in a lush, rich pasture, but claim the grass over the fence is definitely greener. It creeps into your spirit and rots you from the inside out if you let it. But there's a way to beat the big green monster.

The truth is contentment is the key to beating jealousy. Yep, jealousy—envy—is the big green monster. It creeps in when you want more and focus on what you don't have. It grows when you can't stop thinking that something he has is better than yours—and you must have it for yourself! That kind of thinking spreads like maggots through your spirit.

Thankfulness and satisfaction flush envy right out of your system. Focusing on all the good you do have and choosing to be happy with it stomps all over the big green monster. It brings your happiness back and returns fun. Choose contentment and choose the good life.

TRIPLE DOG DARE

- Let go of wanting something a friend has. Choose to enjoy what you have.

- Rediscover an old toy, game, song, movie, book, place, or anything you've forgotten.

- Say "I have enough" and ask your friends to bring toys or money for kids in need to your birthday instead of gifts for you.

What did you do? What did you learn?

MISSION ACCOMPLISHED!

David Kept Looking to God

Are you the youngest or smallest guy in your family? Do you ever get overlooked? King David was that guy. Read about it in 1 Samuel 16:1–13. His own dad almost forgot about him. David was the youngest, so he wasn't considered very important—just the kid who took care of the animals. But God wasn't about to let the greatest king of Israel be overlooked, no matter how young he was. God made sure Samuel anointed David as the next king.

David was no stranger to Triple Dog Dares. He killed lions and bears when they tried to attack his sheep. He had to wait patiently and humbly until God's time for him to be king. He had to play the harp for the crazy king he knew he would someday replace. And of course, there was the whole showdown with the giant that the whole army was afraid of. All those were just the beginning.

The Triple Dog Dare that ruled them all for David applies to us, too: See with God's eyes, not man's. David wasn't afraid of wild animals or enemies because he trusted in God to take care of him. He knew God was with him, and he knew God had plans to use him. David didn't always do everything right—remember Bathsheba? But even when he blew it, he eventually confessed his sins and turned back to seek God's heart.

TRIPLE DOG DARE!

O Read about David in 1 Samuel 16—2 Samuel 24. Also read songs and prayers by David in Psalms.

O What are your biggest, scariest obstacles or enemies? How can God overcome them?

O Make a go-for-it list—things you want to do by looking to God and forgetting any fear.

GO FOR IT!

YOUR PAGE

Summer is ...

TRUTH
Life's not fair, but the wicked will get their due.

NOT FAIR

That's not fair! You'd be rich if you had a dollar for every time you've said that.

The truth is, you're right! Life isn't fair. Better get used to it. You get way more than you deserve while kids in other neighborhoods or countries get way less than any kid should have, including food and housing. Evildoers cheat and steal and kill and get away with all sorts of guilty deeds. And terrible things happen to good people through no fault of their own.

But one day God is going to make everything right. He sees every tiny action and event that goes on. When we meet Him in person, we'll all have to account for every action and attitude. If we know Jesus, we'll receive forgiveness and reward. If we've rejected Jesus, we'll get guilt and eternal suffering. That's when wrongs will be made right. The bad guys won't win in the end. The wicked will get what they deserve.

TRIPLE DOG DARE

○ Make a list of life's "unfairnesses" and thank God for His good in your life in the midst of it all.

○ Write a story or make a movie about twins separated at birth and forced to live in different countries. Will good or evil win in the end?

○ Pay your parents a dollar every time you complain that something isn't fair.

What did you do? What did you learn?

MISSION ACCOMPLISHED!

TRUTH

Humility is much stronger than pride.

TRUE STRENGTH IS HUMBLE

We all want to be respected. We want to prove we're tough enough and show we're strong. And sometimes that gets out of hand when everybody's puffing out his chest and ordering others around. When everybody acts like he's da bomb, somebody's going to blow up.

The truth is God wants us to wear humility, not be too big for our britches with pride. He wants us to be confident because we know He is with us. He wants us to be strong without bragging about it. Don't worry; smart people will recognize strength in your actions, and your humility will speak louder than empty boasts.

Start practicing humility by respecting other people, especially those older than you. That doesn't mean you have to do whatever your older brother says. It means you realize you have lots to learn, and you understand that your parents, teachers, coaches, and other adults have a lot to teach you. Don't be full of yourself. Be full of God.

TRIPLE DOG DARE

- Don't join in when the guys start bragging. Compliment another guy for something good you saw him do.

- Write a note of appreciation to your mom, dad, teacher, coach, or grandparent sharing something you respect about him or her.

- Call or go visit your grandparents. Ask them for advice or about how they learned to do something.

MISSION ACCOMPLISHED!

What did you do? What did you learn?

TRUTH — Pure religion might not be what you expect.

REAL RELIGION

How would you describe religion? Maybe the world's major religions come to mind. You know, Christianity, Islam, Hinduism, Judaism. We often think of religion as a system of beliefs to follow God. Okay, so now describe *pure* religion. You might think of Jesus on the cross, believing in Him for the forgiveness of our sins. Excellent and right thoughts. But wait …

The truth is that the Bible says pure religion is taking care of widows and orphans and keeping ourselves unpolluted by the world. Just what you were thinking, right? James is a Bible writer known for putting muscle where his mouth is. He often emphasizes action—as in, it's not good enough to say or think you believe; you've got to show it with your life.

Jesus taught us to love God and to love our neighbors and enemies. James follows that up by reminding us that God cares about us taking care of the people in the most need. We follow God by doing things He cares about and separating ourselves from the things that don't. Connect your hands with your heart.

TRIPLE DOG DARE

- ○ Do yard work (for free) for an elderly neighbor.
- ○ Get a group of friends together to help old people. Paint their porches, or deliver cookies to them in a nursing home.
- ○ Talk to your parents about how your family can help orphans in our country or around the world.

What did you do? What did you learn?

MISSION ACCOMPLISHED!

TRUTH

Discipline leads us to a better life.

HOW TO GET YOUR GOAL

It's not an easy road to _____. Fill in the blank however you want: Become a pro athlete, fly fighter jets, win a scholarship, become president, own a company. If those sound too far away, try these: Make straight As, learn to play an instrument, make the team, or save money for camp. Sleeping in every day, watching lots of TV, eating an endless supply of junk food, or growing roots into your couch won't get you there.

The truth is it takes discipline to accomplish anything worthwhile in life. To reach any goal, we need commitment, training, practice, and hard work. Discipline is the self-control that keeps us on track. It's the ability to say no to immediate distractions that pull us away from what we want in the long haul.

Discipline can be turning off the TV, doing homework first, practicing scales, going to practice instead of the party, saving money instead of spending it, waking up early to read your Bible, or refusing to look at naked pictures because you want to obey God. Discipline isn't always what you feel like doing; it's what you know will pay off later—and better—in life.

TRIPLE DOG DARE

○ Make a plan: What's your goal? List steps to get there.

○ Practice all week without being told.

○ Set your alarm ten minutes earlier to make time to read the Bible and pray.

MISSION ACCOMPLISHED!

What did you do? What did you learn?

TRUTH

Following Jesus is a life of adventure. It's not always safe, but God is always in control.

DANGEROUS FAITH

Does church ever seem boring? Does reading the Bible rank below clipping your toenails on your list of exciting things to do? Do you secretly think your favorite superhero or action star could beat up Jesus?

Sometimes the ways we do church or the ways we're taught to connect with God are, um, let's say *dry*. That's too bad, because God is anything but stale or boring. Even His Word is full of crazy-exciting stories about heroes, battles, and unusual adventures.

The truth is that Jesus' disciples and the early Christians lived dangerous lives. Devoting their lives to Jesus was far from safe. In fact, many were killed because of their beliefs.

We should be thankful that we can worship God without being killed for it. (Many Christians in other countries still do risk death.) But don't be tricked into false safety and comfort. Sometimes doing the right thing, standing up for what we believe, or serving others should make us a little nervous—because grand adventures always do.

TRIPLE DOG DARE

O Read some crazy Bible adventure stories in Acts and Judges.

O Sign up to go on a mission trip with your youth group or family.

O Do something nice for an unpopular kid in a totally unexpected way.

What did you do? What did you learn?

MISSION ACCOMPLISHED!

MAKE TRIPLE DOG TRACKS

Battle Stations

Battles get a lot of space in the Bible, especially the Old Testament. That's when the nation of Israel was claiming the land of Canaan, then being invaded by other empires. Some of the fights are typical warfare of the times with swords, spears, and bows and arrows. Others wouldn't be attempted by any military leader in a million years—unless God told them to. And of course, there's the ultimate battle of good versus evil.

Check out these unique battles:

- The fall of Jericho—The strangest way to fight or to win without actually fighting. Victory by walking in circles so God could show His power. Read it in Joshua 6.

- Gideon's shrinking army—God keeps telling Gideon to get rid of soldiers because his army is too big. Then He sends them to fight the Midianites armed with trumpets, clay jars, and torches. See what happens in Judges 7.

- The sun stands still—So Joshua and his army have enough time to defeat their enemies. Read about it in Joshua 10:1–15.

- Worst odds—You'd think one versus one thousand wouldn't be much of a fight. It wasn't. The Philistines didn't stand a chance against Samson, who was armed with … the jawbone of a donkey. Check it out in Judges 15:9–17.

- The war to end all wars—There's a lot of symbolism, but it's God versus Satan in the final showdown. Follow the action in Revelation 12—22.

TRIPLE DOG DARE!

- Be ready to stand strong for what's right, and remember that "the weapons we fight with are not the weapons of the world" (2 Corinthians 10:4).

- Draw comic strips or maps of these battles.

- What most inspires you to stand strong?

YOUR PAGE

Write a poem about ... anything.

TRUTH
Just listening to God's Word isn't enough. Do what it says.

DON'T FORGET

You've never forgotten what you look like. You've been looking in mirrors since you were tall enough to stand on a bathroom stool, and you know that's you. You might need to look again to see which direction your hair's sticking out or to make sure there's no broccoli hanging out of your teeth. But you always know what color your hair—and your teeth—are.

Reading the Bible or hearing a lesson but not doing what it says is as stupid as looking in the mirror and forgetting what you look like.

The truth is God wants us to do what He says. He doesn't care if we can quote the entire Bible verbatim—it does no good if we don't *do* the words. Listening to someone shout, "Watch out for that speeding bus!" does you absolutely no good if you don't move a muscle. You're pancaked! Get the spatula to scrape you off the road. Listening is good, but action shows you really believe it.

TRIPLE DOG DARE

- What truth have you been ignoring? Do it.

- Take your favorite Bible verse and do something about it today.

- Write out James 1:22 and stick it to your mirror.

What did you do? What did you learn?

MISSION ACCOMPLISHED!

TRUTH

It makes God happy when we get along, especially with our brothers and sisters.

DID NOT, DID TOO

I know you've waged the he's-on-my-side war—yes, the one in the car. And the did-not, did-too battle—it's a close relative of the he-said, she-said game. They're often combined with each other or with any variation of she's-touching-me, am-not, are-too, or nuh-uh, uh-huh. You're probably pretty good at them, maybe even sorry there's not a pro league. (Your parents are glad there's not a pro league.)

It's usually the people closest to us who can get under our skin the most, and it can feel like your bro or sis was put on earth for the sole purpose of driving you absolutely crazy.

The truth is that God has specially created everyone in your family. Even your swamp-thing brother and squealy-priss sister are gifts—not just to your parents but to you, too. It might take a few more years to feel like that, but you can start working on getting along now. You have the power to refresh and revolutionize your entire home!

TRIPLE DOG DARE

- Refuse to play the next round of am-not, are-too. Move away or share the item being argued about.

- Give your sibling one nice compliment a day for the next week.

- Ask your bro or sis the top three ways you annoy them. Write these down. Then write beside each item one way you can stop doing that.

MISSION ACCOMPLISHED!

What's your plan? What did you do?

PSALM 139:13–18

TRUTH God made you one of a kind.

YOU'RE A MASTERPIECE

No one else on earth has the exact same fingerprint as you. Nearly seven billion people and not one exact match! No one looks exactly like you (unless you're an identical twin). No one sounds exactly like you. And no one thinks exactly like you (even if you are an identical twin). There is only one you—both now and in the history of the world.

The truth is God made you exactly how He wanted: unique and special. Your life is a miracle. God put great care into planning you, and He still takes great care as you walk through your days. He didn't cast you out as a reject; He placed His seal of approval on you—even if you do have some differences from most people. He knows exactly what makes you up and exactly what you need, and He's constantly thinking of you, waiting to help. Don't ever forget that you're God's priceless masterpiece.

TRIPLE DOG DARE

- ○ Look in the mirror and say, "I'm a masterpiece," knowing that's exactly how God sees you.

- ○ Make a list of your flaws that bug you. Burn it in the fireplace (with permission), or shred it.

- ○ Take a picture of your fingerprint with your phone. Or color your thumb with a marker or ink pad and press it onto this page for a thumbprint. Look at it when you feel bad about yourself and remember how God sees you.

What did you do? What did you learn?

MISSION ACCOMPLISHED!

PSALM 62:10

Keeping your heart free from your stuff keeps you free.

HOLD ON LOOSELY

Have you ever lost a favorite belonging? It's no fun. When I was five I lost my favorite blanket, the blanket I carried *everywhere* like Charlie Brown's friend Linus (yes, sucking my thumb the whole time). I was devastated. I cried. I moaned. I wailed. I was brokenhearted—because my heart was set on my blankie.

Stuff wears out. Stuff breaks. It gets lost or broken or stolen. It's our responsibility to take care of what we have. Tuning up a bike or cleaning off cleats will help them last longer and work better. But ultimately, it all just doesn't last.

The truth is that God wants our hearts to be focused on what lasts—Himself. You'll have more money and more stuff as you get older. You'll have lots of opportunities and choices about how to get more and how to use it. Thank God for that. Ask for His advice. Use your stuff to make Him happy, and keep your heart free from latching on to what won't last. Start now.

TRIPLE DOG DARE

- Clean up. Get your skateboard out of the dirt and your gear off the ground. Take care of the stuff you have.

- Clean out your closet. Give away anything you haven't used or worn in the past year.

- Share some favorite gear with your brother or sister.

MISSION ACCOMPLISHED! *What did you do? What did you learn?*

TRUTH

Hotheaded friends will rub off on you.

AVOID THE HOTHEADS

There's a reason we call them hotheads. First they get red in the face as if mercury in a thermometer were rising past their eyes. Then the steam starts shooting out of their ears (okay, it just looks like it). Then they blow like a volcano, and spit and sweat, and sometimes bad words spew from their heads like lava. It can be funny to watch—from a safe distance.

The truth is that hanging out with hotheads can rub off on you—not in a good way. No one's immune to other people. Your friends affect you. And the more you're around a guy who's always raging, the easier it is for angry attitudes to creep into your system. Before you know it, you're flying off the handle too when somebody looks at you the wrong way.

God wants us to be filled with patience and peace. Look for friends who will influence you in those directions.

TRIPLE DOG DARE

O Stop hanging out with that hothead.

O Ask your mom who she thinks is a good and bad influence on you. Trust and follow her judgment.

O Adjust your attitude. What's setting you off so quickly? Ask your parents or youth leader for help.

What did you do? What did you learn?

MISSION ACCOMPLISHED!

MAKE TRIPLE DOG TRACKS

How to Build Up Your Body

The ways our bodies work are amazing! And the Bible has a lot to say about how we use our bodies. They are gifts from God, put together just the way He wants them, and we are responsible to use them with self-control and to glorify God. Taking care of bodies is one way to do that. Eating right and exercising teach us discipline that we can also use for our spirits. Staying fit and healthy helps us to be ready and able to serve God.

TRIPLE DOG DARE!

Exercise regularly—at least every other day if not every day. Here are some basic tips to follow.

1. Build strength. But save heavy weights until you're at least a teenager. Try these basic exercises instead. You can do them every morning or night.

Warnings: Make sure you use correct form to avoid getting hurt. Ask your dad or a coach to show you—or have them help you look online for the right techniques. If you feel pain, stop. And drink water before, during, and after a workout.

- Push-ups: Go for twenty-five straight. Then build up to three sets of twenty-five. These will build your chest and arm muscles.

- Pull-ups: Do as many as you can in a row. Do that three times. Use the playground if you don't have another sturdy bar. These build your back and arm muscles.

- Crunches: Aim for twenty-five straight. Take a break; then do two more sets of twenty-five. Too easy? Do more. These build your abdominal muscles around your stomach and waist.

- Squats: Start with three sets of ten, with breaks in between. These exercises look like you're sitting up and down in an invisible chair—make sure you get the form correct to avoid injury. You'll be building the muscles in your legs and rear end.

- Lunges: These big stretching steps also strengthen your legs. It's important to do them the right way. Start with three sets of ten, with rests in between.

2. Build lung power. Your cardiovascular system—heart and lungs—is the key to keeping going. Run, bike, or even walk fast. Anything that makes your heart beat faster and your breathing harder is giving you cardio work. Set a distance (start with a mile) and time yourself. Write down your times and distances and keep aiming for faster and farther over time.

3. Eat healthy. Here's a good rule of thumb: Eat a rainbow. Is the food on your plate mostly brown or white? Then it's probably fried or processed, and not too good for you. Add color with fruits and vegetables. Choose colorful snacks too—carrot sticks instead of chips, for example. Better foods will fuel better workouts and allow you to maximize the exercise you're doing.

TRIPLE DOG BONUS

Write or print out the following verses and hang them up in your workout space.

1 Timothy 4:8

1 Corinthians 6:18

1 Corinthians 9:25

YOUR PAGE

Today I'm feeling...
⟨draw a picture⟩.

TRUTH
Run away from lusts. Run toward God's goodness.

RUN AWAY

Your body says, *Gimme, gimme, gimme! Right here. Right now!* It says, *You don't matter, just me.* It says, *I want it all. I don't care about the consequences. And I'll destroy whatever's in my way to get it.* That's lust.

Lust is a craving that makes you blind to anything except what it wants. It's raw selfish desire. You can lust for money, power, revenge, popularity, or more. It's very human, and it's hurricane-force-strong, especially while you're growing up.

The truth is God calls us to run away from lusts and run toward His goodness, instead. It's not enough for us to stand still and try to dodge lust's temptations. There are too many flying at you—especially images and opportunities that have twisted God's vision for relationships between guys and girls. That's why we've got to get up and get away—flee, run—away from temptations that trigger our selfish cravings. Even then we can't outrun everything. We need a destination, a goal of God's goodness, love, and peace. Fill yourself up with His ways so there's less room for greedy lusts.

TRIPLE DOG DARE

- Get as far away as possible from your biggest temptation.

- Fill your mind with God's Word. Memorize 2 Timothy 2:22.

- Reject any thought that you wouldn't want someone else to have about your sister or mom.

What did you do? What did you learn?

MISSION ACCOMPLISHED!

PSALM 19:1–6

TRUTH

God's creation shouts out His glory.

GO OUTSIDE

Nature is amazing. You're not too impressed by it? Try watching the National Geographic or Discovery channels sometime for inspiration. Shark Week's not a bad place to start. But even better, go outside.

The truth is that God's amazing creation points to an even more amazing Creator. Surrounding yourself with what He's made can focus your attention on Him in new ways. Getting away from man-made distractions can help you be quiet on the inside, and that helps you listen to God. Seeing the ways God made nature fit together can bring new insights into how God works. Jesus often used lessons from nature, probably from animals and plants nearby as He taught. His Spirit still reveals wonders.

Get outside. Take a walk or go camping. Go with someone who plays guitar and sing around a campfire. Sharpen your senses. Carry a Bible and notebook. Expect God to have something to say. Be listening.

TRIPLE DOG DARE

○ Go to the darkest place you can find and look at the night stars. Enjoy God's hugeness.

○ Take a walk in nature, praying as you go.

○ Sit outside and listen. Write down what you hear.

MISSION ACCOMPLISHED!

What did you do? What did you learn?

TRUTH

Faith is believing what we can't see.

DON'T STOP BELIEVING

Let's say you found a crystal ball that really worked for your own life. It showed you every step of your future: what grades you get, what teams and clubs you make, where you go to college, what you major in, what jobs you take, whom you marry, how many kids you have, where you live, how sick or well you stay, when you die. It's a vision of your entire life. It answers every question.

What reason would you have to use your faith in God?

The truth is that faith is believing in what we can't see. Yes, faith is believing and trusting that Jesus rose from the dead to give us eternal life. But faith is also trusting that God is in control of our lives—and that He's guiding us even when we're not sure what to do. That kind of faith we have to choose every day. That kind of faith God rewards. Don't stop believing!

TRIPLE DOG DARE

○ Pray, ask for advice, and make your decision trusting God's guidance.

○ Write your doubts and put them in an envelope. Then take each one out and replace it with a promise from God out of the Bible.

○ Make a creed—a list of everything you believe.

What did you do? What did you learn?

MISSION ACCOMPLISHED!

TRUTH

Your job is to listen to your parents.

IT'S A HARD JOB, BUT SOMEBODY'S GOTTA DO IT

Your parents have a big job. No, not doctor, lawyer, mechanic job. *Big* job! As in job from God. As in it's their big mission. Their job is to teach you and guide you the ways of life and the ways of God. It's to care for you physically, emotionally, and spiritually to get you ready to live on your own one day.

Sound easy? Yeah, right. You didn't come with instructions. You came out screaming. The doctor handed you to your mom, said congratulations, and it was go-time for your parents. It's a job they don't always get right, but it keeps them leaning on God.

The truth is that you have a job too: to listen to your parents and obey them. You could have Albert Einstein as your teacher but still fail science class if you didn't pay any attention. Same goes for your parents. You can hear their advice and instruction but fail to listen. *Hearing* is passive—sounds like sirens and dogs barking just hit your ears. *Listening* is active—it's paying attention to the sounds. Hearing is registering the sound; listening is doing something with it in your brain. Sound easy? Yeah, right. Sounds like a job to keep you leaning on God.

TRIPLE DOG DARE

- Obey your parents the first time all day today.

- Cut your parents some slack. Forgive them now for what you're holding against them.

- Don't understand what they're saying? Repeat back what you think they're telling you to do, like this, "So you want me to move my bike then clean my room, right?"

MISSION ACCOMPLISHED!

What did you do? What did you learn?

TRUTH
Laziness will break you.
Diligence will make you.

MAKE SOME MOMENTUM

Inertia keeps you stuck still. Momentum keeps you going. The more you have of one, the easier it is to get more of the same thing. Think of a train. It takes a lot to get it moving, but once it's rolling, it takes a lot to slow it down.

The truth is laziness will break you, but diligence will make you. They're inertia and momentum. The more you lie on the couch, the harder it is to get up. The more you stay busy doing your homework and chores, the easier it is to get them done and still have time for fun.

Where do you want to be ten or twenty years from now? Now is the time to build the habits that will take you there. The first step is often the hardest; take it today. Get out of bed. Jump up from the couch. Click the TV off. Shake off laziness. Get moving and keep moving. Ride your own momentum.

TRIPLE DOG DARE

- Brainstorm three ways to make some money. Choose one and do it.
- Tackle the project you've been putting off. Today!
- Got free time? Learn a new hobby or skill (a new video game doesn't count).

What did you do? What did you learn?

MISSION ACCOMPLISHED!

MAKE TRIPLE DOG TRACKS

Dads and Dudes

"Children, obey your parents because you belong to the Lord, for this is the right thing to do. 'Honor your father and mother.' This is the first commandment with a promise: If you honor your father and mother, 'things will go well for you, and you will have a long life on the earth.' Fathers, do not provoke your children to anger by the way you treat them. Rather, bring them up with the discipline and instruction that comes from the Lord" (Ephesians 6:1–4 NLT).

It's a two-way street between fathers and sons, even in the instructions God gives in the Bible. It's a relationship that needs give and take. The way to achieve that is to get to know each other and to build trust and communication. Your relationship with your dad is one of the most powerful earthly relationships you'll ever have. Do your part to make the most of it.

Some dads are better than others when it comes to expressing love or affection, but you can be sure there's a special place in your dad's heart that's just for you and no one else. Reach out to your dad today.

TRIPLE DOG DARE!

Make time to hang out with your dad. Ask him to spend time together and put in on your schedules.

Things I want to do with Dad:

Ways I want to be like Dad:

Ways I don't want to be like Dad:

Ways I'm already like Dad:

Things I can learn from Dad or ask him about:

TRIPLE DOG
BONUS

Show your dad these lists and talk about them.

YOUR PAGE

When my dad was a kid my age, he liked to ...

1 TIMOTHY 6:9–11

TRUTH
Loving money will make you crazy—and ruin you.

DON'T LET MONEY BREAK YOUR HEART

People in love do some crazy things. They buy flowers and candy and gifts. They write poems, notes, and songs. They climb the highest mountains and cross the widest seas—at least the songs say so. They'll stop at nothing to prove their devotion and win the girl's heart.

Some people will do the same for money. It's the object of their affection. It's all they want. But they can never get enough. That's the way money love goes. The more you want, the more you want more—until you're willing to do anything to get it. Ever wonder why millionaire CEOs get busted for illegal dealings? Money love.

The truth is that loving money pulls us away from God and happiness and into wrecking our lives. We need to fall in love, but with God—not money. What we love is what we think about and act like. Don't worry about getting rich. Focus on God and thank Him for the money He's given you. That's the way to real happiness.

TRIPLE DOG DARE

- Have you cheated to get more money? Give the money back.

- Break up with your money. Discover how good it feels to give it to help someone in need.

- Make a list of all the things God has given you. It'll probably be a long list.

What did you do? What did you learn?

MISSION ACCOMPLISHED!

TRUTH Jesus wants to change us from the inside out.

A WHOLE NEW YOU

Get stronger! Look better! Feel happier! Smell sweeter! Lose more! Gain less! Eat this! Play that! Have it all! A whole new you!

Advertisers promise us the world. They pull crazy stunts, shout loudly, and spend millions on innovative technology. Can you imagine what it would be like if everything they promised came true? What if all those products really worked? Humanity would be perfect—and we wouldn't need to buy their products anymore. Hmmm, wonder if they've thought of that? Oh, wait, they know those products can't really solve all your problems.

The truth is that only Jesus can truly fix us, and He completely changes us on the inside. When we give our lives to Him, He makes us alive. He makes us a new creation. Our new spirit is alive. He gets rid of the old one. Sometimes we notice it right away: Temptations or fears are gone immediately. Sometimes we notice over time as God's Spirit helps us grow stronger. We won't fully see or realize our new selves until we see God, but in the meantime we can catch glimpses of the "whole new you" God is making.

TRIPLE DOG DARE

- Turn off or skip every advertisement you see this week.

- Shake off the old. Get rid of old temptations and habits, and live like you're new.

- Make a list of old and new traits, ones you've seen change and ones you want help with changing.

MISSION ACCOMPLISHED! What did you do? What did you learn?

TRUTH

Dig in and experience God's goodness.

DIG IN

Imagine a heaping plate of your favorite food. Maybe it's twelve scoops of chocolate ice cream or six slices of extra-cheesy pizza. You can see the steam rising from it. You can smell it. You can plunge your hands or face into it, but that won't do much good. You want to taste it! Dig in and chow down!

The truth is you've got to dig into God to truly taste how amazing He is. Don't hold back. Devour His Word. Dive into worshipping Him with all your heart. Dig into serving Him and other people like you can't get enough. Smear Him all over your face so others see His joy. Don't just know *about* God—*know* God. You won't be sorry. He will leave you full and satisfied.

TRIPLE DOG DARE

O Help your mom cook dinner tonight and tell her about this lesson.

O Get candy bars for yourself and a friend and explain it's an example of digging into God's goodness. You can even eat them while you read the Bible.

O List what you merely *know* about God. Ask Him to help you dive in and see for yourself.

What did you do? What did you learn?

MISSION ACCOMPLISHED!

TRUTH

God makes us strong, even when we're weak.

GET STRONG BY GETTING WEAK

We usually don't notice the safety backup until we need it. Think about a spare tire, a fire escape, or the safety net below a trapeze. You might not even notice these until you're stranded on the side of the road, running from the flames, or plummeting toward the ground. But all those backups can help you go for it because you know you can get bailed out.

The truth is we see and experience God's strength in us when we're weakest and most vulnerable—when we need a backup. It's like we're sick and He is the only cure. We're drowning and He is the life ring. We're dying of thirst in the desert and He is the water fountain. Our weakness reminds us that we need Him. Then we turn to Him and find that God gives us His strength. He gives us what we need when we need it. That helps us say "bring it on" to whatever challenge is in front of us!

TRIPLE DOG DARE

O Memorize 2 Corinthians 12:9–10.

O Write a story about a time when God came through for you.

O Thank God for your weaknesses, insults, hardships, persecutions, and difficulties. Ask to Him to be strong in each one.

MISSION ACCOMPLISHED!

What did you do? What did you learn?

1 JOHN 4:7–12

TRUTH Love is an action.

DO LOVE

You can probably sing a zillion pop songs about love—how love feels, how it rocks your world, how it makes you high, how it breaks your heart, how you can't fight it, how you can't find it, how you fall in and out of it. It's got to be the most popular theme for songs in the world. And there's no doubt we all need love.

The truth is love is much more than a feeling; it's a choice and a verb. It's a commitment and a way of life. Yes, it is an emotion, too, but the feelings aren't always strong or noticeable. God calls us to love much deeper than we feel like.

Love is choosing to be patient when someone bugs you. It's forgiving when your feelings get hurt. It's staying true when someone or something else looks more exciting. It's sacrificing when you know you can make someone else's day instead of your own. It's choosing God's ways when it seems like everyone else isn't. You have hundreds of opportunities each day—choose love.

TRIPLE DOG DARE

- O Listen closely to lyrics. Are they talking about empty feelings or godly, lasting love? Fill your brain with the ones about real love.

- O Show your mom and dad you love them with three sacrificial acts this week.

- O Give your brother or sister a hug and offer to clean his or her room.

What did you do? What did you learn?

MISSION ACCOMPLISHED!

FROM THE TRIPLE DOG POUND

Jeremiah: Not Too Young

"Too young" is never a good excuse. When God calls you to a plan, He'll give you what you need to get it done. Just ask Jeremiah.

Jeremiah was one of ancient Israel's greatest prophets, and God had special plans for him before he was even born. Jeremiah was a boy when God called him. It was the biggest Triple Dog Dare of his life so far. Jeremiah couldn't believe it and definitely didn't feel worthy. "I don't know how to speak. I'm only a child!" Jeremiah told God. But God wasn't worried about Jeremiah's excuses. "I am with you and will rescue you," God replied, and He put His words in Jeremiah's mouth.

Next God gave Jeremiah what he needed: some prophet training and confidence. God showed Jeremiah two visions and walked the new prophet step-by-step through what they meant. It not only gave Jeremiah practice, it also helped him realize that he could do it with God's help. It didn't matter how young or inexperienced Jeremiah was. What mattered was that God helps His servants do whatever He wants them to do.

TRIPLE DOG DARE!

O Read Jeremiah 1.

O What do you sense God asking and calling you to do?

O Fill in the lists on the next page.

MY EXCUSES:

WAYS GOD HELPS ME
OVERCOME THEM:

If I could solve one big problem for
the whole world, it would be ...

TRUTH
God gives us the armor and a different way to fight.

GET DRESSED

It's a common bad dream. Maybe you've had it. Suddenly you're standing in front of a large crowd. Lots of people are staring at you. Then they start to chuckle and snicker. Now they're pointing and laughing—yes, at you. You look down and realize: You're naked! Or maybe in your underwear. Either way, you're totally underdressed and you can't move. That's the way many of us face the battles of life and the attacks of the Devil—naked and unprepared.

The truth is that God's armor gives us the protection we need. Our real war isn't against other people; it's against the Devil and his evil spirits. The way to fight is to learn God's Word, get to know Him, and pray. And the way to prepare is to get dressed. Your armor won't do any good hanging in your closet. Put it on!

TRIPLE DOG DARE

○ Draw a picture of your spiritual armor. Use Ephesians 6:10–18 as your guide, but be creative for the style. Modern? Ancient? You choose.

○ As you get dressed each day this week, picture yourself putting on the pieces of God's armor. Use a checklist if you want to.

○ When you face a battle or struggle today, pray first. Ask God to handle the fight and give you wisdom.

What did you do? What did you learn?

MISSION ACCOMPLISHED!

TRUTH

God says get in or get out.

GET IN OR OUT

Hot chocolate is yummy, and cold chocolate milk is delicious. Coffee is best hot, and tastes good iced, too. Milk tastes best cold, and it can be soothing hot. But any of them lukewarm? *Bleh.* You'd rather spit them out.

The truth is God wants us to be spiritually hot. And He'd rather we be spiritually cold than to talk the talk without walking the walk. Lukewarm Christians make Him want to spit them out of His mouth!

There are people who are lazy and apathetic (don't care) about following God. They may go to church and answer the questions in Sunday school, but they go home and act nothing like God's children. They may think they're good with God because they've grown up in church, but they've never given Him their hearts. They may say they love God, but they do nothing to love the people around them. You can't jerk God around. Give Him all you've got or nothing at all.

TRIPLE DOG DARE

○ Quit faking it. Be totally honest with God and surrender what you're holding back.

○ Get God's perspective. Drink lukewarm buttermilk. Use lukewarm milk if it's all you've got. Then make sure you don't act like it.

○ Take a big gulp of water and spit it into a strong wind. Use it as a reminder not to fight God. It just doesn't work.

MISSION ACCOMPLISHED!

What did you do? What did you learn?

TRUTH

When God forgives our sin, it's gone.

GOING, GOING, GONE

You can't head west and ever be going east. You can go around the world and pass through the eastern and western hemispheres, but you're still headed west. East and west are opposites, like darkness and light, good and evil. Where there is one, there's not the other. You can fly through the universe in one direction and never reach the other.

The truth is that's how far God removes our sin when He forgives us. It's gone. Done. Finished. You're never going to get it back. You should feel guilt after you sin; that's God's Spirit letting you know you've stepped out of bounds. You should feel sorry about what you've done; that helps you to change and avoid more sin. You might suffer consequences; that's the way the world works. But your guilt is gone; that's the way God works.

Don't take back what God has taken away. Pray and confess your sin; then stop beating yourself up. You are forgiven. Let it go like God has.

TRIPLE DOG DARE

○ What do you keep feeling guilty about? Write it and tie your note to a helium balloon. Let it fly away.

○ Make a list of as many opposites as you can while you realize that's how far your sin is from you now.

○ Look at the stars in a dark night sky and blow your mind with how far away God has taken your guilt.

What did you do? What did you learn?

MISSION ACCOMPLISHED!

TRUTH

God can use whatever you have to give.

THE POWER OF PENNIES

You've got pennies between the seats in your couch and car. They're probably under your bed and in the corners of every drawer in your house. You might have a jar filled with them. And you probably don't even care. Pennies are puny. One cent each? *Pshaw.* It's all about the big dollars for us. How much? How many zeroes? You can't do anything with pennies, right?

The truth is God can use whatever you have to give. He would rather have the last few pennies from a poor widow—or a kid—than thousands of dollars from a millionaire. That's because it's not about the amount to God. He doesn't need our money. But our money shows where our hearts are. Do we give God whatever's leftover that we don't need? Or do we give everything because we know it's His anyway and that He will take care of us?

Give whatever you have to give. Give your silver and copper coins, and give your time and ability. Give and watch what God does with it.

TRIPLE DOG DARE

- Give more money than usual to church or a ministry this week. Make it more than your leftovers.

- Round up all the loose change in your house and give it to a group such as Loose Change to Loosen Chains (kids helping to end modern-day slavery).

- What do you have the most of: time, musical or artistic ability, an outgoing personality? Give it to others.

MISSION ACCOMPLISHED!

What did you do? What did you learn?

TRUTH
God gives us a way to fight differently.

HOW TO FIGHT

Maybe you've taken karate lessons. You've at least seen kung fu, judo, jujitsu, or tae kwon do. Masters of the martial arts are impressive to watch. They control their bodies to exploit an opponent's weakness. With his bare hands, a martial artist can overpower a foe armed with heavy firepower. And a master knows that his true art is used to stop a fight before it begins. Martial artists have a different way of fighting.

The truth is that God gives us a different way to fight. Our real enemies aren't people, even the ones who bug us and disagree with us. Our real battle is a different one, and we win it in our minds and spirits. Our war is spiritual, and our enemy is the Devil.

Train for the battle by sharpening your spirit and strengthening your mind, especially learning God's Word. Fight with prayer. Wear God-vision goggles to stay focused on the real enemy, and avoid the fight with people by disarming them with Jesus' love. You are a young warrior. Learn to train in the ways of your Master.

TRIPLE DOG DARE

- Pray instead of complain.
- Spread God's peace by showing God's kindness and love to everyone.
- When you're tempted by a lustful thought, tell God you're taking it captive for Him.

What did you do? What did you learn?

MISSION ACCOMPLISHED!

MAKE TRIPLE DOG TRACKS

Be a Triple Dog

Dogs make the best pets. Sorry, cat-lovers. Cats have their strengths, but dogs rule. They're just cool animals. And while the main idea of this book is the *dare* of the Triple Dog Dare, we can learn a few things from the *dog* part too.

Do you have a dog? What's its name and breed? Draw or stick a picture of your dog on the next page. Then let's compare dog notes.

Dogs are always eager and ready to go. I have two yellow Labrador Retrievers named Bailey and Baxter, and they love to go with me for a run, walk, or hike. They have a special dog superpower. They can be in the backyard, but they know whenever I put on my running shoes and grab the leashes—without ever seeing me. Then it's dog excitement city, jumping and barking and running in circles like it's the greatest day in the world. *Yo Dawg, what can you be more excited and enthusiastic about?*

Dogs are loyal encouragers. They're always happy to see you, and they're not afraid to show it. They greet you with a wagging tail and a big wet kiss. They'll lie down beside you when you're bummed out and try to nose you into playing and feeling better. *Yo Dawg, how can you hang out and encourage a friend who is feeling bummed out?*

Dogs are fearless (usually). They'll bark and growl to defend you against a bear or other bigger animal. They'll go head-to-head against a meaner, tougher dog if they have to, and they'll sound the alarm to warn you of any intruders. Okay, sometimes they'll hide under the bed from thunder, but when it comes to defending you, they'll do whatever it takes. *Yo Dawg, what fear can you overcome? Who needs you to stand up in their defense?*

Dogs rely on each other. They're social pack animals who know they need each other. In the wild, dogs work together to survive like their cousins the wolves. They know they can't make it alone. Dogs are also good judges of character. They can sense who is honest and trustworthy, and they don't trust a two-faced person who says one thing but does another. *Yo Dawg, who makes up your pack? Whom can you rely on to help you make it through good and bad times?*

Dogs live for their purpose. My labs' ancestors were bred to hunt and retrieve, and my dogs will play fetch all day long. They love it. They live for it. They're fully alive when they're chasing a ball or a stick. It's what they were made to do. *Yo Dawg, what makes you feel alive inside? What can you do to live out praise for God?*

TRIPLE DOG BONUS

Take your dog (or a friend's) for a run, walk, or hike. Watch and learn.

YOUR PAGE

People I want to talk to in heaven:

TRUTH
Exercise your faith to make it stronger.

MUSCLE MAN

You don't get muscles lying around on the couch. Lifting weights builds muscles. You've got to use and test your body to make it stronger.

The truth is you've also got to work out your faith to make it stronger. Shake off spiritual laziness and build some muscle in your spirit. How? Learn more by reading and studying the Bible. Trust more by putting yourself in situations where you need God, like talking to a friend about Jesus or volunteering for a service or mission project. Understand more by talking and listening to God; give Him your problems and ask for His help. See more by looking for God and ways to follow Him every day. Go pump some spiritual iron!

TRIPLE DOG DARE

- Schedule on your calendar fifteen minutes each day to read your Bible, pray, and write to God.

- Do twenty-five push-ups and twenty-five abdominal crunches every day this week.

- Get sweaty serving someone. Mow a neighbor's lawn or walk an elderly person's dog—for free.

What did you do? What did you learn?

MISSION ACCOMPLISHED!

TRUTH

God is at work in your life. Take the opportunity you are given.

YOUR TIME

It's probably happened to you. You've been in the right place at the right time—maybe to make a game-winning catch, maybe to save someone from running in front of a car. Sometimes the results are small. Sometimes they're life-changing. Some people call it luck. Some call it coincidence.

The truth is that God is at work in our lives, and sometimes He puts us in just the right place at just the right time. It's up to us to act in order to take advantage of the opportunity before us. Sometimes doing so can be scary—as it was in Esther's situation—but that's where our faith comes in.

When you're facing an opportunity or choice, ask yourself and someone wiser, like your parents, these questions: Will my action line up with God's Word? Will it hurt me or other people? Will it glorify God? Is it wise? Do I trust God? Unless there are good reasons not to, make the most of the opportunities you're given.

TRIPLE DOG DARE

○ Ask the questions above about a decision you're facing.

○ Write your autobiography and trace God's work through your life.

○ List your opportunities. Start with education, music, and sports.

MISSION ACCOMPLISHED!

What did you do? What did you learn?

TRUTH

Jesus came to bring healing and freedom to everyone.

FREE FOR ALL

Look around church sometime. Most of the people probably look like you—not like your twin, but they're probably dressed similarly. Their families most likely make about the same money and live in similar houses to yours. They might even be mostly the same color. That's not all bad, but it's not all good.

The truth is that Jesus came to bring healing and freedom to everyone, and He calls us to do the same. That's hard to do when everyone in church is so similar. Where are the poor people and prisoners?

It's true that without Jesus we're all spiritually poor, brokenhearted, held prisoner, grieving, and in despair. We all need rescue and hope from God. But there are many literally poor people and prisoners in our towns and world. God hasn't forgotten them, and He wants us to remember and help them too.

TRIPLE DOG DARE

○ Get your family or class to volunteer at a local food pantry.

○ Find a ministry in your church or city and volunteer to help.

○ Gather some money with family and friends and loan it to a person in another country to start a business through an organization like Kiva.

What did you do? What did you learn?

MISSION ACCOMPLISHED!

TRUTH
God wants us to measure our media against His Word.

YOUR MEDIA MEASURING STICK

Look around your room. The walls are straight. The corners are square. The floor is flat. The windows and doors are even. It'd be pretty funny if one window was sideways and the other touched the ceiling. Ever wonder how construction workers build things so straight? You probably know. They measure. And they look at their blueprints—the master plan.

With all the media flying around us, it can be hard to know what's good and what's not. Some is healthy. Some is junk. If we judge by what's popular, we can swallow movies, songs, and games that make God sick—and that will rot our own spirits. If we go only by what looks or sounds good, we easily end up sucking on candy-coated poison drops. We need something to measure against.

The truth is we have a media measuring stick and an ultimate blueprint: the Bible. God's Word tells us God's priorities. It tells us things He wants us to do and not to do. It doesn't say "Thou shall not play *MegaWars*," but it gives us guidelines we can use. Philippians 4:8 is one of those guidelines. Do its words describe your media? It'll help you know what measures up.

TRIPLE DOG DARE

- Make a Philippians 4:8 checklist. Measure your favorite games, songs, and movies.

- Create your own entertainment. Film your own movie. Sing your own song. Produce your own play. Get friends and family to help.

- Try some new entertainment. Take a poll from friends, parents, and adults you trust for their favorites to try.

MISSION ACCOMPLISHED!
What did you do? What did you learn?

JAMES 1:2-4

TRUTH God wants to use our problems and trials to make us stronger.

THANKS FOR WHAT?!

Thank you for *what?!* Thank you for my annoying brother or sister? Thank you that I got the really hard teacher this year? Thank you for the mean comments people make about me? Thank you that my dad lost his job? Thank you that my team always loses? You've got to be kidding!

The truth is that God wants to use our problems to help us grow stronger. Understanding that is the first step to persevering and overcoming our trials—because that understanding changes our attitudes.

It's not easy to shift our thinking. Usually we whine and complain when we have problems. But instead of focusing on how bad our problems are, God wants us to focus on Him. When we do, He can help us see how He's working in our lives. That doesn't mean He'll always take away our problems; it means He'll help us deal with them, learn from them, and grow stronger. And in the middle of it all, we can feel God's peace and joy.

TRIPLE DOG DARE

○ Ask God to help you keep going through a problem you're facing.

○ Write a story about someone dealing with a problem you're having. How would your hero get through it?

○ Prove you can persevere. Fill a bucket with ice water. Hold your hand in it for five minutes.

What did you do? What did you learn?

MISSION ACCOMPLISHED!

Bezalel and Oholiab Were Good with Their Hands

We all like to be recognized for our work. But do you ever feel like no one notices? That can be discouraging, especially when you're trying to work hard and do the right things. The good news is that God always notices.

Take Bezalel and Oholiab, for example. Never heard of them? They were Israelite crafts-men with a Triple Dog Dare. God chose them to build the tabernacle and all its furniture and objects for worship. It was a big deal. The tabernacle was more than a church; it was where God met with Moses and the priests and where the Israelites offered sacrifices. And God gave specific instructions for how to build and use everything. Not just anyone could make this sacred place. God wanted Bezalel and Oholiab to do it.

We don't know much about the two guys. Maybe their work had made them famous. Or maybe they had labored and carved crafts for years and wondered if anybody cared. Whatever the case, God made it clear in Exodus 31:3–6 that He had filled these two and other craftsmen with their skills, abilities, and knowledge. God also wanted them to use those gifts for Him. God wants the same from you with whatever talents He's given you.

TRIPLE DOG DARE!

O Read Exodus 31:1–11.

O What do you wish other people would notice?

O Fill in these lists.

THINGS I'M GOOD AT:

WAYS I CAN USE IT FOR GOD, INCLUDING HELPING OTHERS:

TRIPLE DOG BONUS

Use your hands to create a craft you can give to someone as an unexpected gift. Try carving, sculpting, or woodworking. Sketch some ideas here.

YOUR PAGE

My biggest fears are ...

TRUTH
God wants you to have nothing to do with pornography.

PLAN TO BEAT PORNOGRAPHY

Someday it's going to happen if it hasn't already. I wish it weren't the case, but somebody is going to show you some pornography. Porn is pictures or videos of naked people. It might be on a phone or computer or in a magazine or book. You're going to want to look it, out of curiosity, excitement, peer pressure, or all three. But don't be caught off guard.

The truth is God wants you to have nothing to do with pornography. It's natural to be curious about women's bodies, but porn disrespects what God has made beautiful. God made every detail of our bodies and gave husbands and wives a special gift to enjoy called sex.

But pornography is an imposter that twists and cheapens that gift. It turns women into objects instead of real people and pollutes what God made pure. Looking at these kinds of pictures can be addicting, and it warps users' understanding of God's plans. Talk to an adult you trust if you have questions. And do yourself and your future wife a favor—plan now to say "no" to porn whenever it pops up.

TRIPLE DOG DARE

- Write and rehearse an action plan for how you'll say no and turn away from pornography when someone tries to show it to you.

- Talk to an adult you trust about avoiding porn.

- Make a pact with your close friends that you're going to fight porn, not use it.

What did you do? What did you learn?

MISSION ACCOMPLISHED!

TRUTH

Your words have power. Use them for good.

YOUR SUPERPOWER

Spider-Man's Uncle Ben said it so well: "With great power comes great responsibility." You have power—the power of words. But it's a power that can go both ways, and you have a superhero's choice.

The truth is our words can build a person into a strong skyscraper or tear him down to a pile of rubble. You know. You've been on both sides. Praise or encouragement from a friend, parent, teacher, or coach can fill you up and set you sailing like a hot-air balloon. But a dis from one of the same people can deflate you faster than a machine gun to that balloon—especially if the insult happens in front of other people.

Harness your great power. Fill your speech with positivity. Practice the art of the compliment. Launch uplifting balloons all around you. Turn people's piles of rubble into tall towers. Express gratitude. Release the power of your words on the side of good. Consider it your superpower.

TRIPLE DOG DARE

- Give a compliment for every insult the guys are flinging.

- Compliment or encourage three total strangers today.

- Find ways to brag on other people in public—in front of a person's friends, teachers, parents, and others.

MISSION ACCOMPLISHED!

What did you do? What did you learn?

EPHESIANS 5:19–20

TRUTH
Make music for God, no matter what the style.

ROCK IT

There are hundreds, if not thousands, of styles of music. And thanks to technology, you can find anything from Tibetan-monk chants to Gypsy polka on iTunes or the Internet. Your favorite style is probably a little more mainstream than that. But whatever it is, you can use it to praise God.

The truth is we should worship God with all sorts of songs and styles of music. And not just alone, but with other people. That helps to unite us while it focuses our attention on God. Music has a way of touching our hearts and connecting with our spirits. Music can move us and get us over ourselves. It opens us up to God's Spirit.

Sing to God with every style of music you like. Thank and praise Him in your heart and out loud. Don't worry about how you sound; God cares more that your song resonates in your heart than that it's crystal clear on your lips. Sing it out!

TRIPLE DOG DARE

- Make a playlist of your favorite worship music and crank it up.

- Make up your own song saying thanks to God.

- Invite friends over for your own praise session. Play instruments if you can, or just sing along with a CD.

What did you do? What did you learn?

MISSION ACCOMPLISHED!

TRUTH

Sink your roots deep by putting your trust in God.

ROOTED

Banyan trees are cool because you can see their swirling, tangling roots growing from above the ground down into the soil. Sometimes their roots are as big as tree trunks. They almost look alive. Wait, they are alive! They are the anchor of a living, growing organism. And to be healthy, a tree must have healthy roots.

The truth is we need healthy spiritual roots that come from trusting God over and over again. We grow them by choosing to trust God day by day and decision by decision. Sometimes that's easier than other times. But a secret about roots is that they grow deeper when it's dry. Sure, they like lots of rain and water that is easy to drink and nourish their tree. But when drought and scorching heat hit, they burrow down deep for nutrition. The deeper the roots go, the stronger they are at holding the tree solid. Send your roots down deep in good times and bad.

TRIPLE DOG DARE

- Draw your spiritual tree. How's your root system?

- Choose to trust God in a hard situation you're experiencing.

- Go for a walk and examine tree roots, including some by a river or lake. Look for God's lesson.

MISSION ACCOMPLISHED!

What did you do? What did you learn?

TRUTH
Too much of a good thing will make you sick.

DON'T PUKE

Can you really have too much of a good thing? Too much candy will rot your teeth. Too much sleep will make you feel lazy. Too much video gaming will change your brain. Too much water will drown you. Too much sunshine will fry your skin. Too much speed will make you crash and burn. Too much ice cream will make you puke.

Yep. The truth is you can get too much of a good thing—and it can mess you up. Don't grab more than you can hold. Don't buy more than you can use. Don't take more than you really need. Ask God to help you know what you can live without. Be content by focusing on *enough* instead of *more*. Store the Bible in your mind and heart and let its words make you unselfish. Then you can use just what you need and share with others.

TRIPLE DOG DARE

○ Eat all the food on your plate before taking more.

○ Go on a stuff diet. What are you getting too much of? (Ask your parents for help if you can't figure it out.) Set a time or amount limit for this week.

○ Practice a contentment test. Before buying a new item, ask *Do I have enough already? Will I die without this thing?*

What did you do? What did you learn?

MISSION ACCOMPLISHED!

MAKE TRIPLE DOG TRACKS

Sing Out Your Psalms

Ever get a song stuck in your head? Psalms can stick in your heart like that. Psalms are both songs and prayers. Some are happy; some are sad. They are great examples reminding us that we can pour out our hearts honestly to God no matter what we're feeling, and find hope, comfort, and strength.

Read these samples: Psalm 1, Psalm 8, Psalm 31, Psalm 51, Psalm 142.

TRIPLE DOG DARE!

Write your own psalm to God. Thank Him. Praise Him. Ask Him. Tell Him. Write whatever you're thinking and feeling. You can even think of a tune to go with the words.

YOUR PAGE

Write some funny jokes.
⟨Ask people if you can't think of any.⟩

TRUTH

Reminders of God are everywhere.

LOOK UP

People have been climbing mountains as long as, well, the mountains have been there. The mountains have a way of calling to us. The journey up focuses our energy and attention. Whatever's bothering us at the bottom slips away the higher we go. And standing on the summit changes our perspective in more ways than one. Nothing blocks our view for miles. Big things below now look small. Challenges that almost kept us down are defeated. Silence sings around us with the wind. Our bodies stop on the peak, but our spirits soar even higher.

The truth is God has been using mountains to remind and inspire people for centuries. He called Moses and other prophets and leaders up high to meet with Him—talk about a change of perspective! Mountains are some of God's biggest creations. They're big, strong, and solid, yet God is infinitely bigger. Need help? Look up high. Let the creation remind you of the Creator.

TRIPLE DOG DARE

○ Climb the mountain closest to your house. No high peaks? Look on Google Earth for the highest point near you. Go there to pray and get a new perspective.

○ Put up a picture of Mount Everest. Look at it when you read Psalm 121, and remember God's incredible power is there to help you.

○ Find a place to rock climb, even if it's indoors. Picture God protecting you in every part of life, guarding you and keeping you from falling.

What did you do? What did you learn?

MISSION ACCOMPLISHED!

TRUTH

Your friends influence you for good or bad.

CONTAGIOUS COMPANY

You are what you eat. Garbage in; garbage out. Remember those sayings from earlier in this book? They make sense. What you put into your body and mind becomes part of you, and it's what comes back out in your actions. Here's another saying I'm creating: You are who you hang out with.

The truth is our friends rub off on us. So choose your friends wisely. It's kind of like they all have germs. No one is immune to germs, but you can pick whether you're getting good friend germs that will make you stronger and wiser or bad friend germs that will make you weaker and foolish.

Have your parents expressed concern about you hanging out with a certain kid? Listen up. Have you been getting in trouble every time you hang out with a guy? Consider it a warning. Do you feel mad, guilty, or rebellious when you're around some friends? Get out while you can. It might hurt a little now to limit your time with a person who's dragging you down, but it will save you worse pain later. Stick with the friends who lift you up.

TRIPLE DOG DARE

○ Ask your parents which of your friends they like best. Hang out more with those guys.

○ List your friends' decisions. Do they lead to trouble, punishment, and hurt … or recognition, reward, and happiness?

○ Be contagious. Make wise choices and obey God even when your friends don't.

MISSION ACCOMPLISHED!

What did you do? What did you learn?

TRUTH Life is short but filled with God's love. Embrace it!

SEIZE THE DAY

Your life looks like a road that stretches as far as you can see and keeps rolling into an infinite horizon. The end? That's so far out there that it doesn't even seem real. *Dying is for old people,* you think. *It'll never happen to me.*

The truth is that every single one of us will die someday. Hopefully the end will come after we've lived long, fulfilling lives. But there are no guarantees. We get to live much longer than the grass and flowers that die every year, but even the longest human life is incredibly short in the overall span of eternity.

That's why every day counts! Once the sun goes down, there's no going back. What are your dreams? What are your hopes? What do you think God wants you to accomplish? There's a time for patience and learning how to progress, but don't put off taking steps to get you started. Seize each day and make the most of it!

TRIPLE DOG DARE

- What have you been putting off? Do it today.

- What have you been afraid to try? Give it a shot. Then try it again.

- Make a life list of things you want to do before you die. Take it out each year and update it with accomplishments and new ideas.

What are you going to do? What did you learn?

MISSION ACCOMPLISHED!

TRUTH
Scripture is the way to beat temptation.

FIGHT LIKE JESUS

The Devil kicks us when we're down. He pours on his heaviest temptation when we're weak or tired or discouraged. He doesn't exactly play fair. He probably really thought he could get Jesus after Jesus hadn't eaten for forty days. The first temptation he threw at Jesus was food. Smart choice if you're going to be a tempter; you'd probably have turned the rocks into hamburgers on day two if you could.

The truth is Jesus used the best weapon against Satan's temptations: the Word of God. He didn't rely on His own strength. He didn't try to one-up Satan. He didn't even pray. He turned to the source of truth and quoted it word for word. Not only did it work, it also gave us an example of how to beat the Devil. When you're tempted, don't try to argue it out in your brain. Turn to the Bible. Memorize some verses so you're armed and ready on the spot. Or if you've got your Bible handy, open it up and start reading. Use it like your go-to weapon.

TRIPLE DOG DARE

- Memorize one verse this week related to an area you struggle with. Use the concordance in the back of your Bible.

- Carry a small Bible with you and take it out when you're tempted.

- Treat your Bible like your sword. Draw a picture of a sword and stick it on your Bible cover.

MISSION ACCOMPLISHED!

What did you do? What did you learn?

TRUTH

God has told us what's good: justice, mercy, and humility.

WHAT GOD WANTS

Ever wonder what God's will for your life is? Where will you go? What will you be? Some people agonize over those questions, trying to find just the right path. Sometimes God might call you to specific tasks. If He does, He'll make them clear. In the meantime, you don't have to look too far to find out what God wants for all of us all the time.

The truth is God wants us to live out justice, mercy, and humility before Him. Justice means we act fairly to others and try to right wrongs. Mercy means we forgive people and show them kindness they don't deserve—even when they treat us badly. And humility means we don't brag because we realize all we have and can do comes from God. Think of that as your basic training!

TRIPLE DOG DARE

- ○ Stand up to a bully on behalf of someone else.

- ○ Cut someone some slack who doesn't really deserve it.

- ○ Pray instead of brag. Thank God for the abilities you have.

What did you do? What did you learn?

MISSION ACCOMPLISHED!

MAKE TRIPLE DOG TRACKS

Fire!

Fire is cool. Yeah, you definitely have to be careful with it—no playing with matches. But it's awesome to burn sticks in a campfire, getting the tips glowing and smoking. Or to watch the flames dance in a raging bonfire—that's a hypnotizing sight.

Fire shows up in the Bible in some pretty miraculous ways. Check these out:

- God gets Moses' attention by talking to him from a bush that burns without burning up. Read about it in Exodus 3.

- Elijah has a contest with the priests of Baal. Whichever god sends fire from heaven to burn up the sacrifice wins and is the true god. Nothing happens for Baal's 450 prophets. Elijah makes his sacrifice soaking wet, then God blasts it with raging flames so hot that they even burn up the rocks of the altar. God takes the victory in a shutout, and the people worship Him. Read it all in 1 Kings 18:16–40.

- Elijah is taken into heaven (without dying) by a burning chariot pulled by fiery horses. Pretty sweet ride! Read about it in 2 Kings 2.

- The fiery furnace that Shadrach, Meshach, and Abednego were thrown into is heated up seven times hotter than normal. It is so hot that it kills the soldiers who throw the three rebels in. Check it out in Daniel 3.

TRIPLE DOG DARE!

Help your dad build a campfire or fire in the fireplace. Burn sticks and talk about life and God. Draw or write about it here.

YOUR PAGE

I can listen more to ...

TRUTH God picks you back up to soar.

FLY WITH THE EAGLES

Have you ever gotten a second wind? Just when you thought you couldn't go another step, when every muscle in your body was screaming *Stop!* and when your lungs felt like a deflated balloon, everything kicked into a higher gear you never knew you had. Ah, the second wind. It's like your power cord gets plugged back in. It's like your gas tank gets refilled. It's like you reach the mountain peak and soar off the top.

The truth is God's strength is our second wind when we feel like giving up. And there will be times when you feel like giving up. We all do. But keep going! Call out to God in your weariness and despair. He sees your struggles. He hears your panting. He understands the course better than you, and He can see the finish line. He wants to fill your spirit back up and launch you like an eagle. That's an amazing ride!

TRIPLE DOG DARE

○ Draw yourself soaring on eagle's wings over your troubles.

○ Go run a mile.

○ Take a rest stop with God. Get in a quiet place and tell Him what's weighing you down.

What did you do? What did you learn?

MISSION ACCOMPLISHED!

TRUTH
Loyalty means sticking beside a friend even in hard times.

STAND BY ME

It hurts to have a friend turn his back on you. If you've been there, you know. But it's an awesome feeling to have a buddy stick up for you right when rejection is about to swallow you up.

The biggest part of having a good friend is being a good friend. Sometimes that's hard. Sometimes friends make you mad or annoy you. Sometimes they make bad decisions or do something uncool. But sometimes so do you.

The truth is that a good friend doesn't turn his back on a bro. A loyal friend has his friend's back in good and bad times. That doesn't mean you let a friend drag you into activities you know are wrong or cover for his bad decisions. Being loyal means being there for him. It means caring enough to call him on taking the wrong path and to offer help to get back on track. It means expecting the best of a friend and not giving up.

TRIPLE DOG DARE

○ Apologize to a friend whose feelings you've hurt.

○ Text or call an old friend and ask how things are going.

○ Stick up for a friend when you see he's getting hassled.

MISSION ACCOMPLISHED!

What did you do? What did you learn?

TRUTH

God is the only thing you can absolutely count on to never let you down.

WHEN THE BOTTOM DROPS OUT

You hear adults talk a lot about the economy. Your parents might argue about money—with you or with each other. Your mom or dad might have lost a job. You might know someone who couldn't afford to keep his house. It all sounds like an economic crisis is a big deal.

But go back a few years and people were giddy over how much their houses were worth. Stock prices were soaring. Companies were spending and building and making and growing. People were buying, buying, buying. Maybe you got more Christmas presents or went on an exotic vacation.

The truth is wealth can come or go; only God will always, consistently, absolutely be there without fail. Money may seem safe like the "fortified city," but only God is the true "strong tower." He's the one to run to. He's the one who can really help. He's the one to build your life on.

TRIPLE DOG DARE

○ Don't take your blessings for granted. Make a list and thank God for them.

○ Try to live on $10 a day for a week—not just 10 bucks spending money, $10 total for *everything*. Get help from your parents to figure food and housing costs. You'll be glad it's just an exercise.

○ Do a brain check. When you need something, do you think of God first? Put a note in your wallet to remind you.

What did you do? What did you learn?

MISSION ACCOMPLISHED!

TRUTH

Our biggest tests reveal what we're made of.

STAY STRONG

The integrity of the steel matters when you're driving over the Golden Gate Bridge. The integrity of the aluminum matters when you're cruising in a plane at thirty thousand feet. The integrity of the rope matters when you're climbing five thousand feet above the ground on the face of Half Dome. Failure in any of those situations would be catastrophic.

The truth is we reveal what we're made of in our biggest tests. Integrity is consistent strength, and it's proven over long periods of time. Psalm 15 gives a good list of integrity's characteristics: truth, honesty, generosity, and faithfulness even when it hurts. Stay strong. Stay true. Bend, but don't break. Build integrity in your life that spans across deep chasms, soars through stormy skies, and belays you to the highest heights.

TRIPLE DOG DARE

- Keep your word. If you say it, mean it, and follow through. Write a list or use a calendar if you need reminders.

- Prove to your parents that you're trustworthy. Do your chores without being asked and look for ways to help your younger brothers and sisters this week.

- Look up *integrity* in the dictionary and copy the definitions.

MISSION ACCOMPLISHED!

What did you do? What did you learn?

TRUTH
Remembering God saves you lots of trouble.

REMEMBER

If you forget the answers on a test, you fail. If you forget where you live, you're lost. If you forget the rules, you foul out. If you forget to do your chores, you're grounded. If you forget God, you're headed for trouble.

The truth is we always need to remember God and His faithfulness. To remember, we've got to know. To know, we've got to learn. And to learn, we've got to listen.

The Israelites got themselves into trouble because the new generation didn't know God. They didn't listen and learn from the people who came before them. They didn't know or remember all the amazing things God did for their ancestors. There's a famous saying that says, "Those who cannot remember the past are condemned to repeat it" (George Santayana). The Israelites kept forgetting, turning away from God, getting into deep problems, turning back to God, and finally being rescued. They kept taking the hard way and suffering for it. You don't have to.

TRIPLE DOG DARE

○ Write all the good things God has done for you.

○ Take a poll of adults you look up to. Ask them the biggest lesson they ever learned about God.

○ Trace God's work through your ancestors. Ask your relatives for help.

What did you do? What did you learn?

MISSION ACCOMPLISHED!

Friends with Backbone

Check out the cool Bible story in Mark 2:1–12. These guys had their friend's back—quite literally, since his own spine didn't work. We don't know much about the paralyzed man, except that he couldn't walk—and he had good friends.

Maybe he was born that way. Maybe the guys carrying him were brothers or cousins who had known him their whole lives. Maybe he was a stonemason or fisherman who had recently fallen and now had no way to earn money to feed his family. One thing is sure: He needed help.

Okay, two things are sure: He needed help and he got help. Even when the crowd was too big to get near Jesus, the friends found a way. Picture it. They worked their way close enough to the building, climbed onto the roof—while carrying a paralyzed man, remember—cut a hole through the ceiling, and lowered their friend down to Jesus to be healed!

Sooner or later, we all need guys we can count on no matter what. Sometimes we just can't carry ourselves, and we have to lean on others. Be ready to go the extra mile to make sure your friend gets help when he needs it. Surround yourself with guys you can trust to do the same for you.

TRIPLE DOG DARE!

◯ Read Mark 2:1–12.

◯ What friends can you count on to always have your back? Whom are you ready to stand beside no matter what?

◯ You probably know somebody who needs some help. Step up and do whatever it takes to make sure he or she gets it. Make a list. Who needs help? What's one thing you can start with to help? Go do it.

WHO NEEDS HELP: WHAT I CAN DO:

YOUR PAGE

Someday ...

1 CORINTHIANS 9:24–27

TRUTH

Being a Christian is like being an athlete. It takes training and practice.

RUN TO WIN

The Olympics are awesome. Athletes from all over the world represent their countries and try to be the best on the planet. These guys and girls have spent hours and days and years practicing—many of them at unusual sports like biathlon (skiing and shooting), curling (think shuffleboard on ice), or live pigeon shooting (well, that one was canceled after the 1900 games).

It's these athletes' number one goal: Be the best they can at their sport. They practice over and over again, sometimes botching a start or falling, sometimes nailing a perfect landing or new personal best. They put the healthiest foods in their bodies and resist junk even if it smells tempting. They get big-time satisfaction out of winning, but even their gold medals won't last forever.

The truth is we should train our hearts and spirits like an Olympic athlete, focused on winning the ultimate prize. So keep going. Don't stop even when life's junk looks tempting. Build good training habits, and get up when you fall—because the only prize that will last forever comes from God.

TRIPLE DOG DARE

O Read your Bible every day this week.

O Wake up fifteen minutes early every day to read your Bible.

O Give up some spiritual junk for a week—maybe a video game or some music that distracts your spirit.

What did you do? What did you learn?

MISSION ACCOMPLISHED!

TRUTH We are called to season and shine.

SALTY AND BRIGHT

Popcorn with no salt is awfully plain. Same goes for potato chips. Beef jerky? Wouldn't even happen without the salt. Salt brings the zing. It's the seasoning and the flavor. Our nation gets too much of it in our food, but back in Bible days it was vital. It preserved food and kept it edible before there was such a thing as refrigeration. If the salt went bad, all the meat went bad.

The truth is God calls us to be salt—and light—in the world. He wants us to be the seasoning that preserves life. He wants us to be the light that shines in the darkness to brighten the way.

When the crowd around you is huddled in bland darkness, stand up and shine. Shake out some salt and be different. Don't know what to do? Obey God and choose actions of love to shine through you. Others will be attracted to your glow and your flavor. It's what God has put you here for.

TRIPLE DOG DARE

- Do a taste test. Make some popcorn with and without salt. Or try low-sodium versus regular soup.

- Go in your closet with the light off. Turn on a flashlight and notice the differences it makes.

- When all your friends are doing something you know is wrong, stand up and do something different. Invite others to join you.

MISSION ACCOMPLISHED!

What did you do? What did you learn?

PROVERBS 17:17

TRUTH A real friend stands by you even in trouble.

THE WINGMAN

A fighter pilot needs his wingman. Without him, a pilot might as well be wearing a bull's-eye. Both pilots have to be just as good of flyers, and they're both committed to the same mission. But the wingman's job is to protect his partner, to intercept enemy planes, and to make sure his partner reaches the target. The wingman is an extra set of eyes and wings. Together the pilots are a team. And wars are won by teams, not individuals.

The truth is we all need a wingman in real life. A true friend has your back and sticks beside you even when things get rough. It can be hard to listen to and obey God's Word, but a good friend can remind and encourage you. It gets hard to blast through enemy distractions that come from pride, anger, TV, and music, but a wingman can help you stay focused.

Sometimes you'll be the squad leader. Sometimes you'll be the wingman. Find solid friends you can count on. And be a true friend to others.

TRIPLE DOG DARE

- Who are your wingmen? Spend more time with the guys who are trustworthy.

- Who needs a wingman? Encourage a friend and let him know you have his back.

- Who's going down in flames? Invite over a friend who's hurting or facing some hard times.

What did you do? What did you learn?

MISSION ACCOMPLISHED!

TRUTH

Planning ahead beats laziness and want.

ARMY OF ANTS

Ants are amazing little creatures. I'm sure you've stepped on an anthill and seen the army of little insects pour out to defend their territory; at that point you probably surrendered and let them have their turf back. But have you ever had an ant farm? If so, you've seen their network of tunnels that looks like something out of Middle Earth. Don't forget ants' incredible strength—they can lift one hundred times their body weight!

The truth is the Bible tells us we can learn a thing or two from the ant, especially this: Planning ahead beats laziness and want. Ants work hard and prepare for the future, gathering and storing food for when there isn't any that's easy to grab. Ants don't lie around feeling lazy; they keep moving and get their work done. Ants know what they need and keep going to make sure they get it. They also rely on help from each other.

What do you want? Make a plan and keep going toward it.

TRIPLE DOG DARE

O Watch an anthill and learn. Take notes on your observations.

O Set your alarm fifteen minutes earlier this week. Accomplish something with your extra time.

O Set three goals. Add an action that will help you achieve each goal. Then make them happen.

MISSION ACCOMPLISHED!

What did you do? What did you learn?

TRUTH

You reflect God. You were made in His image.

IMAGE IS EVERYTHING

Image matters. That's what the advertisers tell you. You've got to look cool, smell cool, smile cool, eat and drink cool, drive cool, sleep cool, and make sure your dog eats cool dog food. Advertisers spend billions to convince you their products are the key to cool. They're right that image matters. They're just wrong about where true image comes from.

The truth is you were made in God's image. You reflect God. That's cool! And that makes you cool. Image is just a reflection of who you really are and what you're about on the inside. If all you care about is having the coolest clothes and stuff, you might impress people for a while. But sooner or later they'll realize you're nothing but empty on the inside. Instead, take to heart that you reflect God; you bear His mark as His child. That means you really matter. You have purpose and depth and identity. Don't worry about your own image being cool. Enjoy the image God gave you.

TRIPLE DOG DARE

- Look in the mirror every morning this week and say, "I'm God's son, and I matter."

- Keep a list of what advertisements are really trying to sell you. For example, product: hair gel, promise: popularity.

- Whenever someone insults you, remind yourself that God made you just the right way in His image.

What did you do? What did you learn?

MISSION ACCOMPLISHED!

Create a Comic

Comic books are all about the art and action. They're fun to read. They can also be fun to draw. Good comics use a variety of angles and sizes to show the excitement in different and interesting ways.

TRIPLE DOG DARE!

Draw in the panels below to create your own comic strip of a favorite Bible story. Choose key events and important details to show the action moving along. Be sure to color your comics too!

Here are a few story ideas to get you started.
Get others from the movie-making lists in
this book. Or come up with your own.

- David fights Goliath (1 Samuel 17)
- The fall of Jericho (Joshua 6)
- Jesus calms the storm (Matthew 8:23–27)
- Jesus raises Lazarus from the dead (John 11:1–43)
- Saul encounters Jesus (Acts 9:1–19)

YOUR PAGE

My biggest mistake I'd like to erase is ...
⟨Write it down. Talk to God about it. Then erase it.⟩

TRUTH

Our neighbors are all around the world. Love them.

LIKEWISE

The hatred is mutual between Yankees and Red Sox fans. Imagine this: One day a Yanks fan is beaten by muggers. Along comes a pastor, then a worship leader. Both are from New York. Both cross the street and ignore the beaten man. Finally a Sox fan comes by. He stops, carries the man to the hospital, and pays for his medical care. Is this story sounding familiar?

The truth is God calls us to love our neighbor as much as ourselves—and our "neighbors" are all over the world. Sure, the people in your neighborhood count, but in our small world, so do the people who live in other cities and other countries. With the way news and information get around these days, it's easy to find out about catastrophes and big problems people are facing around the world. It's also easy to find ways we can help.

The good thing is there are many groups helping neighbors in other countries. And you can help too. Raise money. Volunteer your time. Spread the word and raise awareness. Write letters to political leaders. Sponsor kids to go to school. Now you know who your neighbors are. Go and do likewise.

TRIPLE DOG DARE

- Write a letter to the child your family sponsors. Talk to your parents or teacher about getting a pen pal if you don't sponsor a child.

- Pick a problem in the world and do something about it.

- Talk to your parents about providing a microfinance loan to an entrepreneur in another country.

What did you do? What did you learn?

MISSION ACCOMPLISHED!

TRUTH
Stay strong even when your friends turn away.

STAY STRONG WHEN OTHERS TURN AWAY

It might come out of nowhere. It might be a guy you know really well. You might have grown up together in church. He used to love Jesus. He used to serve God. Then one day he turns his back on God and says he doesn't believe.

It happened to Jesus and the disciples. It will happen to you.

The truth is you can stay strong when others fall away by focusing on what you know is true. Peter had the right idea. "Where else are we gonna go?" he said to Jesus. "We know that You are God." He clung to his most basic belief. We can do the same.

Don't give up on a friend who turns from God. Pray for him. Talk to him. Love him with God's love. Stay true and be a real example of faith in action in his life. You may just change his mind.

TRIPLE DOG DARE

- O Pray for a friend who doesn't believe in God.

- O Talk to an old friend you used to go to church with but haven't seen in a while.

- O Remember how you first believed in God. Renew your commitment to Him today.

MISSION ACCOMPLISHED!

What did you do? What did you learn?

TRUTH *Jesus will win in the end.*

YOUR COMMANDER IN CHIEF

Have you ever thought Jesus looks like a wimp? It's okay; you can admit it. Many of the pictures and paintings of Christ look passive and weak and just plain wimpy. You've probably seen some in Sunday school or maybe art class.

No one knows exactly what Jesus looked like. That was *waaay* before cameras, and it's likely that no one even drew a picture of Him back then. So the images we get have more to do with the artists' styles and perceptions than anything else.

The truth is that Jesus is no wimp; He is the ultimate conquering warrior. His strength is greater than we can fully understand. That doesn't mean Jesus looks like a comic-book power lifter. But you don't want to be on the other side when He brings down the final hammer of justice. One day He'll reveal His full power and glory and finish God's ultimate work of restoring His creation and kingdom. You'll see Him then and be left speechless.

TRIPLE DOG DARE

○ Draw a picture of Jesus based on Revelation 19.

○ Think of obeying Jesus as taking orders from your wise and battle-tested commander in chief.

○ Get rid of a habit that you don't want to have when Jesus returns. Ask for help if you need to.

What did you do? What did you learn?

MISSION ACCOMPLISHED!

TRUTH

It's okay to get angry, but there's a right way to do it.

GET MAD

Some things should make us mad: bullying, murder, rape, injustice, unfair treatment of others, slavery, genocide, prejudice, killing babies, blatant destruction, and waste. The list could go on. These things and more make God angry.

The truth is even Jesus got angry at the way people mistreated the temple. He turned over tables and threw out the culprits, but He didn't sin. That tells us there's a time and place for us to get mad too. But we need to learn the difference between pitching a fit about losing a soccer game and getting so upset about global poverty that we take action to change it.

Start with these guidelines. Are you mad because you didn't get what you wanted, or because you saw God's ways being violated? Do you want to defend yourself or another person being mistreated? Will your action cause more trouble, or is it a legal, legitimate way to help?

TRIPLE DOG DARE

- Get mad about something good—and get involved to change it.

- Deal with your anger. Cool off and talk with the person you're mad at. Apologize and forgive.

- Learn to cool off before you lash out. Find an activity to help, such as throwing a ball off a wall or running.

MISSION ACCOMPLISHED!

What did you do? What did you learn?

TRUTH

When you're sad, it's time to remember what God has done for you.

SINGIN' THE BLUES

Some days you're just singin' the blues. We all have those days. Sometimes we simply feel sad, down, blue, or lonely. Maybe a friend said something mean. Maybe a girl you like ignored you. Maybe a pet died—or maybe it was a person you loved. Maybe even God feels far away. Whatever the reason, feeling sad and lonely sometimes is part of being human.

The truth is that's the time to remember all the good things God has done for you. The writer of Psalm 42 was pretty bummed out when he wrote his song, and he didn't hold back letting us know. But he also starts to remember and begin to see the way out of his funk. He thinks about how he used to join his friends going to church and worshipping God. Then he starts to think about how God loves him and has taken care of him. By the end, the psalmist starts to feel some hope and to praise God. You can do the same.

TRIPLE DOG DARE

- Write your own psalm. Start with how you're feeling. Then remember God and start praising Him.

- Make a list of ways God takes care of you and your family.

- Make good-day and bad-day jars. Add a dollar or candy to a jar if it's an overall good day. Add a slip of paper describing how you feel to a different bad-day jar. At week's end, shred or burn (safely) the bad day papers and start over. Celebrate with the good-day symbols.

What did you do? What did you learn?

MISSION ACCOMPLISHED!

MAKE TRIPLE DOG TRACKS

Stars Sing Out

God's fingerprints are all over science. Humans still don't understand everything about our universe or even our own bodies. God's creativity and work can blow our minds—from the teeniest molecular detail to the biggest and most amazing galaxy. Looking at the stars is an awesome way to explore and appreciate God's creation. Psalm 19:1 says, "The heavens declare the glory of God; the skies proclaim the work of his hands."

TRIPLE DOG DARE!

Go outside at night. Lie down in a dark place. Look up. Be amazed. Here's a minichart of some basic constellations to look for. Check 'em off when you find 'em.

PISCES

ORION

URSA MAJOR

SCORPIUS

GEMINI

DRACO

BIG DIPPER

TRIPLE DOG BONUS

Get a star chart and telescope or binoculars and keep exploring. Also catch the Perseid meteor shower for an awesome show!

YOUR PAGE

People I admire:

TRUTH Jesus is God's Son.

DON'T BELIEVE THE HYPE

Everybody—even Satan—believes Jesus lived and died. There's no denying that in history. But a lot of different people have a lot of different opinions beyond that. The most common is that Jesus was a great teacher but not God's Son who rose from the dead. They respect some of what He said, but they don't want to give Him control of their lives.

The truth is Jesus is God's Son. He meant what He said—all of it. He is the way to God and true spiritual life that never ends. Don't believe anyone who tries to tell you different, but expect them to. Watch out for lies about Jesus.

How can you tell what's true? Look to the Bible. Read Jesus' words and learn what He taught. Get help to understand the parts that sound confusing. Ask lots of questions of your parents, youth leaders, Sunday school teachers, pastors, and other older Christians. But for starters, don't believe anything that denies Jesus' God-ness or resurrection.

TRIPLE DOG DARE

- Pick one of the Gospels—Matthew, Mark, Luke, John—and read it all this week.

- Write a list of your favorite sayings of Jesus. Memorize three.

- Give Jesus your life. Check out The Ultimate Triple Dog Dare at the back of this book if you're not sure how.

What did you do? What did you learn?

MISSION ACCOMPLISHED!

TRUTH
Look at God and never give up.

NEVER GIVE UP

You know England was in trouble if you've studied World War II. Hitler's Nazis had stormed through western Europe, defeating every nation in their way. And the British Isles just across the English Channel were the next target. The Nazis seemed unbeatable, but England fought back and repelled them under the leadership of Prime Minister Winston Churchill.

After England had turned the tide against Germany, Churchill made a famous speech at his old school that still applies to us: "This is the lesson: Never give in, never give in, never, never, never, never—in nothing, great or small, large or petty—never give in except to convictions of honour and good sense. Never yield to force; never yield to the apparently overwhelming might of the enemy."

The truth is God wants us to never give up no matter how bad the situation looks. In fact, He wants us to not look at our situation—that will only discourage us. Instead we should look at God and the promises of the Bible. One day all our problems will be gone. One day Jesus will rule. Victory is ours. Never give up!

TRIPLE DOG DARE

O Fight back. Take one step to stand up to your problem.

O Draw a picture of God defeating your problem.

O Write out 2 Corinthians 4:18 on a note card, computer, or phone wallpaper.

MISSION ACCOMPLISHED!
What did you do? What did you learn?

PSALM 100:1-2

TRUTH
You can worship God with whatever noise you can make.

SHOUT IT OUT

There are some funky sounds in the animal kingdom: whoops and hoots and squawks and warbles. They come from animals just being animals, but don't you think it makes God happy to hear a zebra braying or a howler monkey whooping it up? After all, He's the one who made them to sound so weird.

The truth is you can worship God with whatever noise you can make. You don't have to be an amazing singer. You don't even have to be able to carry a tune. God understands if you're a little, or a lot, off-key. He gave you your vocal cords. And He cares more about the attitude in your heart than the pitch flowing from your lips.

So let out your joyful noise. Send out a worshipful shout. Sound your barbaric yawp. Cheer with wild abandon like you're at the Super Bowl. And howl at the top of your lungs. It's all God's kind of sound.

TRIPLE DOG DARE

○ Go outside or down in the basement—just somewhere you won't startle your mom—and let loose with a joyful noise to God.

○ Sing from your heart. Close your eyes. Forget anyone else is around, and let loose your song to God.

○ Play your instrument to God or use homemade drums while you make up your own praise song.

What did you do? What did you learn?

MISSION ACCOMPLISHED!

TRUTH

God can and will forgive every wrong thing you do.

WRONG IS GONE

Something changes when a person apologizes. That is, when they say they're sorry for what they've done wrong to you and you can tell they really mean it. Sure, sometimes you still feel mad. You might not even want to forgive them. But "I'm sorry" opens the door to making things right.

When it's the other way around, sometimes you think you've gotten away with something, and you're glad. Other times you're truly really-feel-bad sorry—especially when you realize you've hurt someone you love. Then it can feel like there's a wall between the two of you.

The truth is that no matter what you've done wrong, God promises to forgive you when you ask Him to. No matter how big or how bad your sin, He'll keep His promise. Even more, He'll make you cleaner than your white laundry and purer than mountain water. That doesn't mean you won't get in trouble from your parents or teachers. Our actions always have consequences. But it means there's nothing—no guilt—between you and God.

TRIPLE DOG DARE

○ Write a list of things you're sorry for. Read it to God. Then burn it in the fireplace or grill (as long as it's okay with your parents). That's the way God sees your sins—gone!

○ Whose feelings have you hurt? Apologize to them today.

○ When your brother, sister, or friend apologizes to you, forgive them as you remember all you've been forgiven for.

MISSION ACCOMPLISHED!

What did you do? What did you learn?

TRUTH

You're never too young to serve God.

NEVER TOO YOUNG

Sometimes it's convenient to be too young—like when it gets you out of work or something you don't want to do. *Who me? I'm too small. I can't do that!* Just don't try that excuse with God.

Jeremiah tried it. God said, "Uh, no. You can do it." Why was He so sure? Because God created Jeremiah and chose him before he was born. God knew just how He'd made him. He knew Jeremiah's abilities, strengths, and weaknesses. Even more, God knew what God could do, and He promised to be with Jeremiah in whatever He called the prophet to do.

The truth is you're never too young to serve God. God created and chose you, too. He has promised to always be with you. He's given you His Spirit to live within you. You're His son. And you're never too young to speak His Words and share His love. You can accomplish anything God calls you to do.

TRIPLE DOG DARE

- O Lose your excuses. Use what you love to serve God and make the world better.

- O Make no excuses all week when your parents ask you to do something.

- O What is God calling you to do? Do it.

What did you do? What did you learn?

MISSION ACCOMPLISHED!

Abraham: Give It Up

Abraham is the original faith father. Check out the stories about his life in Genesis 12—25. He's the one God first made the ultimate covenant with to bless and restore His people to the original relationship God created. But from the start, God came to Abraham, or Abram as he was named then, with a Triple Dog Dare: Leave his homeland and head out to a new country.

More dares followed, including waiting and trusting God to deliver His promise of a son even though Abraham's wife, Sarah, was ninety years old and hadn't been able to have any children. Abraham didn't always get everything right, especially when he jumped the gun and had a son with Sarah's servant. But he kept trusting that God would do what He said.

Abraham's biggest Triple Dog Dare came after his son Isaac was born. God had finally delivered on His promise, and Abraham loved his son. Then God told him to sacrifice his boy. It must have torn Abraham's heart apart, but he didn't hesitate. God had promised to make a great people out of Isaac, but killing him sure seemed like a crazy way to accomplish that. Abraham must have held onto God's promise as he built the altar, tied Isaac to it, raised his knife, and—God came through. He stopped Abraham and praised him for being willing to hold nothing back.

God gives the same Triple Dog Dare to us today: Hold nothing back from Him. God didn't take away Abraham's beloved son, and He won't necessarily take away things you love. But He wants us to love Him more and put Him first above everything.

TRIPLE DOG DARE!

○ Read Abraham's story in Genesis 12—25.

○ What do you need to surrender to God? Make a list on the next page.

○ Make a "sacrifice" to God. Line up a ring of small stones on your floor. Place an object in the ring that symbolizes what you're offering to God, maybe your basketball, skateboard, or video game controller. Tell God you love Him more than whatever that thing is, and ask Him to help you use it wisely and in ways that glorify Him.

TRIPLE DOG BONUS

Ask your parents for help setting healthy limits on activities like video gaming and movie viewing.

YOUR PAGE

Things that bug me:

TRUTH

We must stay connected to Jesus to truly live and accomplish anything worthwhile.

YOUR ORGANIC LIFE

Look at any tree or bush around you. You've studied plants and photosynthesis in science class, but you knew this before you started kindergarten: Branches must stay connected to the plant to stay alive and grow fruit, flowers, or leaves. The trunk must stay connected to its roots to take in nutrients from the soil. If not—dried-up, dead plants.

The truth is we are branches who must stay connected to Jesus' trunk to live spiritually. Jesus called Himself the vine and us the branches. Stay connected to Him like your life depends on it, because He's where your life comes from. Get nutrients by talking with Him, reading the Bible, learning and talking about God, worshipping Him with music, glorifying Him by using the talents He's given you, obeying His commands, and serving other people. Those things will lead you to actions—fruit—that shows God's work in your life and loves people around you with His love. And the more you stay connected to the Vine, the more natural those actions will become for you. Who knew your spiritual life was so organic?

TRIPLE DOG DARE

O Pick a branch off a bush in your yard. Keep it and compare it over time with one on the bush.

O Draw a spiritual-photosynthesis diagram. Copy the framework from a science book to get started.

O Check your harvest. What kind of crop are you producing? Reconnect to God's life source.

What did you do? What did you learn?

MISSION ACCOMPLISHED!

TRUTH

There's a battle inside you that only Jesus can win.

FLESH VS. SPIRIT

The story from the 1800s is so famous that we still refer to it today: Dr. Jekyll and Mr. Hyde. You know it: One man, two personalities. One is good. One is bad. The two battle for control of the body, and the good Dr. Jekyll loses control of turning into the evil Mr. Hyde.

The reality is that we're all Dr. Jekyll and Mr. Hyde. Our flesh was born sinful and evil. Our spirits were reborn when we gave them to Jesus. One day we'll be completely transformed into the spiritual beings Jesus is making us. Until then, we live on earth with new spirits in old bodies. And the battle for control rages on. We make mistakes. We do what we say we won't. We lose control.

What can we do? Stay close to Jesus. Fight sin with all your might. Confess sin when you fail. Get help from family and friends. Grow stronger over time. Rejoice when you win a battle. Learn from when you lose. And remember there's a long war ahead.

TRIPLE DOG DARE

- Draw a picture of your flesh and label it with sin. Crumple it up and draw a picture of your spirit and label it with God's traits.

- Make a list of sin's opposites. When you're tempted, do the opposite good act instead.

- Offer yourself as a slave to God's law. Remember that you must obey.

MISSION ACCOMPLISHED!

What did you do? What did you learn?

TRUTH The only real security is God.

LIVE LIKE IT'S THE END

Let's say you won the lottery. *Bam.* Winning ticket. Big bucks. You're in the news. Man, you've got it made. You quit school, buy an island and a private jet to get you there. No more school. No more taking out the trash. No worrying about getting a job—ever. You plan on kickin' it the rest of your life. Instead, you kick the bucket the next day.

The truth is the only thing you can rely on to last is God. All that money and the things it can buy? Worth nothing, nada, zip, zilch, a big round goose egg the nanosecond you check out of this life. *But I can still live it up with my island and private jet while I'm around,* you think. Maybe. Your life could end today. There's no guarantee you'll make it to your next birthday, much less your eightieth.

So live like the end is near. Enjoy the stuff God has allowed you to have, but enjoy Him more. Focus on loving God and loving other people. All that comes out of that will be built to last.

TRIPLE DOG DARE

○ Write a letter to your eighty-year-old self. Remind yourself what you want to live for and what's worth living for.

○ Make a list of the ten most important goals you want to accomplish before you die.

○ List three ways you can be rich toward God.

What did you do? What did you learn?

MISSION ACCOMPLISHED!

TRUTH
You don't have to wait to be a leader.

DON'T WAIT—LEAD NOW

What are you waiting for? Who says you can't? Who says you're too young? Kids and teenagers have accomplished great feats: climbed Mount Everest, sailed around the world, created artistic masterpieces. They've also started organizations and raised money to end modern-day slavery, provide clean water, and fight poverty.

The truth is you can set an example and make a difference, no matter how old you are. That doesn't mean you have to break a world record. But you can follow God's leading and the dream He's placed in your heart. Even your "small" efforts can make a world of difference to your neighbor who needs help or your classmate who doesn't fit in.

You'll probably need some help and support from your parents or other adults. That's okay. Tell them your plans. Show them you're serious. Obey God, and live like you mean it. It's time to step up. Take the lead. Be an example. Other people will notice and be inspired.

TRIPLE DOG DARE

○ What opportunity have you been afraid of? Go for it.

○ Set an example for your brothers and sisters—obey your parents.

○ Suggest and plan a project your whole class can do to help someone in need.

MISSION ACCOMPLISHED!

What did you do? What did you learn?

TRUTH

Listening to good advice from people you trust will lead you on smart paths.

TAKE MY ADVICE

Want some good advice? Listen to good advice. Refusing to listen or listening to bad advice is like following a faulty onboard-navigation system. You'll end up sidetracked or lost—in the wrong place and probably without a clue to get out.

The truth is listening to good advice from trustworthy sources will take you to positive places. It will make you wise. You're probably surrounded by sources of good advice: parents, grandparents, teachers, coaches, youth workers, and pastors. Many of those people already give you instructions. You might not like that, but pay attention. Think about what they're trying to teach you and why.

But don't automatically assume that all relatives or adults can steer you straight. Tell the difference between good and bad advice. Start by comparing it to the Bible. Does it agree with God's Word? Look at your advisers' lives. Would you, and, more importantly, God want your life to look like theirs? Wisdom can save you pain and trouble—take my advice.

TRIPLE DOG DARE

- Make a list of good advisers in your life. Go to them and ask questions, especially when you face tricky situations.

- Write about the best and worst advice you've ever received. Why? Where did it take you?

- Choose your destination. What do you want in life? Who do you know who has it or is there? Study him. Ask questions about how he got there. Don't know him personally? Read about his life and note the choices along his path.

What did you do? What did you learn?

MISSION ACCOMPLISHED!

Noah and the Big Crazy Boat

Noah's ark must have brought on some awesome insults. It was probably the first time in the history of humanity when insults were elevated to an art form. Think about it—what was that thing?! A big behemoth of a boat nowhere near the water. It was at least a football field and a half long, maybe longer depending on the exact length of the ancient cubit. So there it was, the world's first cruise ship—sitting in a dude's backyard.

Talk about being laughed at. People must have come from all over the country to check out Noah's big boat. "Hey, Noah, what's that? A barn that floats?" "Hey, Noah, Atlantis called. They want their navy back." "Aye, aye, Captain Crunch!" Okay, so nobody knew who Captain Crunch was back then, but come on—can't you imagine the sailor jokes? And then the animals started showing up. Oh, man!

But Noah was up to the challenge. He did just what God said no matter what anybody else said. Did their mocking bother him? Maybe. But Noah focused on what God said and the mission he'd been given. Noah's Triple Dog Dare was to obey and build a huge boat—oh, yeah, and to ensure the survival of the human and animal races as a result. Definitely a God-sized task, but with God's help Noah was up to it. Genesis 6:22 gives us his key: "Noah did everything just as God commanded him."

TRIPLE DOG DARE!

- Read Noah's story in Genesis 6—9.
- What do you need to do "just as God commanded" even if people are laughing?
- Draw blueprints of the ark, using the measurements in Genesis 6:14–16. Use the next page to designate areas for certain animals, and don't forget room for Noah's family and food storage.

TRIPLE DOG BONUS

Build a scale model of Noah's ark out of wood, cardboard, or LEGOs.

I want to be ...

TRUTH

Jesus came for the poor, sick, oppressed, and imprisoned.

NOT WHO YOU'D THINK

It's easy for us to think Jesus likes the good people best. After all, we think of church as a place for good, clean, maybe even dressed-up, people. We're supposed to hang around people who are a good influence, right? So it's easy for us to think of those people as ones like us: with nice homes, nice cars, nice clothes, nice stuff. But while Jesus loves those people, He also loves dirty, grimy, addicted, violent people just as much.

The truth is Jesus came for the poor, sick, oppressed, and imprisoned people—the ones who need a Savior. And the truth is that includes you and me, too. Even if we look a little cleaner on the outside, we are just as sinful on the inside. When it comes to our spirits, we're no different from the drug dealer in prison or the pastor at church. We all need Jesus. And Jesus wants us to reach out to those who are poor, sick, oppressed, and imprisoned on the outside, too—just like He did.

TRIPLE DOG DARE

- Don't talk about hurting or needy people as "them." Talk about and treat them as fellow humans.

- Volunteer to help prisoners' families through Prison Fellowship.

- Talk to a kid at school whose family might not be well-off.

What did you do? What did you learn?

MISSION ACCOMPLISHED!

TRUTH
You can do anything with Christ's strength.

YES, YOU CAN

You can get along with your pesky brother or sister. You can get a better grade on that test. You can become a better striker, passer, receiver, batter, free-throw shooter, or defender. You can land that kick flip. You can make that speech. You can remember to take out the trash. You can make your own lunch so your mom doesn't have to—you can even do your own laundry. You can stand up for what you believe. You can make a friend. You can endure that teacher you don't like. You can get used to your new home and school. You can obey your parents. You can make it through their divorce. You can feel better after the death of a loved one. You can make it to college. You can outlast the embarrassment when people laugh at you. You can be happy again. You can experience the awesome life that Jesus promises.

The truth is you can do everything through Him who gives you strength. That doesn't mean you won't have to practice—a lot. It doesn't mean you won't fail—or that you'll always succeed on the first try. It does mean Jesus will always be with you. It does mean things that are part of God's will. It means you will make it.

TRIPLE DOG DARE

- Make a list of three goals for this year.

- Make a list of ten goals for your life. What do you want to work toward?

- Memorize Philippians 4:13. Say it out loud when you feel discouraged.

MISSION ACCOMPLISHED!

What did you do? What did you learn?

DEUTERONOMY 10:18–19

TRUTH God wants us to reach out to the new kid.

NEW KID IN TOWN

It can be like walking through a dimly lit tunnel into a dark, cavernous room. You hear sounds—voices—echoing in front of you. Suddenly you're squinting into a giant spotlight that could guide a space shuttle. You're blinded. The light is hot. Sweat beads on your forehead. Your mouth is getting dry. Then you realize it: You're standing on a stage … in a stadium … filled with people … who are now staring … right … at … you! You have no idea what to do. You want to run but it's like your feet are nailed to the floor. *Help!*

That's what being the new kid can feel like. Coming to a new school or neighborhood can be crazy scary. Maybe you've been the new kid and know.

The truth is God wants us to reach out to the new kid. Talk to him. Smile at him. Show him around. Introduce him to your friends. Sit beside him. Eat lunch with him. Ask questions about him and his old school. Listen to him. Think about how he must feel. And remember: Someday the new kid might be you.

TRIPLE DOG DARE

- Go over and meet your new neighbor.

- Introduce yourself to someone you don't know every day this week.

- Look around the lunchroom. Invite an alone kid to sit with you.

What did you do? What did you learn?

MISSION ACCOMPLISHED!

TRUTH

God cares what comes out of your mouth. Keep it clean.

CUSSING ISN'T COOL

Have you ever had your mouth washed out with soap? *Yuck!* Tastes gross, but the punishment fits the crime. It's a good reminder to clean up your language.

Cuss words have become much more common all around us. Part of that's because entertainers are always pushing their boundaries. Shocking people is a way to get attention, and swearing is an easy way to shock people. The more we hear rude language, the more we all use it. The cycle goes around, and it takes more to shock us. Before we know it, curse words and raunchy jokes are slipping into our vocabulary.

The truth is God cares about what comes out of our mouths, and He's called His people to reflect Him with our speech. *But what's wrong with cussing?* It's rude, offensive, and bad-mannered. It's usually used to insult or tear someone else down. *What about crude jokes?* Yes, the human body can be funny sometimes, but raunchy jokes often tear down other people. None of those is God's way. Keeping your speech clean is way to stand out of the crowd for God.

TRIPLE DOG DARE

- Pay your parents $10 every time a swear word or raunchy joke comes out of your mouth (whether they hear it or not).

- Don't tell a joke you wouldn't tell your mom.

- Walk away if a friend begins telling a dirty joke.

MISSION ACCOMPLISHED!

What did you do? What did you learn?

TRUTH
God gave you a conscience as your guide.

KEEPING YOUR CONSCIENCE CLEAR

Many shipwrecks happen when boat captains don't heed the warnings. Maybe they don't see the lighthouse in the fog, or maybe they ignore their maps and charts. Somehow they sail too close to dangerous rocks or lurking obstacles. All it takes is a small puncture in the hull, and water seeps in and sinks the vessel forever.

The truth is God has given us a conscience to keep us from shipwrecking our faith. You know, it's that feeling you get when you know something's not right. It's the sense of right and wrong God has put in your spirit, and it's often what His Holy Spirit uses to remind and guide us.

Consider your conscience your lighthouse. Listen to its foghorn warning. Do what it's telling you. When the guys are egging you on, but you know inside something's just not right, don't do it. Steer clear. Keep your conscience clean and your faith sailing strong.

TRIPLE DOG DARE

○ Don't use somebody else's answers even if other students are.

○ When you have the feeling something's not right, stop, back away, and leave.

○ Speak up when your friends are considering something wrong. You're probably not the only one who thinks so. Tell them you won't do it, and encourage them to do something else with you instead.

What did you do? What did you learn?

MISSION ACCOMPLISHED!

Make a New Testament Movie

Making movies can be fun and a great way to learn. A good producer keeps the big picture in mind and also focuses on the details. He sees creatively beyond the script and understands what the characters are feeling. Making a movie is an awesome way to go deeper into a story and bring it to life. So …

TRIPLE DOG DARE!

Make a movie based on a story in the New Testament. Consider changing the time period; for example, tell the Prodigal Son story in modern times or during American pioneer days. Use props and actors. Film from different angles, and edit with software such as iMovie or Windows Live Movie Maker. Don't forget the credits.

Here are some starter ideas. Look through the Bible for more.

- The Good Samaritan (Luke 10:25–37)
- Paul and Silas in jail (Acts 16:16–40)
- The Prodigal Son (Luke 15:11–32)
- Jesus calms the storm (Matthew 8:23–27)
- Peter walks on water (Matthew 14:22–32)
- Jesus' crucifixion and resurrection (John 18—20)

Add your own ideas.

TRIPLE DOG BONUS

Use action figures to make a stop-motion animated movie. Start writing the script here.

YOUR PAGE

Know music? Write a song here.
Don't know music? Just hum it; then add some words.

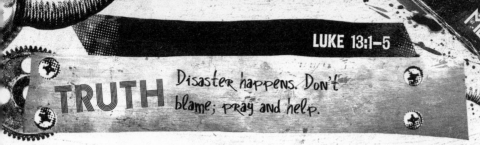

TRUTH
Disaster happens. Don't blame; pray and help.

WHOSE FAULT IS IT?

The world is filled with natural disasters: earthquakes, hurricanes, floods, landslides, tornadoes, forest fires, and more. Usually after the biggest catastrophes there are some people saying it's God punishing somebody for something. Are they right? No.

The truth is that accidents happen. Bad things happen to good people. It's easy to point a finger and blame someone else. People were doing the same thing back in Jesus' day. When people were persecuted and when a building collapsed, they looked for someone to blame whom God must be punishing. But Jesus said no—catastrophes happen. They're part of our broken world.

Instead of pointing fingers, we all need to make our hearts right with God by confessing our own sins and following Jesus. When disasters strike, pray for those affected, give money, or help how you can. Thank God that you were spared, get involved to fix problems that can avoid repeat accidents, and keep your heart humble and right with God. That's the way to deal with disaster. Whether it strikes your life personally or not, you're emergency-prepared.

TRIPLE DOG DARE

- Don't forward sensationalized or blaming stories after catastrophes. Speak up for truth when you hear those rumors.

- Get your friends to pray and raise money and supplies for victims of disasters.

- Check your heart. Are you ready to meet God if your life ended suddenly?

What did you do? What did you learn?

MISSION ACCOMPLISHED!

TRUTH God wants more than robots.

NO ARMY OF ROBOTS

ASIMO is the world's most famous robot. He's a four-foot humanoid that can walk, talk, run, dance, and even conduct an orchestra. Honda made him and hopes to one day produce robots as companions for the elderly or disabled. Scientists have been able to create and program robots to do amazing feats, but they can't program them to feel. Robots don't have emotions.

The truth is we act like robots when we go through the motions without giving our hearts to God. God doesn't want robots. He wants our hearts. He doesn't want us to simply go to church; He wants us to join other people to worship with all our hearts and learn with all our minds. He doesn't want us simply to follow the rules on the outside while we rebel on the inside. He wants us obey Him even when we don't feel like it, because we love Him and trust that He knows best. He doesn't want us to talk about what we're going to do for Him; He wants us to do it. Be God's human child, not His robot.

TRIPLE DOG DARE

○ Plug into church. Think about the words you sing. Read along in the Bible. Ask questions about anything you don't understand.

○ Change your heart to match your words the next time you have to apologize.

○ Make your actions say "Jesus loves you" at school this week.

MISSION ACCOMPLISHED!

What did you do? What did you learn?

TRUTH

You can shine like a star by avoiding complaining and arguing.

QUIT COMPLAINING

Complaining wears you down. It's like a vulture pecking out your eyeballs or a piranha nibbling at your liver. It's ancient Chinese water torture killing you one drip at a time. It's a flesh-eating disease gobbling your body one cell at a time. It's maggots burrowing their way through your heart.

The truth is complaining rots you and everyone around you, but thankfulness warms and glows like the brightest stars in the universe. Each breeds more and more of itself. Each is contagious. Complaining, arguing, and nitpicking curdle you like sour milk; they are the ways of death. Thankfulness, gratitude, and positive words bloom like roses; they are the ways of life. Leave behind the death of complaining. Spread the life of positive thankfulness.

TRIPLE DOG DARE

○ Quit complaining. Do twenty push-ups every time a complaint escapes your lips.

○ It takes two to argue. Refuse to be the second. Stay silent or walk away when a sibling or friend tries to pick an argument.

○ Play *Things would be worse if…* When you're tempted to complain, think of ways the situation could be worse. Then be thankful that it's not.

What did you do? What did you learn?

MISSION ACCOMPLISHED!

TRUTH
Be confident, but don't brag.

NOBODY LIKES A BRAGGER

Nobody likes the guy who can't shut up about himself. It might be true that he's the best player, or it might not be. He might be so full of himself that he thinks he's the next Tim Tebow, or he may know he's not so he tries to sound like it. Either way, you get sick and tired of listening to him brag about himself.

Everybody likes the guy who's really good but doesn't talk about every detail of every play he made. He might have hit a grand slam in the bottom of the ninth, but he gives credit to his teammates for getting hits to get on base. That makes you admire him all the more.

The truth is our deepest confidence comes from God, and He doesn't want us to brag about it. Some translations of the Bible use the words *quietness* and *trust* in Isaiah 30:15. They put them together as ingredients that make us stronger. Trust God for His strength. Do what He's given you the ability to do, and let others do the talking about your accomplishments.

TRIPLE DOG DARE

- Answer with a simple thank you when other people praise you.

- Look for ways to praise and compliment teammates.

- Walk away when a guy starts bragging. Tell him, "I don't like bragging."

MISSION ACCOMPLISHED!

What did you do? What did you learn?

TRUTH

Worship God by keeping your mind and body pure.

TAKE CARE OF YOUR TEMPLE

You wouldn't pet a hungry tiger. You wouldn't walk into a burning building. You wouldn't crouch on an NFL line of scrimmage with no pads—or take a nap on a NASCAR track. Not if you have even one ounce of common sense. You'd stay as far away as possible to preserve your health and life. If you've got any spiritual sense, you'll do the same when it comes to temptation.

The truth is God wants us to run away from temptation, especially those temptations that pollute our minds and bodies. God created sex as a great and powerful gift for married couples, and He's happy when husbands and wives enjoy it together. But lots of pictures, movies, music, jokes, language, and even people twist this gift in ways that make God sad. Run away from those kinds of sex-related temptations. If those aren't tempting to you yet, be glad—they probably will be in a few years. Make your battle plan now. Your best strategy is avoiding this kind of temptation wherever possible.

Your body is a temple where God lives, and you can worship Him by using it inside the boundaries He's created. You—and your future wife—will be glad you did.

TRIPLE DOG DARE

- Get rid of anything you have that tempts you.
- Talk to your parents and get Internet filtering software on your computer and phone (if you don't already have it).
- Commit yourself now to honor God by keeping your body pure. Write down your goal and review it every year.

What did you do? What did you learn?

MISSION ACCOMPLISHED!

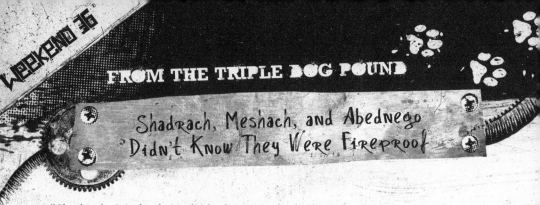

FROM THE TRIPLE DOG POUND

Shadrach, Meshach, and Abednego Didn't Know They Were Fireproof

"Shadrach, Meshach, and Abednego replied, 'O Nebuchadnezzar, we do not need to defend ourselves before you. If we are thrown into the blazing furnace, the God whom we serve is able to save us. He will rescue us from your power, Your Majesty. But even if he doesn't, we want to make it clear to you, Your Majesty, that we will never serve your gods or worship the gold statue you have set up'" (Daniel 3:16–18 NLT).

Have you ever moved to a new town or school? How about a new country? Man, you want to fit in! And that can be tough when people just don't do things the same as you're used to back home.

That must be what Shadrach, Meshach, and Abednego felt like. They'd been taken away to Babylon when Israel was conquered. Thankfully, they weren't put in prison. Like Daniel, they were put in a Babylonian school to learn the ways of their new country, and they became leaders.

That's when their biggest Triple Dog Dare came: Bow down to the ninety-foot golden idol and live—or stay true to God and die. Of course, they weren't going to worship any other god. They told the king, "Nope, God can save us if He wants, and even if He doesn't we're still not disobeying Him." So into the inferno they went—where they hung out safely with God's angel and didn't even get smoky. The king was amazed. He praised God, promoted Shadrach, Meshach, and Abednego, and commanded everyone to respect their God. Instead of giving in to the wrong pressures of their new land, they stayed true and influenced others around them for good.

TRIPLE DOG DARE!

○ Read Daniel 3.

○ What pressures are you facing from the people around you?

○ List ways you can say no and other people who will stand with you for God.

YOUR PAGE

My favorite songs, movies, and games:

TRUTH
Nothing is too small for God to use.

GIVE WHAT YOU'VE GOT

It was one water drop in an ocean. It was one grain of sand on a beach. It was one snowflake in an arctic blizzard. It was one stalk of wheat in the prairies of the heartland. It was one—make that two—small fish from the huge schools in the biggest lake in the region. It was one young, small boy out of five thousand people. But it was a God-sized act of faith.

The truth is God can use whatever we have to give, no matter how small. What could that boy have possibly been thinking? People must have laughed at him—the disciples probably laughed at him. He had a lunch for a boy, not a feast for a stadium crowd. But he gave what he had. And it was more than enough in the hands of God.

What are you holding on to? What seems too small to make a difference? Offer it to God.

TRIPLE DOG DARE

- O Volunteer at church, school, or with another organization. Let God use you.

- O Share your gift with other people.

- O Never say never. Make a list of things too small to use, then find a way to use them for God.

What did you do? What did you learn?

MISSION ACCOMPLISHED!

TRUTH

Use your strength to help the weak.

STRONG FOR A REASON

We all need help sometimes. You included. All of us are good at something, but none of us is good at everything. What would you learn without a teacher? How would you improve without a coach? How could you survive without parents? And how far could you get without teammates?

The truth is that God wants us to use our strengths to help those who are weak. Our lives are not all about us. They're about God using us to love and help others for Him. When something is easy for us, we can be patient with others who have a hard time. We can encourage them and use our skill and knowledge to help. A school subject, a talent, a sport, a musical skill—use yours to help someone else.

TRIPLE DOG DARE

O Volunteer to tutor students who need help.

O Help a friend practice. Rebound, pitch, or chase fly balls. Practice lines for a play together.

O Encourage a friend to make good choices. Explain that you won't watch or listen to certain things because they don't make God happy.

MISSION ACCOMPLISHED!

What did you do? What did you learn?

TRUTH *The only true treasure is God's.*

GET RICH FOREVER

A moth is the apocalypse to a sweater. The little paper-thin varmint can turn your favorite shirt into Swiss cheese. Rust can do the same to a car. The metal fungus can freeze up the most powerful earthmover or rot the strongest gates. Ever try to ride a bike with a rusted chain? No go. And then there's the thieves. Get hit by a robber and stuff that was there last night is gone in the morning. Vanished.

It's the way our world works. You science geeks know you can thank the second law of thermodynamics. (The rest of you can look it up.) Everything is breaking down. Nothing will last forever, including all of our earthly treasures: our money, our gadgets, vehicles, houses, you name it.

The truth is that only spiritual stuff lasts forever. It's weird because we can't see it, but God can. The most valuable treasures come from Him—things like love, forgiveness, life, relationships. Somehow our actions that reflect God last—forever, eternally, after we're dead on earth. In the meantime, what we value and try to get shapes who we are. Get rich with what will last longer than your body.

TRIPLE DOG DARE

O Instead of buying a new song, buy a drink for a kid who looks lonely.

O What thing can you not live without? Don't use it for a week.

O Invest in heaven. Serve your parents, a friend, and a neighbor today.

What did you do? What did you learn?

MISSION ACCOMPLISHED!

TRUTH

You are a mighty warrior who can accomplish awesome deeds.

YOU—YES, YOU— ARE A WARRIOR

Look in the mirror. Picture your helmet. Pull back your bow. See the light glint off of your blade. You are a warrior, a mighty warrior.

You might not always feel like it. You might not feel brave or strong. You might not want to be a warrior. Sometimes it just seems easier to go with the flow. That's just what your enemy wants you to think. Oh, yeah, you definitely have an enemy, the Devil, who wants to take you out.

But the truth is you also have a more powerful Commander, and His strength never changes. Even when we're weak, we can rely on Him to be strong.

Being a warrior doesn't mean we go looking to pick a fight. And we're never going to beat somebody into believing in God. Being a warrior means we have a quest: to serve God and to live out His life and kingdom around us. It means we're ready to stand for truth, to defend the weak, and to fight to right wrongs. Those are awesome things!

TRIPLE DOG DARE

O Who's the outcast in your class? Tell your friends you're done joining in the put-downs. When insults start, give the targeted kid a compliment and ask him to hang out.

O Volunteer with a group that's helping people in need.

O Treat girls with respect. Don't pick on or hit them.

MISSION ACCOMPLISHED!

What did you do? What did you learn?

TRUTH Everyone needs a second chance.

SECOND CHANCES

You've done something you regret. You might have realized it immediately and tried to grab back your words even as they flew out of your mouth. Or maybe you looked back later and saw you really blew it. Maybe you were a real jerk for a real long time. You wanted another try, a second chance, right?

The truth is God gives everyone a second chance. He knows we blew it, and He offers forgiveness and grace that we don't deserve. That goes for us and for everybody else. That's what Paul was writing to ask Philemon: Give Onesimus a second chance.

Are you willing to give a second chance to the kid who picked on you all last year? He says he's changed. He seems to be acting different. What about your brother who apologized? He sounds sincere. Make sure the kid follows up on his promise, but give him another chance—just like you would want. And don't forget that kid who got a mean nickname or bad rap. Give him a chance.

TRIPLE DOG DARE

- ○ Give someone a second chance this week.
- ○ Talk to the kid nobody liked last year. Give him a second chance.
- ○ Tell a friend you want him to give another friend a second chance.

What did you do? What did you learn?

MISSION ACCOMPLISHED!

MAKE TRIPLE DOG TRACKS

Ways I Can Worship

Worship can happen any time, any place, any way. Worship is expressing thanks and praise and wonder to God. Where are you most struck by a sense of God's power? What makes you think of God most? What activities make your spirit feel like it's flying? Why do you burst out singing praise songs? Those answers are good signals of worship. Turn your attention to Him in the middle of those experiences. Give a simple thank you or think more deeply about Him. Worship is an attitude of our hearts and a natural expression of our lives.

TRIPLE DOG DARE!

Worship God by doing one or more of the items on this list. Add your own ideas to the list. You'll come up with your own that are more powerful for you.

- Make up a song.
- Run.
- Swim.
- Bike.
- Write a poem.
- Walk in the woods.
- Climb a mountain.
- Skate, surf, or snowboard.
- Stargaze.
- Watch the sun rise or set.
- Look at the moon through a telescope.
- Paint.
- Build.
- Help your mom cook your favorite meal.
- Eat your favorite meal.
- Cry.
- Climb a mountain and enjoy the view.
- Put your feet in the mud.
- Visit the zoo.
- Visit old people who can't get out.
- Chop wood.

Your turn. Keep going …

YOUR PAGE

The coolest thing I've ever learned in school is ...

TRUTH
God's voice comes quietly. We must listen.

LISTEN FOR THE WHISPER

You want loud? God could give us loud. He spoke the universe into being with a word. Can you imagine if He shouted? It'd make a drag-race tractor-pull with jet engines and a Super Bowl–sized crowd in the middle of an active war zone sound like a whisper.

Sometimes we wish He'd give us directions like that—the kind that would knock us over and that we couldn't miss. We'd know exactly what we should do when we face hard decisions or confusing situations.

The truth is God speaks to us quietly in our spirits. To hear Him we have to listen and pay attention—just like Elijah did. God sent Elijah a wind, probably hurricane-force, then an earthquake and a wildfire, but God spoke in a whisper. Maybe He does it that way to keep us using our faith—you know, trusting Him and believing what we can't see. Maybe it's to keep us turning down the distractions all around us. Pay attention. It won't be an audible sound, but God wants to speak to our spirits. Make sure you're listening.

TRIPLE DOG DARE

- Listen for God by reading His Word. He's given us lots of direction in the Bible.

- Ask your parents, youth leaders, or Sunday school teachers for advice about a confusing decision.

- Start your day with a quiet zone: no music, TV, or texting. Pray and listen to God.

What did you do? What did you learn?

MISSION ACCOMPLISHED!

TRUTH

God wants us to keep on forgiving

CAN I BEAT HIM TO A PULP NOW?

Chances are it's your brother or sister who you get mad at the most. Siblings have a way of knowing just how to press our buttons, and some bros and sisses think it's fun to get your goat (funny expression—whoever came up with that one?). It's because they know you so well. No matter who's bugging you, it gets old when they make you mad or hurt your feelings for the 108th time. Is there a limit where it's okay to just stop forgiving them?

The truth is God wants us to forgive other people endlessly—just like He forgives us. Jesus said seventy times seven or seventy-seven times, depending on your Bible translation. But He wasn't giving a limit; He was making the point that we should keep on forgiving. (Peter was trying to get away with seven times.)

Forgiving doesn't mean we have to keep taking abuse, though. If someone is hurting or bothering you, talk to him and ask him to stop. If he keeps it up, he's not being a good friend, and it's okay to stop hanging around with him. Keep forgiveness in your heart rather than a grudge, and spend your time with true friends.

TRIPLE DOG DARE

- Forgive everyone you're mad at. Ask God for help.

- Call a truce with your brother or sister. Make some rules to avoid intentionally bothering each other. Get help from your parents if necessary.

- Talk with your biggest tormenter and forgive him. If you need to, steer clear of him as best you can.

MISSION ACCOMPLISHED!

What did you do? What did you learn?

LUKE 12:47-48

TRUTH
The more you've been given, the more that's expected of you.

MAKE THE MOST OF IT

Your stuff is more than stuff. Take a closer look at your bike, computer, video-game console, iPod, books, football, and bank account. While you're at it, add your school, church, teams, choirs, and bands. They're all opportunities—opportunities for you to learn and improve and pursue and grow and give and serve. They might lead you to a career or a lifelong hobby. Whether you realize it or not, you're rich in opportunity. You're loaded with choice.

The truth is the more you've been given, the more that's expected of you. It's called responsibility. You might not think you've got anything special because every kid around you has most of the same opportunities. It just seems normal, and thankfully it is in our country. But it's rare when you look at the whole world. Your freedom to go to school and church are gifts. Your right to talk openly about God is a gift. Your choice to become anything you want is a gift. And your ability to own so many goods and gadgets is a luxury. It's all an opportunity to worship and glorify God. Make the most of your chances.

TRIPLE DOG DARE

- Inventory all your possessions. List one way you can use each item for God.

- Go all week without complaining about school. When you're tempted, thank God for your opportunity to learn.

- Dream about your career. What do you love to do now? How could you do it as a job?

What did you do? What did you learn?

MISSION ACCOMPLISHED!

LUKE 6:37-38

TRUTH

The way you judge other people is the way you will be judged.

YOU SET YOUR STANDARD

What goes around comes around. You know that kid who is always criticizing everybody else? It won't be long until he's being criticized. The two-faced girl who talks behind people's backs? They'll be talking behind hers. The guy who holds grudges—they'll be holding grudges right back. The person who never forgives—no one will keep forgiving him. The whiner who always complains—they'll just stop hanging out with him.

The truth is the way you treat other people is the way they'll treat you right back. You hold the measuring tape. You set the standard that you're held to. And it goes the good way, too. Try it. Smile at people, and they'll smile back. Be a friend to all, and you'll always have a friend. Forgive others' mistakes easily, and they'll forgive yours. It all comes back around. Decide how you want to be treated.

TRIPLE DOG DARE

- Do a smile experiment. Smile at everyone today, even strangers, and notice how many people smile back.

- Forgive the person you're holding a grudge against. Apologize to him.

- Do twenty push-ups every time you blame someone today.

MISSION ACCOMPLISHED!

What did you do? What did you learn?

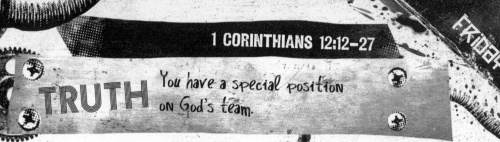

TRUTH

You have a special position on God's team.

TEAM PLAYER

The quarterback can't go long to catch passes. You don't want your catcher chasing down fly balls in center field. And your goalie does no good dribbling down to shoot at the opposing goal. Every player has his position, and every position requires special skills and roles.

The truth is God's team is the same way, and you've been given a special position to play. The Bible compares it to our body. Every part matters. Some get lots of attention, and some work behind the scenes. But a body needs all the parts to work, just like a team needs all its players.

You might still be learning what your role is. That's okay, but don't forget that every position is just as important to the team. Not everyone is good at playing quarterback, and most quarterbacks are lousy on the offensive line. Don't worry about getting attention. Instead of being jealous, realize that you'll be happiest playing the position that uses your strengths. Be a team player.

TRIPLE DOG DARE

- Watch a pro football game and then look around closely at a church service. Make lists of how many different people are doing different things to make it all happen.

- Make a list of all the things you're good at. Note one way you can use each ability.

- Get in the game. Volunteer to help at church and school.

What did you do? What did you learn?

MISSION ACCOMPLISHED!

Isaac Trusted His Dad

Read Genesis 22:1–18, and put yourself in Isaac's shoes. You're walking with your dad into the wilderness to make a special sacrifice to God. Kind of exciting because it's some special time with Dad, and you get to be part of an important event. It makes you feel older, like your dad trusts you. You're carrying the wood for the fire, and you're looking at the torch and ceremonial knife that your dad has when it hits you.

"Uh … Dad?"

"Yes, son."

"We've got the fire and wood, but aren't we forgetting something? Where's the lamb we're gonna sacrifice? That's pretty much the main ingredient of the sacrifice."

"Don't worry, son. God will provide the lamb."

Okay, you'll go with that. But by the time you're tied up and lying on top of the wood, you know something must have gone wrong. This is not what you had in mind when your dad invited you to this sacrifice!

The Bible doesn't give us all the details. It makes sense that Isaac must have been freaking out. And even though Abraham was getting ready to go through with it, he must have been upset and weeping thinking about what was going on. Both of them must have remembered the sound of that angel's voice calling out for the rest of their lives! Talk about relief! Talk about prayers of joy as they sacrificed *that* sheep!

Somewhere in the timing of it all, Isaac must have had a chance to bolt. Instead, he faced up to his Triple Dog Dare: Trust his father. He knew his dad loved him and loved God, and even in a hard and confusing time, Isaac stuck with his dad.

TRIPLE DOG DARE!

- Read about Isaac in Genesis 22 and 24.

- Have you and your dad been butting heads? What do you need to trust your dad about?

- Ask your dad to spend some time together. Make a list of activities you'd like to do together.

YOUR PAGE

The coolest thing I've ever learned outside of school is ...

TRUTH

Honesty builds people's trust in you.

BE A TRUST BUILDER

You've got five hundred dollars cash and you need some supplies. Whom do you trust with the money and send to get the stuff? Your answer shows whom you trust.

The truth is that honesty builds people's trust in you. The more you're transparent with them and follow through on what you say you'll do, the more they know they can count on you. You probably see it with your parents. The more you obey, do your chores, and meet your responsibilities, the more they're willing to let you do—because you've proven you can handle it honestly.

Unfortunately, we hear stories all the time about CEOs of big companies going to jail for breaking laws or about business people taking advantage of customers. There's a lot of dishonesty out there. No matter what business you end up in as a grown-up, start now to build honest habits. Act in ways that people can trust—with their money or their lives.

TRIPLE DOG DARE

O Come clean with any lies or half-truths you've been hiding.

O What have you told other people you would do? Do it.

O Don't sneak into a movie you didn't pay for even if your friends do. Ask them not to because it's dishonest.

What did you do? What did you learn?

MISSION ACCOMPLISHED!

2 CORINTHIANS 9:6–7

TRUTH God loves a cheerful giver.

GET CRAZY CHEERFUL BY GIVING

Have you ever seen a little kid give a gift he thought was the coolest ever? Maybe he took it to a friend's birthday party and was excited when he bought it. But when it came time to hand it over—nothing doing! He cried. He screamed. *He* wanted that superawesome toy. It's funny because a little kid doesn't know better. But sometimes we act the same way.

The truth is God loves for us to give generously and happily, both to Him and to others. He doesn't want to pry our tithes and gifts to church out of our hands. He doesn't need our money, but He knows we need to remember that everything we have is His. He's not impressed if we grudgingly offer our leftovers to someone in need. Neither are other people. We determine how much we get by how much we give—because people remember kindness and generosity. Open your wallet with a smile.

TRIPLE DOG DARE

○ Give money to church this week with happiness. Sing your favorite worship song in your head to help feel good about it.

○ Give a small gift to your mom. Buy it or make it, but get excited about giving it.

○ Surprise a friend by offering to buy a snack or drink for him today.

MISSION ACCOMPLISHED! What did you do? What did you learn?

TRUTH
God uses our problems and hard times to make us more pure.

WHEN THE HEAT IS ON

The purer a precious metal is, the more valuable it is. Pure gold. Pure silver. Pure platinum. Why settle for less than the real thing? Well, if you've ever bought a bracelet for your mom or sister, you might have chosen a lesser purity because it was all you could afford. Can't blame you there.

Precious metals don't come out of the ground in their purest states. They are dug out of mines as part of soil and rock, and they're chemically connected to alloys, other metals and elements mixed into them. The most common ways to separate them all involve heat. Getting the impurities out means meltin' 'em down till they're liquids and skimming off the extra particles that float to the top.

The truth is that God uses heat to purify us on the inside too. Problems and struggles turn up the heat in our lives. They're not easy to deal with, but God is always there. And when we let Him scrape off the extra junk that floats to the top of our spirits, He makes us purer, truer, and more like Him.

TRIPLE DOG DARE

○ What's your biggest problem right now? Let God use it to purify you.

○ Wear a wrist band or necklace to remind you that God is working in your life.

○ Thank God for the struggles you're facing.

What did you do? What did you learn?

MISSION ACCOMPLISHED!

TRUTH

Life flies by. Make it count for God.

NOT MUCH TIME

Time flies when you're having fun. You've heard it a million times, but it's true. Playing your favorite game with friends can make an hour seem like five minutes. It's like you're in some kind of time warp.

God's clock is an actual time warp. It runs totally differently from ours. It's got different rules that we can't even comprehend—like no beginning and no end. (Think about it: Everything we're used to on earth has a start and a finish.) And God can see and be in all that eternity at once. Mind-blowing! Imagine your life against that backdrop. It's a speck, a nanosecond, a breath.

The truth is our lives fly by, but God can make them count. He gives us hope that there is more than just our ups and downs on earth. He makes going to school and training our brains and working hard worth much more. He helps us recognize eternity in our every day. Open your eyes to see it, and make today count for eternity.

TRIPLE DOG DARE

- Count how many days you have to live. Multiply 365 times the number of years you think you'll live. Subtract the number of days you've already lived.

- Make today an eternal quest—because it is. Choose actions that will last.

- Ask God to give you hope in your schoolwork. Look for ways to use what you're learning for His purposes.

MISSION ACCOMPLISHED!

What did you do? What did you learn?

TRUTH
God's kind of strength is filled with love.

GENTLE GIANTS

We call him a gentle giant. He's the mountain of a man with soaring head, barrel chest, tree trunk arms and legs, and a voice that booms like thunder. He can be intimidating and scary at first glance. Looks like he could squash you like a bug! But get to know him and you realize: He's powerful as a grizzly but gentle as a teddy bear. He's fierce as a tiger but kind as a kitten. Maybe you know a gentle giant. Maybe it's your dad or your uncle or a close family friend.

God is like that.

The truth is that God is all unlimited power and unfathomable love. He could destroy the universe in a single breath, but He tumbles and tickles His children. He will defend His own to the death but wipe away each of our tears. That's the kind of mix He wants to fill us with. He wants to build our strong spiritual muscles so we're ready to fight for truth and battle off attacks. And He wants to fill us with overflowing love that helps the helpless and welcomes the weak. Let Him grow you into a gentle giant on the inside.

TRIPLE DOG DARE

○ Tell your dad three things you admire about him.

○ When you play a game or do some work you're really good at, look for a way to help someone who's not as good.

○ Write a story about a giant who chooses love over destruction.

What did you do? What did you learn?

MISSION ACCOMPLISHED!

Get Your Hands Dirty

Some guys love to build and tinker with stuff naturally. But anybody can learn a lot from getting his hands on something to take it apart or build it up from scratch. Believe it or not, you can bring the Bible to life by getting your hands dirty in it. Here's what I mean in this weekend's Triple Dog Dare …

TRIPLE DOG DARE!

Build something out of the Bible. Use modeling clay, balsa wood and glue, Play-Doh, toothpicks, canvas, cardboard, LEGOs, marshmallows, or whatever else you have on hand. Gather the details you can from the Bible, and add your imagination. Think about the reasons behind the design and how and why people used it. Imagine living and connecting with God in or with that building or object, and you'll find yourself connecting with God's Word in a new way.

Here are some starter ideas. Look through the Bible for more.

- Noah's ark (Genesis 6—8)
- The temple in Jerusalem (1 Kings 6)
- The ark of the covenant (Exodus 25:10–22)
- A fishing boat (John 21)
- The manger where Jesus was laid (Luke 2:7)
- The pool of Bethesda (John 5:1–3)
- The Cross (John 19:17–20)
- Jerusalem (Check the maps in your Bible.)

Draw your building plans here or get some graph paper.

TRIPLE DOG BONUS

Go big. Get your dad's help and use plywood and lumber.

YOUR PAGE

Draw your ultimate vehicle.

TRUTH
It's wise to look for more than a pretty face in girls.

GET TO KNOW THAT GIRL

There's probably a cute girl who's caught your eye. You might not admit it, but she probably gives you butterflies in your stomach. Even if you still think girls are gross, there's probably one you think is the coolest, for a girl anyway. It's okay; I won't blow your cover. But within the next few years, you're going to look at girls a whole lot differently, and someday you'll probably even want to marry one.

The truth is that a girl's heart is much more important than her face. Even in your friendships with girls now, it's wise to look for godly character traits. Consider it practice for getting to know girls worth knowing. No, you probably won't meet your future wife in fifth grade, but your relationships with girls will have a big influence on you as you grow older. Learn now to see and respect girls for what's inside, not just get hung up on how pretty they are on the outside.

So what should you look for? Proverbs 31 gives a good list to start with: hard-working, dependable, giving, generous, smart, strong, compassionate, prepared, good-humored, wise, faithful, kind, attentive, and committed to God.

TRIPLE DOG DARE

- Make a list of all your mom's good traits and give it to her with thanks for all she does for you.

- Make a list of traits you hope to find in a wife someday.

- Compliment a friend who is a girl today.

What did you do? What did you learn?

MISSION ACCOMPLISHED!

TRUTH

God helps you tell others about Him.

YOUR MISSION

The most important things can be the hardest to talk about. It's easier to joke around about a guy's goofy blunders than to tell him he's your best friend. It's easier to laugh off a girl's kindness than to tell her you like her. And it's easier to debate video game strategies than to tell a friend about Jesus.

The truth is Jesus wants us to lead people to Him, and He's always with us to help. *Phew! You mean it's not up to me to say just the right words to convince somebody to give his life to God?* Exactly. God wants us to do our part, but it's not entirely up to us. He gives us words to say, and His Spirit works in other people's hearts.

Witnessing is more than words. Making disciples means living with, guiding, and being an example to them. Arguing someone into accepting Jesus doesn't work, but loving and helping them shows God's love in action. And it gives you opportunities to explain Jesus in your life and His love for others. Make sure your life tells about God, and ask Him for the words to use at the right times.

TRIPLE DOG DARE

- Write this quote credited to Saint Francis of Assisi. Think about it and practice it this week: "Preach the gospel at all times; when necessary, use words."

- Talk to a friend about Jesus this week. Start by asking what he believes about God.

- Invite a friend to church or a church youth event this week.

MISSION ACCOMPLISHED!

What did you do? What did you learn?

TRUTH
True success can only come from God.

DON'T COME UP EMPTY

You plan to make your first million by when? You can picture your ginormous crib? You've got all twenty-seven vehicles in your fleet all picked out? Get over it.

The truth is that true success can only come from God. Yachts and private planes can be fun for a while, but eventually they all come up empty. All the successful deals and crazy cash someday lose their ability to pump you up. None of it can really satisfy you on the inside. Only God can do that.

Start now to put Him first in your work. Do your best at school and glorify Him by using the gifts He's given you. Go through each day knowing He's working all around you; join Him by loving your fellow students. Learn His ways by obeying your teachers and listening to their lessons. Sharpen your view of success now. It's not about money and power; it's all about contentment that comes from obeying and walking with God.

TRIPLE DOG DARE

- ○ List your life priorities. What matters most to you?

- ○ Get a job and learn to work hard. Mow yards. Rake leaves. Walk dogs. Or design websites.

- ○ Make three goals about your future career. What matters most to you: working outside, helping people, being creative?

What did you do? What did you learn?

MISSION ACCOMPLISHED!

TRUTH

You died and rose again with Jesus. Now put on His clothes.

BAD OL' ZOMBIE

So there's the old you that was a zombie. Yep, complete with blank stare, rotting flesh, decaying clothes, and Frankenstein walk. You might have even had an eyeball missing or a major organ hanging out. No, none of this was on the outside of you—you've always been a normal, good-looking boy. It was your sinful spirit that was in zombie condition.

The truth is you died and rose again with Jesus, and your spirit got a new life. And here's where things get tricky. One day in heaven you'll be the completed new you, fully sin- and decay-free. For now, the old zombie keeps trying to pop back up from the undead. You have to choose every day to put on the new you, just like you're putting on clean clothes. That starts with choosing where to focus your mind: on God's ways. Next comes keeping off the zombie traits like lying, filthy language, greed, and lust. Instead, it's dressing in God's uniform, which includes compassion, humility, patience, forgiveness, and more. Those will definitely keep all your organs in your body, especially your heart.

TRIPLE DOG DARE

- Set your mind on things above each morning by reading the Bible or listening to worship music.

- As you get dressed, think of the godly traits you want to wear that day.

- Draw a picture of Jesus defeating your sinful old zombie.

MISSION ACCOMPLISHED!

What did you do? What did you learn?

TRUTH
Getting corrected is no fun, but we need it to learn.

DO THEY HAVE TO LOVE ME THAT MUCH?

Our parents would let us do whatever we want, whenever we want—if they didn't love us. Think about it. If they didn't care about us, they'd have let us play in the street when we were preschoolers. If our lives made no difference to them, they'd let us eat candy for every meal. If they didn't mind our brains turning to mush, they'd let us play video games and watch TV 24/7. Instead, our parents (and other authority figures in our lives) give us limits and boundaries—along with unfun consequences to help us remember when we break them.

The truth is that God and our parents discipline us to help us learn. Believe it or not, it's not fun for them either. But they see and understand life better than we can, and they're trying to guide us and help us grow. Their discipline shows they love and care for us. That can be hard to remember on the wrong side of being grounded, but learning to find the lesson will help reduce the frequency of being punished.

TRIPLE DOG DARE

O Apologize to your parents (or teacher) after you've been disciplined.

O Start a life-lessons journal. Record what you get in trouble for and answer, *What can I learn?*

O Examine the rules. Look at what each one is trying to protect you from or help you learn. Talk to your parents about them.

What did you do? What did you learn?

MISSION ACCOMPLISHED!

Ebed-Melech to the Rescue

It often takes help to stop a bully. He'll pick on his victim ruthlessly, especially when that victim isn't strong enough to stop him. But a bully will stop when others stand up and come to the defense of the victim. It's worked that way since Bible times.

Jeremiah wasn't very popular. His job as a prophet was to deliver God's messages, and those messages most often weren't happy in days when the kings and people were disobeying God. So some bullies threw Jeremiah in a well. They wanted him to die, but they didn't necessarily want his blood on their hands. So maybe the well seemed like a good place to suffer and eventually fade away—to death.

That's where Ebed-Melech comes in. He was an official in the palace who knew Jeremiah was a man of God, and he stood up to save the prophet. Ebed-Melech went to the king for help, then took thirty men to get Jeremiah out of the well. He even brought padding for the ropes to make the rescue more comfortable for Jeremiah. Ebed-Melech may be a character hardly anyone knows about, but he saved one of the Bible's most famous prophets by standing up for what's right.

TRIPLE DOG DARE!

- Read Jeremiah 38:1–13.

- Who do you know who is being bullied? Who is the bully?

- Follow Ebed-Melech's example. Get help from someone with authority. Do something to help: Tell the bully to leave the victim alone and reach out to help the victim. On the next page, write down ways you can do that.

YOUR PAGE

I feel closest to God when ...

TRUTH

You've got no reason to be a sore loser or a spoiled brat.

SORE LOSER

It's no fun to play with sore losers. They get mad, kick the ball away, or throw the game board onto the floor. Then they pout and whine and complain like a drama queen. You don't even want to be around them anymore.

The truth is you've got no right to be a sore loser. Instead, you've got every reason to be thankful you can play the game. You've got arms and legs that let you throw and run. You've got eyes to see the field or board and a brain to understand the rules and strategy. You've got money to afford the equipment and team fees. You've got freedom to play instead of dodging bombs.

You don't have to *like* losing, but learn from your losses. Turn your frustration into more practice. And thank God you've got opponents instead of enemies. Above all, don't be a drama king like Jonah.

TRIPLE DOG DARE

- ⭘ Congratulate your opponents even when you lose.

- ⭘ After each loss, write down three things you can practice and improve.

- ⭘ Never blame the refs. Thank them for doing a hard job.

What did you do? What did you learn?

MISSION ACCOMPLISHED!

TRUTH

God wants us to take care of other people's needs.

ACT LIKE A HOTEL MANAGER

It's fun to stay in hotels. They've got big beds, elevators, and snack machines right down the hall. Even better is room service. They'll cook up whatever food you want, whenever you want it, and deliver it right to your door. And the best thing is the pool—oh, yeah! It's usually inside so you can swim in warm water no matter what the weather is. Hotels really know how to take care of you.

The truth is God wants us to take care of each other, especially people in need. That's what hospitality is: generously taking care of others' needs. Hotels and resorts are part of the hospitality industry. And do you notice the same root word in *hospital,* the place people are cared for and treated to get well?

You don't have to have a pool and room service to practice hospitality the way God wants. You can welcome new students at school or church. Share lunch or books with people who forgot theirs. Invite new kids or loners to sit with you and your friends or to come to your house. Spread kind words. Look around and it's easy to see ways to be hospitable every day.

TRIPLE DOG DARE

- Look for someone eating lunch alone and invite him or her to join you.

- Ask you teacher if you can bring a special snack for your whole class.

- Look around and spot one need you can meet each day this week.

MISSION ACCOMPLISHED!

What did you do? What did you learn?

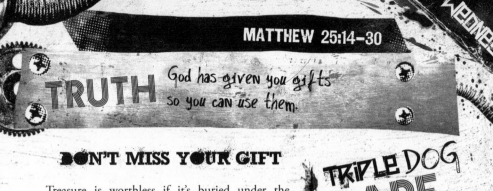

MATTHEW 25:14–30

TRUTH

God has given you gifts so you can use them.

DON'T MISS YOUR GIFT

Treasure is worthless if it's buried under the ground. Money does no good if it rots under your mattress. The cure for cancer won't help if it never leaves the test tube. The secret code can't give you access if you never punch it in. Are you getting the picture?

The truth is you have gifts, and God wants you to use them. Everyone's are different. Some people have more than others. What's important is what you do with what you've got.

What are yours? What are you good at? What do you like to do? What do teachers and parents praise you for? What do you get the best grades in? The answers can help you figure it out, but that's only the beginning. Even the world's greatest and most gifted masters had to practice hours to improve and sharpen their skills. What if they hadn't? The world would have lost out. The gift would've been wasted. That's the way God sees it. Make the most of what He's given you.

TRIPLE DOG DARE

- Practice your instrument or sport and do your homework this week without complaining.

- Give your gift. Share your creativity or ability to help or encourage others.

- Invest your money. You might start with a US Treasury Note.

What did you do? What did you learn?

MISSION ACCOMPLISHED!

ISAIAH 61:8

TRUTH

We get to know God better by doing what He loves.

WHAT GOD WANTS TO DO

You've got a lot in common with your best friends. Your common likes and interests probably helped draw you together. It's the way relationships work. We get to know somebody by spending time doing what he likes to do. Your friend likes bike riding? You probably hang out and ride together. Your friend is a baseball freak? You probably play catch.

The truth is that God loves justice, and He wants us to join Him in doing it. When we do, we get to know Him better. We ask for God's strength and see Him provide it. We learn to see other people through His eyes. We see Him giving us chances to use His love and be His hands on earth. When we do what we can to bring fairness to unfair situations, we meet with God. Do something God likes to do and get to know Him better in the process.

TRIPLE DOG DARE

○ Pick an important topic and find out what you can do about it to make a difference.

○ Collect school supplies to give to other kids in our country or another country.

○ Make a list of poor or needy people. Answer this question about each: What would I do in their situation?

MISSION ACCOMPLISHED!

What did you do? What did you learn?

TRUTH

You can learn a lot from other generations.

STRONGER TOGETHER

Try looking through your grandparents' eyes sometime. You might get sick of the "In my day …" stories, but have you stopped to really listen to them? Your grandparents are living history. They lived through the Vietnam War and the civil rights movement when Martin Luther King Jr. was alive. They saw communism and New York's Twin Towers fall. And they actually existed before the Internet and mobile phones.

The truth is we have a lot to learn from other generations, and we can deepen our faith by worshipping together. The Israelites learned that when they all came together to pour out their hearts to God in celebration. The older people remembered when the temple was destroyed. Some cried and some shouted for joy. Everyone was excited to see it being rebuilt. And it took all of them coming together.

Try to pick up bits of wisdom from older people, and share your knowledge with them. You, your family, church, and community are much stronger together.

TRIPLE DOG DARE

O Make a documentary movie about your grandparents' or parents' lives. Interview them like on a news story.

O Ask your whole family to sing worship songs and pray together one night this week.

O Visit a nursing home and ask residents for stories about when they were kids.

What did you do? What did you learn?

MISSION ACCOMPLISHED!

Hall of Faith

Read Hebrews 11. These are the originals on God's all-time all-stars list. They go way back in the day—before Jesus, before the Bible, some even before the Ten Commandments. They didn't have a lot to go on as far as learning *about* God, but they trusted Him and got to *know* God.

TRIPLE DOG DARE!

Draw lines to match up the hall-of-faither with his or her key play. The answers are at the back of the book.

PERSON		KEY FAITH PLAY	
1.	Noah	a.	obeyed and trusted to become father of many
2.	Isaac	b.	gave a better sacrifice than his bro
3.	Gideon, Barak, Samson, Jephthah, David, Samuel, prophets	c.	were sawed in two and persecuted
4.	Enoch	d.	believed and had a son
5.	early Christians	e.	blessed his grandsons and worshipped
6.	Sarah	f.	gave instructions to take his bones
7.	Israelites	g.	blessed his sons' future
8.	Abel	h.	gave up palace life and led others on a miraculous path
9.	Rahab	i.	pleased God, never died
10.	Joseph	j.	hid spies
11.	Abraham	k.	shut lions' mouths, conquered kingdoms, administered justice
12.	Jacob	l.	built an ark
13.	Moses	m.	brought down walls by walking

MY KEY FAITH PLAYS

If I could fly ...

TRUTH *You get what you give.*

GET A GOOD HARVEST

When you plant an apple tree, you can't wait to eat the—avocados?! *No, that's not right!* You know your strawberry bush is going to grow—cactus flowers?! *Something's wrong here. Try again.* When you slug your brother in the jaw, you know you're going to get—double allowance and rewards?! *Only in some backward universe!*

The truth is every one of your actions grows a specific type of result. You've heard it before: You reap what you sow. You harvest what you plant. You get what you give. Every action has a consequence. In science, Newton's third law of motion says it this way, "To every action in nature there is an equal and opposite reaction."

Your actions are like seeds. You can't change the fact that they will grow something, but you can decide what type of fruit they'll grow. Plant kindness and generosity, and you can enjoy their good results. Plant meanness and greed; then don't complain when that's what comes back at you. Just stay patient and remember: Sometimes good fruit takes a while to grow. But it tastes so much better when it's ripe!

TRIPLE DOG DARE

- Check your crop. Tired of bitter fruit? Trace it down and change your bitter actions.

- Plant. Plan and do three acts of kindness for people you don't like.

- With a few friends, plan and do three acts of kindness or service for your teachers, classmates, and school.

What did you do? What did you learn?

MISSION ACCOMPLISHED!

TRUTH You can't serve God and money.

YOU CAN ONLY WORSHIP ONE

You can't play for the Yankees and the Red Sox. You can't serve in the US Army and the Chinese Army. You can't vote for the Republican and the Democrat. You can't root for Auburn and Alabama, or Michigan and Ohio State, or USC and UCLA, or … (you get the picture.)

The truth is you can't devote your life to both God and money. You've got to choose. You've got to pledge your allegiance to one or you'll be torn in two. Money will buy you some good times and fancy toys, but it can also rob your relationships and leave you empty. And when you die, it's all gone. Buh-bye Benjamins.

God offers joy, peace, love, and satisfaction on the inside. Following Him can be hard, but He always helps us. He might bless us with lots of money, or He might not. But His ultimate payoffs are even richer than we imagine. Choose wisely!

TRIPLE DOG DARE

- What's dividing your heart? Get it out of the way.

- Show God you're devoted to Him by giving some of your money to your church.

- Pick a side. Make up your own pledge of allegiance to God.

MISSION ACCOMPLISHED!

What did you do? What did you learn?

PROVERBS 16:28

TRUTH Gossip tears friends apart.

DON'T PASS IT ON

Rumors are like cartoon snowballs. You know, the ones that start little, then roll down a hill getting bigger and bigger and bigger. They roll over small animals and anything else that gets in their way, and you see bird beaks and squirrel tails sticking out of the snow as it keeps rolling. Faster and faster you can see it coming. Then *BLAM!* it smacks some poor, unsuspecting guy and flattens him paper-thin.

The truth is that's what rumors and gossip do—they can wipe out a person and flatten a friendship. The results aren't pretty. Repeating stories or suggestions about another person leads to trouble and can destroy lives and friendships. Don't do it. Stick up for a friend when you hear lies being spread. If you're not sure what to believe, go to the source; ask the guy or girl concerned if the rumor is true. But don't pass it on. Spreading half-truths or stories at someone else's expense might gain you some quick attention, but it can cost you a long-term friendship.

TRIPLE DOG DARE

- ○ Don't hit Forward. Dump rumor texts, posts, and emails in your trash and ask others to do the same.

- ○ Stand up for the truth. Speak up when you know or suspect a lie is being spread.

- ○ Even if a story is true, would you want it being spread around about you. No? Then don't pass it on.

What did you do? What did you learn?

MISSION ACCOMPLISHED!

PROVERBS 3:5-6

TRUTH
God leads us on the best paths when we trust in Him.

DRIVE THE STRAIGHT ROADS

A straight road is much faster than a curvy road. Has your family ever taken a vacation to the mountains? If so, you probably drove on some curvy, winding roads. It was probably slow going and easy to get lost. It could have been bumpy and rough, and all that switching directions back and forth might have even made you sick.

The truth is we can live our lives on straighter, smoother roads when we look to God for our directions. We do that with the decisions we make: by obeying His Word and trusting more in Him than our own ideas. In every situation, remember God and His bigger picture. It's like He can see the entire world atlas while we can see only a map of a few blocks. Ask God for help in making decisions. Ask Him to point you on His roads. Then step on the gas and enjoy the ride.

TRIPLE DOG DARE

- ○ Ask for God's help making a decision you are facing.

- ○ Practice looking to God for directions. Write "God" or a map symbol on your hand as a reminder to ask what He would do in every situation.

- ○ Trust and go. If your decision lines up with God's Word, give it all you've got for God.

MISSION ACCOMPLISHED!
What did you do? What did you learn?

TRUTH

Jesus sets you free from sin and death.

NO MORE DEATH ROW

You were born on death row. You had a date with the executioner before you got a Social Security number. Your spiritual future looked grim, as in Grim Reaper. What had you done? You were human and guilty by your sin nature. You can thank Adam and Eve.

The truth is Jesus suffered your execution and gave you a pardon. When you gave your life to Him, you got a get-out-of-death card—otherwise known as forgiveness of your sins. All of them. Forever.

The Devil will try to tell you that it doesn't work. He'll accuse you when you sin and tell you you're too bad for God. He'll whisper that God can forgive most people of most stuff, but not *you* of *that!* Don't believe his lies. You will still sin sometimes. When you do, confess it to Jesus and count on the promise of Romans 8:1–2. You'll still face consequences for your actions on earth, including punishment from parents, teachers, or law enforcement. Learn from them, and remember: God forgives you. Forgive yourself, too.

TRIPLE DOG DARE

O Let your guilt go. Write your sin on a scrap of paper. Pin it to a cardboard cross. Then burn them in the fireplace (if it's okay with your parents) as a symbol that your guilt is gone.

O Write a story about yourself as a prisoner pardoned on death row.

O Pray and surrender your life to Jesus. Look back at today whenever you doubt God's forgiveness.

What did you do? What did you learn?

MISSION ACCOMPLISHED!

Stick with It

Most guys love stickers. We've got them on our bikes, notebooks, skateboards, surfboards, snowboards, go-karts, walls, and any other flat surfaces we can find. What makes a good sticker? Sure, we like a cool design. But our favorites are ones we can identify with and get behind—maybe our favorite board or shoe company. Those are the ones we want people to connect us with.

If you could design your own sticker, what would you want it to say about you? How would it show you're connected to God?

TRIPLE DOG DARE!

Draw your own logo and stickers. Make them show you stand for God. Be creative, but here are some tips:

- Use symbols.
- Include a favorite Bible verse somehow, either through pictures or words.
- Get colorful.

TRIPLE DOG BONUS

Ask your parents to help you create and order your own stickers online.

YOUR PAGE

Free Page
⟨Use it however you want.⟩

TRUTH

Treat others with fairness and generosity.

A FAIR DEAL

Sometimes people just need help. And sometimes you have just what they need. Maybe it's lunch money or an extra set of gym clothes. It could be a phone to call for a ride or a spare bike to be able to keep up with the other guys. Are you going to charge a guy to use them?

The truth is God wants us to treat other people with fairness and generosity, especially when we have something they need. Don't try to exploit others when you can help them. That's what Nehemiah called out the Israelites for. They were loaning money but charging interest to newly returned refugees who needed help. They were taking advantage of the people in distress. It was definitely not dealing fairly.

Don't make every situation about you. Don't try to get ahead. Lend generously and help friends and neighbors in need. You'll be repaid when those same people help you when you need it.

TRIPLE DOG DARE

- Find a way to help your brothers or sisters this week.

- Buy fair-trade products when you can, ones that make sure poorer growers and producers in other countries receive a fair price.

- Stand up for fairness. Call out friends when you see them treating others unfairly and ask them to do what's right.

What did you do? What did you learn?

MISSION ACCOMPLISHED!

TRUTH

God is a mighty warrior. You are in His service.

THE COMEBACK OF ALL TIME

The ultimate conflict of good versus evil—it's what makes all the best stories. Think about your favorites. There are probably heroes and villains and some kind of battle. It might even look like the bad guys will win or that the hero has arrived too late to save the girl, or humanity, or the earth, or the universe.

That kind of story rings true deep inside us because it reflects the ultimate story we're all living in. It's easy to forget, but we're all smack in the middle of the ultimate war between good and evil.

The truth is the battle rages around us, and God is the conquering warrior. He's incredibly patient and merciful to us, and we don't usually see His battle face. It can even seem like the bad guys are winning. But that won't always be the case. In the biggest comeback in the universe, God will one day claim victory. Until then, fight with Him as His warrior armed with truth and love.

TRIPLE DOG DARE

O Stand up and say no to something you know is wrong.

O Know someone who's being bullied? Tell the bully to stop today. Get help from friends and a teacher or parent.

O Fill in the blanks with your name and read it out loud. "_____ is God's warrior. _____ the warrior is his name."

MISSION ACCOMPLISHED!

What did you do? What did you learn?

TRUTH

Give everything when it comes to loving God.

GIVE GOD ALL YOU'VE GOT

I like to sweat. It shows me I'm playing hard and doing something worthwhile. My heart is pumping. My muscles are working. And I'm lost in the game, giving it all I've got. You know the feeling?

The truth is God wants us to give it all we've got when it comes to loving Him. He wants us to give it all our heart, soul, and strength. That's the deepest and best of us. He wants us to follow Him like we'd go into the national championship of our favorite sport or activity: focused, committed, and intense.

Unfortunately it's easy for us to get lazy about following God and to act like we're slacking off at practice. That's why God told the Israelites to use lots of reminders for themselves and their children, visual aids to remind them, "Oh, yeah, this is where God came to our rescue," or "That's right; God wants us to serve Him this way." Use the Bible as your reminder to give God all you've got!

TRIPLE DOG DARE

- Read your Bible for as much time as you play video games this week.

- Whenever you feel bored this week, pray, read your Bible, or serve someone nearby.

- Set up some spiritual reminders around you. Post some Bible verses or pictures on your walls, mirrors, computer, or locker.

What did you do? What did you learn?

MISSION ACCOMPLISHED!

TRUTH
God wants us to love our enemies.

HOW TO TREAT YOUR ARCHENEMY

It's easy to love our friends and family. They're nice to us. They take care of us. They make us feel good. And they're fun to be around. It's good to show love, kindness, and appreciation to our friends and family. But Jesus tells us to do more.

The truth is that Jesus tells us to love our enemies. That's hard to do—actually impossible without His help. God wants us to pray for people we don't like and those who bomb us, either with terrorist explosions or harsh words. He wants us to be generous to those who take selfishly from us. He wants us to stay patient with those who explode impatiently at us. It's tough stuff that will take lots of practice. The bottom line is that Jesus wants us to act like Him. To do that means we have to see other people like He does: with love and compassion—and to do that means we need to keep our eyes focused on Jesus for His help.

TRIPLE DOG DARE

○ Look for one good trait in each of the people you don't like.

○ Pray for kids at rival schools and in countries where our nation is fighting.

○ Look for God's best, but don't let a bully go unchallenged. Stand up to him and get help from parents and teachers.

MISSION ACCOMPLISHED!

What did you do? What did you learn?

TRUTH

God wants to give us wisdom and confidence that He's bigger than any problem.

STRONGER THAN THE MONSTER BENEATH YOUR BED

The monster didn't stand a chance against your mom or dad. When you were little, strange noises or even the dark scared you silly. You'd be lying in bed almost asleep when suddenly you could hear the dragon breathing under your bed or see the eyeballs peeking out of your closet. Your spine tingled, and you just knew something was there!

But you also knew who was stronger than the monsters. You'd run like a bullet for mom and dad's room. They could handle whatever was lurking in your room—as long as you could reach them safely.

The truth is that's the way we should turn to God—with full confidence that He can handle anything that's troubling us. He wants us to trust Him completely and confidently, and He wants to give us wisdom—that's the ability to see and understand with His eyes. When we practice His wisdom, we see how much bigger God is than whatever problems are lurking in our lives.

TRIPLE DOG DARE

O Ask God to give you wisdom about a problem you're facing.

O Write down any reasons you're having trouble trusting God. Ask Him to replace your doubts with confidence.

O Draw a picture of God squashing your fears and troubles.

What did you do? What did you learn?

MISSION ACCOMPLISHED!

Joshua Paid Attention

Talk about some big shoes to fill! Moses had been the leader of the Israelite nation since they had left the slavery of Egypt more than forty years earlier. And it had been a miraculous journey that included crossing the parted Red Sea, gathering food supplied from heaven, and receiving the Ten Commandments directly from God. Finally the people were on the verge of entering the long-awaited Promised Land, but Moses wasn't going with them. Joshua was their leader now.

It was a huge Triple Dog Dare: Become leader of the nation and take over an entire land. Joshua must have been at least a little nervous, but he was ready for the big task. We know that Joshua "had been Moses' aide since youth" (Numbers 11:28). Joshua was ready because he had passed his earlier Triple Dog Dare: Pay attention and learn. Moses had taken Joshua along with him most of the time and showed him how to follow God and lead the people. Joshua watched carefully and picked up all Moses' pointers. When his turn came, he was ready to "be strong and courageous" (Deuteronomy 31:6) and to keep his eyes on God to have enough strength for the task.

TRIPLE DOG DARE!

○ Read about Joshua in Numbers 13—14, Numbers 27, Deuteronomy 31, and the book of Joshua.

○ What adult are you close to whom you can watch and learn from? Who loves God and acts wisely? Your dad, mom, grandparents, youth leader? List whom you can pay attention to and what you can learn.

Fill in these lists:

SITUATIONS I NEED TO BE STRONG AND COURAGEOUS	PEOPLE I CAN ASK FOR HELP	BOLD STEPS I CAN TAKE	WHAT GOD CAN DO

YOUR PAGE

Someday I'm going to go ...

TRUTH

Don't worry. God knows what you need.

NO WORRIES

Time travelers have it made. They can go back and push their loved ones out of the way of speeding trains or redo the biggest mistakes of their lives. They can leap into the future to defuse nuclear weapons or tinker with their pro sports careers. You're not a time traveler. So don't waste your time worrying about yesterday or tomorrow.

The truth is God knows exactly what you need, and He has promised to take care of you even better than you could yourself. Worrying gets you nowhere except sidetracked. You can't add an extra hour to your day or your life. You can't make anything happen by fretting over it.

What you can do is seek God. Talk to Him about the stuff that's bothering you. Give it to Him. As you do, make a plan, set goals, and list steps you can take to get there. Then do what you need to do today: go to school, obey your parents, practice, love God, and love people. Get involved in His priorities and your worries will fade. Your stuff will fall in line: the big test, the girl you like, the tryout. God knows.

TRIPLE DOG DARE

- Send God your worries. Type them in a computer file. Pray. Then delete.

- Focus on today. List your priorities and do them.

- Donate your old clothes to charity. Give supplies to a local food pantry.

What did you do? What did you learn?

MISSION ACCOMPLISHED!

TRUTH

Drop everything and come immediately when Jesus calls.

DROP EVERYTHING

My dad had a certain whistle you could hear across the entire neighborhood. He did it through his teeth, and it could have hailed a cab during New York City rush hour. Whenever I heard it I knew it was time to come home—now. Maybe your parents have a certain call or whistle or tone of voice. When you hear it, you know it's time to drop everything and go.

The truth is when Jesus calls, we should drop everything and come—now. Peter and Andrew and the rest of the disciples did. They left their jobs and whole lives, just like that. They didn't know where they were going, but their hearts knew that this was the right way, God's way.

What is God calling you to? What's holding you back? Give it up. Let it go. Don't waste any time. Drop everything and go. To Jesus. Now.

TRIPLE DOG DARE

- Give your life to Jesus—right now. Got questions about how? Check out The Ultimate Triple Dog Dare at the end of the book.

- Give God any activity or habit or desire or relationship or anything you've been trying to keep away from Him.

- Ask your family members to share the stories of when they felt God calling them to follow Him.

MISSION ACCOMPLISHED!

What did you do? What did you learn?

TRUTH
The way to save your life is to give it away.

LIVING IN OPPOSITE LAND

It's like living in the land of opposites. Imagine going to school and finding the push doors opened with a pull, the students made the rules for the teachers and principal, and your one or two academic classes were squeezed in around lots of breaks. The world as you know it would seem pretty backward.

The truth is Jesus calls us to live with a completely different outlook from the world around us. It's like He wants us to see the world spiritually opposite. All the stuff that matters on earth—money, celebrity, cars, sports championships, latest technologies, coolness—doesn't matter to God. It's not that those things are necessarily evil; it's that they can lead us away from God if they're all we care about.

What matters to God is loving, serving, sharing, and looking out for other people. He cares about us obeying His Word and putting Him first, not ourselves. He calls us to sacrifice harmful short-term pleasures—like Jesus did—to gain spiritual rewards that will last forever.

TRIPLE DOG DARE

- Concentrate and live opposite today. How would Jesus see, think, and act?

- Give your life away today. Ask God to show you how and watch for opportunities.

- What's your cross? How do you suffer? Find one way to learn from it.

What did you do? What did you learn?

MISSION ACCOMPLISHED!

TRUTH

God's commands aren't a burden; they keep us from being burdened.

BEHIND THE RULES

Drug addicts are slaves. They have no choice but to take another hit. Their cravings force them to lie, cheat, and steal to get money for more. Their addiction tears apart their bodies and relationships and sucks the life out of them. They are burdened by the drugs that once seemed so fun.

The truth is that God's commands are not a burden; they keep us from being chained and destroyed by sin. That's a good thing to remember when you feel sick of following the rules. God's rules aren't there to keep you from having fun. They're designed to lead you to the best things in all of eternity. God's rules keep you free to enjoy life and free from being addicted to and enslaved by sin.

God's rules are like a guardrail on a mountain highway; they help us not plunge over the edge. They're like a rock-climbing harness or a parachute that keeps us from splattering below. God's rules are written in love. Follow them in love and enjoy the freedom and blessing they bring.

TRIPLE DOG DARE

- Read the Ten Commandments with love in mind. Look for the pain and damage they protect you from.

- Choose to follow that rule that you've been rebelling against.

- Tell your parents you know they make you follow rules because they love you.

MISSION ACCOMPLISHED!

What did you do? What did you learn?

TRUTH Greed is a sneaky sickness.

THE GREED DISEASE

Sometimes it sneaks up on you. You feel tired, like you don't want to do anything. Your body kind of hurts all over but nowhere specific. You feel warm, but before you know it, your teeth are chattering like it's New Year's at the North Pole. You're sweating, but you're freezing cold. You've got a raging fever.

The greed disease is like that. It starts small, wanting just a little bit more. *If only I could buy the latest (fill in the blank)*, you think. *Then I'll be happy.* But then there's a newer model. And some other shiny gadget catches your eye. It's like you're hungry for stuff, but you can't get full. That's the greed fever. Before you realize it, you're burning up.

The truth is you've got to guard against the greed disease. Life is about much more than stuff. Look around at your possessions. Many of them won't last until next year. Lots of them you won't want next year. And none of them will do you a bit of good at the end of your life. Stay healthy by being thankful for what you have.

TRIPLE DOG DARE

- Go around your room thanking God for each thing you see.

- What can you never get enough of? Share it.

- Let your brother have the last piece of pizza.

What did you do? What did you learn?

MISSION ACCOMPLISHED!

More Than Muscles

We all want to be strong. But strength is much more than big muscles. We all are naturally strong in some areas and weak in others. Being able to tell which is which can help us get even stronger. And the best part is that God wants to give us His strength when we rely on Him—even in our greatest weaknesses.

"The LORD is my strength and my shield; my heart trusts in him, and I am helped" (Psalm 28:7).

TRIPLE DOG DARE!

Take some time to think honestly about yourself and fill in these lists:

MY STRENGTHS

What I'm naturally good at: Ways I can use it:

MY WEAKNESSES

What I struggle with:

Ways I can practice and improve:

YOUR PAGE

The best dream I ever had was ...

TRUTH Get some attitude—like Jesus.

SPORTIN' A 'TUBE

Your parents probably talk a lot about attitude. Maybe you get in trouble for yours. Maybe they just remind you how important a good one is. What's the big deal with attitude? Attitude affects how you think and what you do. It can change an experience altogether—a good attitude can make anything fun; a bad attitude can ruin the best adventures. God knows that. He cares about our attitudes.

The truth is God wants us to have attitudes like Jesus. That means being humble, selfless, and giving even to the point of sacrifice. See, Jesus was God. He didn't have to become a weak human. He didn't have to serve others and wash dirty feet. He didn't have to suffer and die—for everybody else's sin—without complaining! He chose to. He gave up what He deserved. His attitude was loving and giving. Make yours the same.

TRIPLE DOG DARE

- Tie something around your finger or wrist to remind you to not complain at all today.

- Choose ahead of time to have fun or learn something new during a task you have to do but would skip if you could.

- Pick an unexpected way to serve each member of your family this week.

What did you do? What did you learn?

MISSION ACCOMPLISHED!

TRUTH

Friendship is about quality, not quantity.

REAL FRIENDS

Friendship is not a contest. Sometimes that's hard to remember if you're not one of the popular kids. Being surrounded by tons of cool kids can look pretty appealing, especially from the outside. What we can't see is the self-doubt and loneliness that we all feel sometimes—even the popular people.

The truth is that friendship is not a contest for the most friends; it's about having deep relationships with people you can count on. Some people are more outgoing and naturally connect with lots of others. Some people are naturally shy and feel closer to fewer people. Don't beat yourself up if you're not naturally the social king. Remember God has made you special and unique, and focus on making one or two good friends.

Look for a good friend who has your back. You know he'll help you when you need it. He's one you can trust. He's someone who likes the same stuff as you and is fun to hang out with. He's a guy who encourages you to follow God. He challenges you to be a better person, but likes you for being you.

TRIPLE DOG DARE

- O Make a new friend today. Introduce yourself.
- O Talk to a trusted friend about a problem that's bugging you.
- O Limit your time with a friend who drags you down or away from God.

MISSION ACCOMPLISHED!

What did you do? What did you learn?

EPHESIANS 4:31-32

TRUTH Forgiveness is the cure to the cancer of bitterness.

FIND THE CURE

Cancer is a terrible disease. Some forms are treatable, but there's no single cure. Cancer is too often a death sentence. It's like a form of terrorism in your body. Cancer cells try to take over, reproducing themselves too fast and invading and destroying good cells in parts of your body. They can keep going and spread through a body until they eventually shut it down.

Bitterness is cancer of the spirit, but forgiveness is its cure. Bitterness gets planted in you as a seed of anger. If that anger isn't dealt with, it begins to grow—first into a grudge, then hatred, and finally into all-out bitterness. Bitterness churns and grows and hurts you much more than the person you were originally mad at; it'll eat up your spirit from the inside out.

But there is a cure: forgiveness. God wants us to forgive others like He's forgiven us—for others' sakes and for our own. No matter how bad the hurt or anger, let it go. You'll be the one who is free.

TRIPLE DOG DARE

- Picture your sins nailed to Jesus on the cross when you're mad at someone else.

- Have spiritual surgery to get rid of any deep bitterness. Talk to your parents and a pastor or counselor for help.

- Write the name or draw a picture of your worst offender. Tie it to a helium balloon and let it go.

What did you do? What did you learn?

MISSION ACCOMPLISHED!

TRUTH

God wants us to do the right thing even when it's hard.

WHEN NOBODY'S WATCHING

Nobody's looking.

Just one glance at your neighbor's test can't hurt—besides, you need a good grade.

Sure, your mom said only one hour on the Wii, but she's not home.

You can cover it up with one little lie; you were the only one there to see what really happened.

Yes, you said you'd watch your little sister, but this is a much cooler option.

The lies the Devil whispers to us are so subtle! And the temptation seems even stronger when no one is looking.

The truth is that God wants to build integrity into our spirits—that's the consistent habit of doing what's right. It means we obey Him even when no one else is around. It means we do what we said we would, even if that gets hard to do. It means other people can trust and count on us. It means we count on God—every day.

TRIPLE DOG DARE

- Ask your parents what they think your biggest area of inconsistency is. Then ask them to help you change it one step at a time.

- Write down everything you tell someone you will do. Use the list to remind you to do it.

- Pay your parents a dollar every time you lie, stretch the truth, or don't follow up on your word.

MISSION ACCOMPLISHED!

What did you do? What did you learn?

TRUTH
God's strength is the secret to life.

THE SECRET

Sometimes you're the windshield; sometimes you're the bug. Sometimes you're the cat; sometimes you're the mouse. Sometimes you're the bat; sometimes you're the ball. Sometimes you're the trap; sometimes you're the bait. Sometimes you're the arrow; sometimes you're the bull's-eye. Sometimes you're the engine; sometimes you're the caboose.

It's the reality of life. You will have ups and you will have downs. If your circumstances are all you look at, life will be one crazy roller-coaster ride flinging you every which way.

The truth is that trusting God's strength brings contentment no matter where you are on the ride. Contentment is satisfaction. It's peace and calm. It's knowing everything will be okay. Its secret is realizing that God gives us strength to handle whatever might come, even if it's hard or painful. It's remembering that He is much bigger than our ups and downs.

TRIPLE DOG DARE

○ Draw a picture of your life as a roller coaster. Label the ups and downs. Notice how there are many of both.

○ Remind yourself it will get better, especially if you're feeling like the bug right now.

○ Tell a friend the secret. Encourage someone that God is even bigger than his or her problem.

What did you do? What did you learn?

MISSION ACCOMPLISHED!

Tell a Biography

Stories are powerful. They stick with us because we identify with characters and remember unexpected twists. Jesus knew that—it's probably why He told so many parables. We can learn from reading or hearing all the stories in the Bible, but we can also add our imaginations to help us fill in the blanks and put ourselves in the characters' positions.

TRIPLE DOG DARE!

Imagine more about these characters. Write their biographies with words or in comic-book form. Or create a short movie about them.

- The rich young man (Matthew 19:16–30)
- Zaccheus (Luke 19:1–10)
- Lazarus (John 11:1–44)
- Woman who washed Jesus feet with perfume (Mark 14:1–11)
- Nicodemus (John 3:1–21)
- The man with leprosy (Mark 1:40–45)
- Add your own on the next page.

Draw your superhero costume.

TRUTH
God has given you a gift to help other people.

GIVE YOUR GIFT

What if Beethoven never wrote music? What if Michelangelo only painted in his room? What if Walt Disney only made home movies or the Wright brothers stuck to bicycles? Just think of Alexander Fleming keeping his penicillin discovery in his laboratory. Or William Wilberforce keeping his opinion to himself that slavery was wrong. Our world would be a different place.

The truth is God has given you a gift, and He wants you to use it to serve and help others. The world wouldn't be the same without you and your abilities—no matter how big or how small. Your songs may not be chart-topping hits, but they can lift a friend's spirits in his darkest moments. You may not discover a cure for cancer, but you might be the teacher who trains the scientist who does. You might not be a famous architect, but you might help build a home for a foreign family living in cardboard. Use what you love to do for others.

TRIPLE DOG DARE

O Discover your gift. List the things you love to do. What are you good at? What do others praise you for?

O Give your gift. Write a song; build a craft; paint a picture; teach your skill to a younger kid; tell jokes in a nursing home.

O Spearhead a family project for you all to serve others together.

What did you do? What did you learn?

MISSION ACCOMPLISHED!

TRUTH
Patience wins the battle.

THE POWER OF PATIENCE

Have you ever seen someone try to fight or argue when the other person won't? While one gets mad, the other stays calm. The longer the patient guy stays calm, the more angry the hothead gets. Angry dude turns red, screams louder, and gets more and more frustrated. Patient guy keeps his cool and can't help but laugh at mad man's antics. Who looks like the fool? Whom is the crowd laughing at? Mad Brad who's lost all control.

The truth is that patience wins the battle every time. The man who can keep his temper under control is stronger than a mighty warrior. Staying calm is hard sometimes, but it gives the upper hand. Patience helps you think clearly and quickly. It takes two to fight, and staying calm helps you avoid the fight altogether.

Learn to think to keep your temper in check. If an opponent can spark your emotions, then he sucks you in and you get blinded by anger. Act, don't react. Use good humor to diffuse tempers. And see the big picture instead of small insults. You can win the battle by keeping it from starting.

TRIPLE DOG DARE

- Count to ten and keep counting when somebody gets in your face.

- Take a step back, breathe deep, and look at the big picture when you're tempted to lose your cool.

- Memorize and repeat Proverbs 16:32 before you lose control.

MISSION ACCOMPLISHED!

What did you do? What did you learn?

HEBREWS 12:1-3

TRUTH

Look to Jesus for focus to reach the finish line.

RUN FOR THE FINISH

It wouldn't help to run a track race wearing your biggest, heaviest snowsuit. It would hurt more than help to carry heavy barbells. And it would be a waste of time to run a marathon without knowing where the finish line was.

But we do it all the time in our spiritual lives. We distract ourselves with mind-numbing entertainment. We weight ourselves down with sin. And we take our eyes off the finish line and forget where it is.

The truth is Jesus gives us the focus to keep running and finish the race. He gives us faith, and He works inside us to make it stronger. He wants to complete God's work in us. By focusing on Him, we are focusing on the finish line and getting as aerodynamic and fast as possible. And when we feel like stopping and giving up, He gives us strength to keep running. Don't stop until you break the tape. The greatest victory celebration in history is at the end.

TRIPLE DOG DARE

- O Confess and turn away from any sin that's dragging you down.

- O What's taking you off course? Get help to break a bad habit.

- O Train your spirit. Memorize a Bible verse a week for six weeks.

What did you do? What did you learn?

MISSION ACCOMPLISHED!

TRUTH

It's not about how strong or smart you are—it's about God.

NOT YOUR POWER

What are you trying to accomplish? What's your big project or goal? Maybe it's an assignment that's been given to you. Maybe it's a cause that you've chosen. Maybe it's a performance, contest, or game that you signed up for. Maybe it's a calling you've felt from God. Whatever you're facing, it does no good to keep trying all on your own.

The truth is we need to rely on God's Spirit to work through us. He is much stronger than our greatest human strength and power—no matter what our task is.

We all need reminders of that sometimes. The words of this Bible verse were originally spoken to Zerubbabel (you can call him 'Rubba, like Bubba). He was leading the ancient Israelites in rebuilding the temple in Jerusalem. But the message applies to us today, too. We still must try our hardest, but only as we look to God as the source of our guidance and strength. We must plug into His Spirit like the source of our electricity.

TRIPLE DOG DARE

- ○ Memorize Zechariah 4:6, and say it when you're working or playing.

- ○ Encourage a struggling friend with the message of this verse.

- ○ Ask God for new eyes to see your project or challenge, and try again with His help.

MISSION ACCOMPLISHED!

What did you do? What did you learn?

TRUTH A true friend is always honest.

NOTHING BUT THE TRUTH

Some people will tell you anything to get what they want. Have you ever had a friend lie behind your back? Maybe he said one thing to you, then told the opposite to someone else. Why? Probably to make himself look better. Or maybe you've had someone flatter you, saying nice things to puff you up—until he got what he wanted out of you. Then bye-bye. It's hard to be friends with someone you can't trust.

The truth is that a true friend is always honest, even when it hurts. Sometimes the truth does hurt. But you'd want a buddy to tackle you if you were running in front of a speeding car, right? You'd thank him for pulling you back if there were a raging bear down the path.

It's the same when a friend tells you that you made a bad decision—or you tell him. He might let you know that some other friends are dragging you down. You might hear that your idea is going to get you in trouble or injured. You might not like hearing the truth, but it will save you from bigger, badder trouble later.

TRIPLE DOG DARE

- O Know a friend making bad choices? Talk to him alone. Let him know you're concerned and want to help.

- O Who made you mad? Is it because he was looking out for your best interests? Apologize if you need to.

- O Look at your friendships. Whom can you trust to be honest and help you follow God's ways? Who is only looking out for themselves?

What did you do? What did you learn?

MISSION ACCOMPLISHED!

Practice Prayer

"Lord, teach us to pray," the disciples asked Jesus in Luke 11:1. So He did, and we can learn from the same lesson. Jesus gave the disciples and us the model of the Lord's Prayer. Read it in Luke 11:2–4. You might have prayed the words in church. And we can follow the same pattern that Jesus used. Many people think of it as the acronym ACTS—an acronym is when the letters stand for something. Here it is:

A: Adoration—a fancy word for praise

C: Confession—saying you're sorry for sins

T: Thanks—pretty straightforward

S: Supplication—another fancy word, this time for asking for things

TRIPLE DOG DARE!

Write your prayers in the following categories. Use the space below.

MY PRAYERS

_A_DORATION (*praises*)

_C_ONFESSION

_T_HANKS

_S_UPPLICATION (*requests*)

YOUR PAGE

Questions I want to ask God in heaven:

TRUTH

The way we treat Jesus is the way we treat people in need.

JESUS ALL AROUND YOU

Jesus is standing on a corner with a "Will work for food" sign. He's locked up in the state prison. He's an immigrant who doesn't speak English. He's a kid your age living in a garbage dump. He is an amputee with no home after an earthquake. He is speechless and staring in a nursing home. He's drinking diseased water from a mud puddle. Jesus is all around us in need.

The truth is however we treat the lowliest people on earth is how we treat Jesus. Jesus said it's superimportant. It's superimportant to Him that we help people with big needs, especially the poorest, dirtiest, sickest, and loneliest. Those are the people it's easy to forget about. Those are the ones we *like* to forget about. But they are all around our cities and our world. Don't turn away from them. Follow Jesus to them. See Jesus in them. And reach out.

TRIPLE DOG DARE

- O Pack and carry snack bags in your car to give to homeless people.

- O Use your allowance to give a kid good food and education through Compassion International or World Vision.

- O Get your family to help build a home for someone who doesn't have one through Habitat for Humanity or by going on a mission trip.

What did you do? What did you learn?

MISSION ACCOMPLISHED!

TRUTH You get a fresh start every day.

TODAY'S GIFT

Wake up! Today is a gift. It's a one-of-a-kind treasure that you'll never have again. It's a new chance. It's unexplored opportunity and untapped potential. It's the chance to master that new trick that's been eluding you. It's time to make a new friend. It's time to start a new journey. It's time to shake off your doubt and overcome your fear. It's time to start over.

The truth is God's mercy and goodness are new for us every day. His faithfulness never runs out. His love keeps flowing. God is there with us in the morning, and He stays with us all day long. His forgiveness and patience are an ocean that never ends. God is the most priceless treasure we could ever receive, and He gives us an invaluable gift with each new day.

So unwrap your present. Make the most of today. Breathe deep with thankfulness. Fill up with God's strength. Offer your plans to God. Then charge!

TRIPLE DOG DARE

- Do something new today.

- Turn on your watch chime and thank God for all that's going on when it dings every hour.

- Confess any sin to God. Then punch the air with an invisible "Forgiven" stamp every time guilt from that past sin starts to drag you down.

MISSION ACCOMPLISHED!

What did you do? What did you learn?

TRUTH

Jesus understands because He's been there, done that.

BEEN THERE, DONE THAT

If you want to become the best chess player, you don't go to a hockey coach. If you want to improve your math skills, you don't ask a chef. You want training from a master. You want coaching from somebody who's played the game and knows what to watch for. You want tips from an insider who's been there and done it.

The truth is Jesus understands our temptations because He became a human. He's lived on our earth. He put on our skin and all its limitations. He faced our temptations. And He mastered our world, staying sin-free so that He could be the perfect sacrifice for us. That's great news because now Jesus sits with God in His glory and invites us into the King's chambers. He understands firsthand what we're struggling with, and He gives us mercy and help. Come see the Master Teacher any time.

TRIPLE DOG DARE

- ○ Set a spiritual goal. What do you want to overcome, improve, or practice? Ask for help from a wiser Christian.

- ○ Beat temptation the way Jesus did: turning to Scripture.

- ○ Talk to God about anything. There's nothing He doesn't know or understand.

What did you do? What did you learn?

MISSION ACCOMPLISHED!

TRUTH Don't forget to say thank you.

NO THANKS

Imagine you had never been able to walk or talk and see. Suppose you had an extra arm or a tail. What if you were dying of cancer or AIDS? Now picture someone coming along and completely healing you—in a nanosecond. Do you think you'd remember to say thank you?

Seems kind of like a no-brainer. But in Luke 17 only one of the ten men with leprosy came back to thank Jesus for healing him. What's up with that?

The truth is it can be easy to forget to say thank you, but showing our thankfulness is ginormous. Those two simple words can make all the difference to people doing something generous for us—or in them ever helping us again. Showing appreciation shows that we care and that we realize it might have taken some sacrifice by the giver. The more thankful we are, the more generous others usually are to us. Don't forget to say thank you.

TRIPLE DOG DARE

- Count how many times you can say thank you today (for real reasons).

- Write a thank-you note for a gift you received recently.

- Make your mom a gift to say thanks for the things she does for you every day.

MISSION ACCOMPLISHED!

What did you do? What did you learn?

TRUTH We all need help from others.

LEAN ON ME

LeBron James joined a team with superstars Dwyane Wade and Chris Bosh. Michael Jordan didn't win his championships until he had Scottie Pippen and other strong teammates. Frodo had Sam to carry him when he couldn't go any farther. Peter, Susan, Edmund, and Lucy all needed heroic acts from others to save Narnia.

Moses was the leader, but he needed Aaron and Hur to hold up his arms, literally. Without them he got too tired. Joshua was the warrior, but he needed Moses' hands held up. Without them his army started losing. They all needed God to win the battle, and God used each of them to help the others.

The truth is we all need help from others. We are stronger together than alone. Sometimes we need our hands held up. Sometimes we are holding up others' hands. Surround yourself with friends you can count on. Don't be afraid to ask for help. And look for ways to give it. Together you can win the battle!

TRIPLE DOG DARE

- Who's got your back? Build a couple friendships with other guys committed to living for God.

- Who needs your help? Stand by a friend who's struggling. Encourage him and offer to help.

- Don't give up on a friend in trouble, even if you don't know how to help. Talk to a parent for advice.

What did you do? What did you learn?

MISSION ACCOMPLISHED!

Put It in Your Head

To do God's Word, you've got to know God's Word. And one great way to learn it is to memorize it.

TRIPLE DOG DARE!

Memorize parts of the Bible. Here's a list of ten verses to start with. Learn one each week, but review older ones. Copy them out of this book. Practice writing and saying them, and use them often. (All of these are from the New International Version, but memorize whatever translation you read.)

"I have hidden your word in my heart that I might not sin against you" (Psalm 119:11).

"Trust in the LORD with all your heart and lean not on your own understanding; in all your ways acknowledge him, and he will make your paths straight" (Proverbs 3:5–6).

"No temptation has seized you except what is common to man. And God is faithful; he will not let you be tempted beyond what you can bear. But when you are tempted, he will also provide a way out so that you can stand up under it" (1 Corinthians 10:13).

"I can do everything through him who gives me strength" (Philippians 4:13).

"Create in me a pure heart, O God, and renew a steadfast spirit within me" (Psalm 51:10).

"Therefore, I urge you, brothers, in view of God's mercy, to offer your bodies as living sacrifices, holy and pleasing to God—this is your spiritual act of worship. Do not conform any longer to the pattern of this world, but be transformed by the renewing of your mind. Then you will be able to test and approve what God's will is—his good, pleasing and perfect will" (Romans 12:1–2).

"Don't let anyone look down on you because you are young, but set an example for the believers in speech, in life, in love, in faith and in purity" (1 Timothy 4:12).

"So do not fear, for I am with you; do not be dismayed, for I am your God. I will strengthen you and help you; I will uphold you with my righteous right hand" (Isaiah 41:10).

"'Love the Lord your God with all your heart and with all your soul and with all your strength and with all your mind'; and, 'Love your neighbor as yourself'" (Luke 10:27).

"And whatever you do, whether in word or deed, do it all in the name of the Lord Jesus, giving thanks to God the Father through him" (Colossians 3:17).

TRIPLE DOG BONUS

If you memorize all of these, you will have formed a good habit. Keep going! Find verses you like, and learn a new one each week. Write them here.

YOUR PAGE

This week I will ...

TRUTH *God wants us to shine His light.*

LIGHT UP THE CHRISTMAS NIGHT

What do you see when you look at Christmas lights? They're pretty decorations on trees and houses, festive and bright. But there's more than that. Lights have often been used as signals. They point the way; think airport runway lights. They serve as a warning; think lighthouses. They give us guidance; think traffic lights. Light always helps us to see, often things we didn't see before. Christmas lights do the same.

The truth is that Jesus is the Light of the World, shining to show us the way to life in God. Our Christmas lights remind us of Jesus shining in our world. John 1 tells us Jesus is God and has been forever. He came into our world to show and shine God's love. And He wants to shine God's love through us, too. Remember that when you see Christmas lights this year, and shine God's light through you to everyone you come in contact with.

TRIPLE DOG DARE

- Help hang your family's Christmas lights this year and think about what they signal.

- Speak kind words to cashiers and store workers everywhere you go.

- Be God's flashlight, pointing your friends to Jesus this Christmas.

What did you do? What did you learn?

MISSION ACCOMPLISHED!

TRUTH

God wants us to watch out for what we watch.

WATCH OUT

It's hard to look away. We want to see the car crash, the burning house, or the pretty woman. It's part of human curiosity. Our eyes are drawn to the extreme, unusual, and beautiful. That's not all bad.

But marketers and entertainers use it against us. Pop stars create spectacles, pushing to be the most outrageous and to grab the most attention. Video game designers add more blood, more guts, more disgusting ways to die and kill. Even news outlets follow the guideline "If it bleeds, it leads." They all want to get our attention however they can so they can make more money.

The truth is God wants us to guard our eyes. He wants us to control the visuals we let into our hearts. He knows that the imagery we store in our brains shapes how we think. He knows staring at sin helps us get used to it, accept it, and allow it in our own lives. And He knows how it can destroy us. It can be hard to look away, but God will give you strength. Guard your eyes.

TRIPLE DOG DARE

- Put on God-glasses. Get some sunglasses to put on as a reminder when you need to look away from sinful scenes.

- Turn off the tube. Go a day without TV. Go a week.

- Can the commercials. Advertisers love to manipulate your mind. Turn off the screen when the ads come on.

MISSION ACCOMPLISHED!

What did you do? What did you learn?

TRUTH

Contentment is knowing the difference between what you want and what you need.

WANT VS. NEED

You need a house to live in. You don't need a Beverly Hills mansion. You need wheels to get around. You don't need a Lamborghini. You need food to eat. You don't need filet mignon every meal. You need clothes to wear. You don't need the latest hot brand that costs three times more. You need something to do. You don't need to be entertained 24/7.

We confuse our *wants* and *needs* all the time. It's easy to do. There are basics we all need: food, clothes, shelter, love. There are other things we might *like* to have but that we'd still live without. Believe it or not, you would *not* die without your PSP. But advertisers blast us with messages designed to convince us that we *cannot* live without their drink, burger, shirt, skateboard, soap, boat, game, etc., etc., etc. They want to make us discontent—discontent enough to spend money on their product.

The truth is contentment brings us happiness. It comes from listening to God's voice instead of commercials. It comes from looking past the hype and seeing what's really *want* and what's really *need*. It comes from understanding what's really life and death. It comes from being thankful for what you have.

TRIPLE DOG DARE

O Practice asking, *Do I really need this or only want it? Will I live or die without it?*

O Look at all your stuff. Where will it go when you die?

O Skip the commercials. Hit mute or off when the sales pitch begins.

What did you do? What did you learn?

MISSION ACCOMPLISHED!

TRUTH

God wants your heart more than your offerings.

MERCY MATTERS MORE

It doesn't do any good to walk out of church and then kill someone. That's an extreme example, I know. But you've probably given money at church, then refused to share any money or stuff with people the next week. You've probably asked God to forgive some sin, then held a grudge against somebody who wronged you. And you've probably sung your heart out in worship, then gone a few days without thinking about God.

The truth is God wants your heart more than your offerings and worship at church. He wanted the same from the Israelites, too. They were good about offering their sacrifices, but their hearts weren't into it. They forgot about God. It's the same for us. It's easy for us to go through the motions, but then our worship is empty.

Church is important, but offering God our hearts and actions every day is more important. Saying you're a Christian is good, but only if you're living like it. Singing you love God is great, but only if you're showing Him.

TRIPLE DOG DARE

- What did you learn at church last week? Do it.

- Make a list of all the ways God can use the money you give and get excited about giving to Him.

- Show mercy to somebody you should be mad at. Forgive him and give him kindness.

MISSION ACCOMPLISHED!

What did you do? What did you learn?

TRUTH Christmas is about believing

NOTHING IS IMPOSSIBLE

Put yourself in her shoes. You're a young teenage Hebrew girl who's already had her marriage arranged because that's the custom of the day. There's nothing extremely special about you. You're an everybody and a nobody. Like other girls your age in your small town, you probably spend your days fetching water, making meals, and taking care of your house and family. Most days are the same, until—

The angel alone would have been enough to freak you out. But then the things he tells you! It's staggering trying to wrap your brain around just part of it. A baby?! You know it's biologically impossible. Then not just any baby: God's Son, the Messiah the Jews had been awaiting for centuries, the Savior of the world! Talk about blowing your mind! But Mary's response couldn't have been more awesome.

The truth is Christmas is about believing, just like Mary did. She trusted God and chose to believe what made no logical sense. She gave in to God's miracle. We can do the same. As the angel said, "Nothing is impossible with God." Focus on believing that this Christmas season.

TRIPLE DOG DARE

○ Make "Nothing is impossible with God" your motto this Christmastime.

○ Pray Mary's words from Luke 1:38.

○ Walk through the Christmas story in your mind, putting yourself behind the eyes of each character.

What did you do? What did you learn?

MISSION ACCOMPLISHED!

Crazy Christmas

Christmas is an awesome time of year—the most wonderful time of the year, as the song says, right? But let's face it. Christmas can get crazy. We've got Santa and Rudolph and Black Friday and Cyber Monday, and every store is having sales and telling us to buy, buy, buy. Don't get me wrong. The gifts aren't the problem, but we let them crowd out the real, biggest, most important Gift—Jesus.

But we don't have to let greed and materialism crowd out the meaning of our season! We can celebrate giving like never before. We can give our hearts and discover the joy God must have felt that quiet night in Bethlehem. We don't even have to have money to do it! Give time. Give *presence* instead of presents. Give of yourself. Don't worry, you'll get, too. You just might be surprised that you have more fun giving instead.

TRIPLE DOG DARE!

Go crazy giving this Christmas season—but don't spend a lot of money. Use this list of ideas and add to it. Be creative and ask God for ideas.

- Shovel snow for someone who can't or doesn't expect it—and don't take payment.
- Bake cookies with your family and take them to neighbors.
- Buy a gift for a prisoner's kid through Angel Tree.
- Pack shoeboxes full of gifts for kids around the world through Operation Christmas Child.
- Buy gifts through Toys for Tots or volunteer to help sort them.
- Donate change to Salvation Army kettles.
- Go caroling in a nursing home or a children's hospital.
- Write notes to your family members telling them why you think they're special.
- Paint pictures.
- Volunteer to cook dinner for your family.
- Create personalized playlists.
- Take and print pictures. Glue them on heavy paper to make custom photo notecards.

- Edit family videos to make a highlights movie of the last year.

- Build or sculpt something useful: soap dish, cutting board, key-hanging rack.

- Write songs for loved ones.

- Make a scarf or beanie.

- Make a calendar using photos of friends or family.

TRIPLE DOG BONUS

Ask your parents to check out AdventConspiracy.org and give money to build a well so a family and village can have clean water. Write some other ideas here.

YOUR PAGE

My recent highlights: My recent lowlights:

TRUTH
Christmas is the time to obey humbly.

GET OVER YOURSELF

You'd be furious and heartbroken. How could she do this to you?! You trusted her. You thought you knew her. You had saved yourself for her even when it was tempting not to, and you thought she was doing the same for you. Now this?! Your fiancée is pregnant—by someone else! It's a scandal, especially in ancient times. It's crushing you, and worse, people are pointing and blaming you! How humiliating!

Welcome to Joseph's life. It's a life suddenly turned upside down. It's a situation he wanted nothing to do with, so he planned to break off his coming marriage. But God had other plans.

The truth is God wants us all to obey humbly like Joseph did. Everything about the first Christmas was humble, and Joseph and Mary had to swallow their pride over and over again: showing up pregnant, marrying a pregnant girl, giving birth in a stable. None of it was the way anyone would have expected God to enter the world. Everyone involved had to get over themselves to receive God's miracle. So do we. Get over yourself this Christmas. Obey God even when it feels embarrassing. It will be worth it!

TRIPLE DOG DARE

- Give up your Christmas demands. Shorten your wish list by at least half.

- Humble yourself and give a gift or nice gesture to someone you don't like.

- Get over your embarrassment and obey God.

What did you do? What did you learn?

MISSION ACCOMPLISHED!

TRUTH

Following and living God's Word maintains purity.

DON'T EAT YELLOW SNOW

Snow is a great canvas. Just after it falls it's white, clean, soft, and pure. But it also shows its history because everything leaves a mark. People footprints and animal tracks sink in and show who's been there and maybe what they've done. Colors stain and leave clues. Red is the blood of freshly caught prey. Pink is fungus that can make you sick. And yellow is … well, you know what they say—don't eat yellow snow.

Our hearts are like snow. They get marked and tainted by what we let cross them.

The truth is that following and filling our hearts with God's Word maintains our purity. It keeps us free from getting tangled in sin. It guides us on safe, healthy paths. It guards our minds and bodies from pain and scars. It refreshes our spirits and refills our hearts.

Our world is full of many temptations that will dump us into yellow snow. Keep your way pure by living by God's Word.

TRIPLE DOG DARE

- ○ Memorize a new Bible verse each week.

- ○ Read a little of God's Word every day. Get a translation that's easy to understand. Try the comic-book style *Action Bible*.

- ○ Tape a new verse on your bathroom mirror every week—or ask your mom if you can write it on the mirror with erasable marker.

MISSION ACCOMPLISHED!

What did you do? What did you learn?

ACTS 20:35

TRUTH
It's better to give than to receive.

BETTER THAN AN ACTION FIGURE

You've probably heard it at Christmas every year since you were little—and you've probably thought *No way!* After all, you've always had a long list of things and stuff you wanted: important things like new action figures and LEGO sets and video game consoles. How can it get better than that, right?

The truth is that it really is better to give than to get. Have you tried it? There's a warm glow inside that can only come from seeing someone else's face light up with surprise and delight because you took the thought, time, and effort to remember them. It's a feeling that runs deeper than getting another DVD for yourself. It's a satisfaction that lasts longer than the batteries in your electronic toy. Giving taps into God's heart. Try it and see—at any time of year.

TRIPLE DOG DARE

○ Make a giving list *first*. Then jot down a few items you'd like to receive.

○ Give to someone who really needs. Try a local homeless shelter or food pantry. Join Operation Christmas Child or Angel Tree.

○ Don't let money stop you. Make gifts for family and friends.

What did you do? What did you learn?

MISSION ACCOMPLISHED!

TRUTH

God gives us wisdom to think before we act.

AVOID A WRECK

If only life had a reset button. Then we could go back in time and take back the mean words that came flying out—or the stupid statement that was so embarrassing. We could check out the landing and avoid breaking that arm. And we could choose to stand up and say no instead of letting our friends egg us on to break rules and get in big trouble. Yep, a do-over would be cool.

The truth is that God wants to help us gain wisdom to think about what we're doing before we need a do-over. Being hotheaded and reckless is like driving a real car as if it were a bumper car at one hundred miles per hour. It's going to cause problems, and it's going to hurt—us and others.

Wisdom helps us see the big picture, realize where our actions will lead us, and choose to take God's route. We get wisdom partly from experience, partly from reading God's Word, and partly from listening to people like our parents and teachers who have lived more life than we have. Start listening!

TRIPLE DOG DARE

- Count to ten before you say something mean or smart-alecky.

- What usually gets you in trouble? Write a list of your actions and what results will follow with either choice.

- Ask for help. Get some ideas from your mom and dad about how to make smart choices *before* it's too late. Then do them.

MISSION ACCOMPLISHED!

What are you going to do? What did you learn?

TRUTH

Stop and seek. Don't let the real Christmas pass you by.

BE A WISEMAN

Not many people were paying attention, but the Magi were. Of all the people in the world, these three guys from far away in the East were paying attention. The Jews had been promised the Messiah for centuries, but these Gentiles were watching for the signs. They were looking to the skies and searching for God's work. We don't know exactly what they saw, but we know God revealed to them the arrival of His Son. And while the Jews were going about their everyday lives, the wisemen dropped everything and took a great journey to find and worship God.

The truth is it's easy to get sidetracked, but don't let the truth of Christmas pass you by. Keep your eyes open. Watch for God's work. Follow His guidance. Worship like the wisemen. Give like they gave, sharing their treasures with the lowly and humble. And expect miracles.

The crowds will carry on with shopping and partying, and the meaning of Christmas will fly right over their heads. You can do it differently. Drop everything and seek your King. He will change your Christmas—and your life.

TRIPLE DOG DARE

- ○ Help your family slow down this Christmas. Do extra chores and ask your parents for a slower, quieter holiday.

- ○ Worship God with music and prayer every day this season.

- ○ Ask your family to bring Christmas to another family in need this year.

What did you do? What did you learn?

MISSION ACCOMPLISHED!

Hall of Judges

Judges are kind of the superheroes of the Bible. They came through for the people of Israel in hard times to defeat enemies and save their civilization. They accomplished heroic deeds. And some, such as Samson, had superpowers and a mortal weakness.

TRIPLE DOG DARE!

Read through the book of Judges. Draw in the panels below to create your own comic strip of a favorite judge. Use the details in Scripture—plus your imagination.

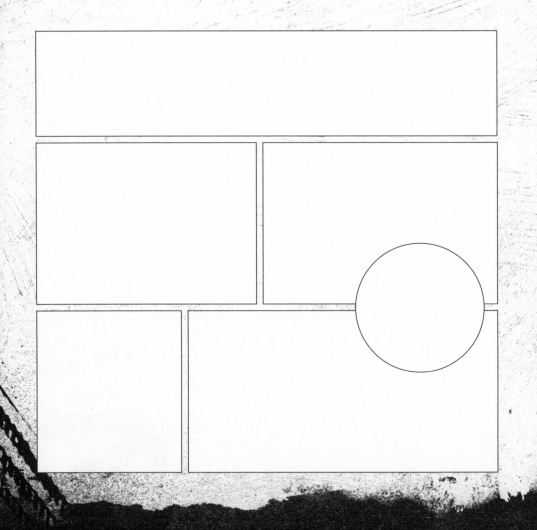

YOUR PAGE

The best news I've heard in a long time is ...

TRUTH

God is patient. Come back to Him.

COME BACK

Even your parents run out of patience. Sometimes you just wear them down and *snap*, they've had enough. They're angry, and you're in trouble. You had your chances to obey but you just didn't do it. The thing is they still love you and you know it. Even when they're frustrated, you know they're there for you.

The truth is God is patient and forgiving and always welcomes us back to Him. He's even better at it than your parents. He showed it to the Israelites time after time when they kept trashing His laws, and He shows it to us when we do the same.

What's been keeping you from God? Come back to Him. Tell Him you're sorry. Ask for His help. God is waiting with open arms.

TRIPLE DOG DARE

- Spend some time with God today. Go for a walk and pray or write a letter to Him in your journal.

- Apologize to God for your sin and ask for His help to overcome it.

- Give this message to a friend who's been drifting from God. Offer to pray with him.

What did you do? What did you learn?

MISSION ACCOMPLISHED!

TRUTH

We show God we love Him by obeying His commands.

HEAD OVER HEELS

Now you can laugh at it all: the googly eyes and dreamy stares, the mushy messages and silly nicknames like Honey Muffin and Pookie Darling, and the cross-the-widest-ocean poetic proclamations. But someday you will fall in love—and you will do all those silly things for another person.

It's part of being in love. Suddenly the most important person in your life isn't you; it's someone else, who you also happen to think is the most beautiful girl in the world. And there's nothing you won't do to prove your love and make her heart sing like yours is.

The truth is God wants us to love Him so much that there's nothing we wouldn't do for Him. That doesn't mean buying Him boxes of chocolates. It means obeying His commands. He doesn't want our obedience just because we have to or because it will protect us from painful consequences. He wants our obedience because we love Him so much that we'd do anything to make Him happy.

TRIPLE DOG DARE

- Show your parents you love them by obeying them.
- Read and obey Luke 10:26–28.
- View your next temptation as a choice to love or hate God.

MISSION ACCOMPLISHED!

What did you do? What did you learn?

TRUTH Jesus wants everything

GIVE IT UP AND GAIN

Do you own your iPod or does it own you? Do you have a hold of your game console or does it have a hold of you? What if your parents asked you to give away your comic book collection? What if Jesus asked you to give up your computer or your bike or all your favorite stuff?

The truth is that our money and stuff can get in the way of our relationship with God. Our wealth buys us lots that makes us feel safe: nice houses, fast cars, good food, cool clothes. We have most of what we want, at least what we need. And we get comfortable from it all and forget that we need God even more.

Nice stuff isn't evil. God won't necessarily ask us to sell everything we have and give it to the poor. But He wants nothing to be more important to us than Him. He knows the real life that He wants us to experience often seems strange when compared with the ways our world works. But He knows how much better His spiritual life is. Don't let your things get in the way.

TRIPLE DOG DARE

- Give away something you like to someone who needs it more.

- Put yourself last somewhere—maybe in a line, maybe at the dinner table.

- What has a hold on you? What scares you most when you read "Sell your possessions and give …"? Find a way to let it go.

What did you do? What did you learn?

MISSION ACCOMPLISHED!

TRUTH

You can give the powerful gift of a blessing.

WAY TO GO

Everybody wants to hear "good job," "well done," and "I'm proud of you." Those kinds of words really pump you up. They build your confidence and recognize your efforts. They put a stamp of approval on you that says you matter. They refocus you and help you keep going.

Consider the alternatives: "Bad mistake, loser," "you're stupid," or "you'll never make it." Just reading words like that is a downer.

The truth is that we have the power to bless other people with our words and to inspire them to great strength. Blessings were an important part of the culture in Bible times. God blessed Adam and Eve in the Garden of Eden. Angels visited men to bring special blessings from God. The priests spoke God's words of blessing to the people, and fathers spoke blessings to sons to pass on important rights and status. Your words are powerful too. Use them to spread strength, encouragement, and life.

TRIPLE DOG DARE

O Before your next game or performance, give each teammate a personalized word of encouragement.

O Write down all the things your mom does for you and your family and read them to her with a thank you.

O Pray out loud for a friend who's facing a problem.

MISSION ACCOMPLISHED!

What did you do? What did you learn?

TRUTH Christmas is all about Jesus.

CHRIST IN YOUR CHRISTMAS

Christmas is an awesome time of year. It's fun. It's festive. It's filled with family and parties and music and desserts. And, of course, there are the gifts. All the cool stuff you've been wanting all year you can put on a list and actually get it, at least some of it. Is it any wonder Christmas is many people's favorite time of the year?

The truth is there's nothing necessarily wrong with all those things, but the most important thing about Christmas is Jesus. Jesus is God becoming one of us and walking in our shoes. Jesus is the pinnacle of all history and the future. Jesus is the most incredible gift there could ever be. And receiving this gift is supposed to change us.

Santa, Rudolph, and Frosty are all fun, but don't let them distract you. Giving is meaningful, but don't let gifts blind you with greed. America spends about $450 billion every year at Christmas! And tons of that stuff is returned to stores because we don't like it. Make your giving really matter. Make your season about what's truly important. Make your Christmas all about Jesus.

TRIPLE DOG DARE

- Think about the words of Christmas songs and worship God when you sing them.

- Shop less and spend more time with your family this season.

- Donate lifesaving gifts, such as clean water, medicine, education, or farm animals, to people around the world who need them. Talk to you parents about giving money to a ministry who provides that kind of help.

What did you do? What did you learn?

MISSION ACCOMPLISHED!

FROM THE TRIPLE DOG POUND

Timothy Wasn't Too Young

Going on a mission trip can be an eye-opening experience. Have you done it? Going into a different country with different customs and language has a way of making you rely on God. It also helps you see different perspectives and ways of serving God. And it can help you see how much you have in common with people all over the world, along with how much material blessing you've been given.

Timothy might have gotten a taste of all those things when he went with the apostle Paul on his missionary travels. It was a great honor to be invited along, but it also meant some difficult journeys, including prison. But all of it helped to shape and strengthen young Timothy's faith.

Paul gave Timothy his first Triple Dog Dare: Get out and serve God no matter how young you are. And Timothy rose to the challenge. He remained a special helper to Paul and the church, showing that he must have followed through on Paul's encouragement to not let his age keep him from being a good example. The same Triple Dog Dare stands for you. Serve God with all your heart. Don't be afraid to go wherever God leads, and be an example even to grown-ups. No one is too young in God's eyes.

TRIPLE DOG DARE!

- Read 1 and 2 Timothy.
- When do you use age as an excuse? How can you use your age as an advantage instead?
- Talk to your parents about taking a family mission trip. Where do you want to go and serve in your home country and around the world?

PLACES I WANT TO GO FOR GOD

YOUR PAGE

My favorite things about Christmas are ...

TRUTH
We should bring Christmas to everyone.

CHRISTMAS IS FOR EVERYONE

The shepherds stank. You can't blame them. They hung out in the wilderness, with lots of animals. Deodorant was millennia from being invented, and it's not like they could pop into town for a hot shower any time they wanted. Other people didn't exactly flock to ancient shepherds. (*Ha, ha, flock—get it? flock?*)

But God sent a sky full of angels to, you guessed it, shepherds. Not kings and important VIPs, not priests and spiritual leaders, not good law-abiding, middle-class families. God made the grandest announcement of the most important birth in the history of the universe to … the shepherds. Lowly, stinky shepherds.

The truth is that Christmas is for everyone, including the lowly, poor, broken, and homeless. It's especially for them, and it's up to us to bring it to them. Don't be blinded by getting or even giving meaningless stuff. This Christmas, give like God gave. Look around your town and around the world and give to those who don't have. Give gifts, food, personal supplies, helping hands—and give joy, respect, and love. Be one of the unexpected angels. Be a bringer of real Christmas.

TRIPLE DOG DARE

○ Find and play the song "Give This Christmas Away" by Matthew West.

○ Fill a shoebox or two for kids around the world through Operation Christmas Child.

○ Ask your parents to serve as a family at a soup kitchen or homeless shelter.

What did you do? What did you learn?

MISSION ACCOMPLISHED!

TRIPLE

TRUTH Motives matter big-time to God.

MOTIVES MATTER

How long is your Christmas list? One mile? Two? Does it fill whole notebooks of paper? Probably not, but take a closer look. Who is it all about— you? When you hear *season of giving,* do you think, *Yep, everyone giving to me!?*

Keep thinking. Are you constantly wanting what your friends and classmates have? Do you get sick of new stuff quickly because someone else has something newer or better? Do you wonder why God doesn't answer your prayers the way you want Him to? These questions are more closely related than you might think.

The truth is God cares a lot about the motives behind our requests. He's not a Santa Claus in the sky who gives whatever we ask with a jolly *ho, ho, ho.* He loves to give us good things, but He knows that truly good things will last, like love, peace, and generosity. He knows that toys and gadgets will break, but that satisfaction from giving to others will last into eternity. Don't be afraid to ask God for what you want. Go for it! But check your motives and ask God to help you keep them from being all about you.

TRIPLE DOG DARE

- Make a giving list that's longer than your get-list.

- Cut your Christmas list in half. Ask yourself why you want each item and get rid of the ones you don't really need.

- Make gifts. Start with music playlists, videos, or coupons for chores.

MISSION ACCOMPLISHED!

What did you do? What did you learn?

TRUTH You can break free from the pack and become like God.

MORE THAN COOL

Who defines cool? Who sets the standard? There's always a new trend catching on. There will always be a new "it"—the hot brand, the latest fashion, the in slang, the must-see movie, and the can't-miss gadget. Or so they say. But who are *they?* Often, *they* are the people making money off of the latest "it." You can go crazy trying to keep up, and keeping up can consume your life.

The truth is God wants to break you out of the world's empty patterns and transform you into much, much more. The way begins with you tuning into God's channel instead of the distracting static being broadcast by the world around you. The more you do, the more renewed and refreshed your mind becomes. You get better at fine-tuning your reception. The static fades, and you hear God's signals more clearly. You can break free!

TRIPLE DOG DARE

O Tune into God's channel by reading an entire book of the Bible this week.

O Worship God with your body through your sport or activity. Offer it to Him.

O Rise above the crowd. What's the coolest trend at your school right now? Do without it for a week.

What did you do? What did you learn?

MISSION ACCOMPLISHED!

LUKE 1:46–55

TRUTH Let Christmas bring a fresh perspective to your praise.

WORSHIP WITH ALL YOU'VE GOT

The music is one of the best parts of Christmas. Maybe it's special because we only listen to it during one season a year. I think it's mostly because Christmas songs grab our emotions and remind us of what matters most. Our hearts join the instruments and sing praise to God! Just like Mary did in the first Christmas season. Her song praised God for His faithfulness, power, and mercy. When she sang, Mary appreciated her small place in God's big plan, and she sang with all her heart.

The truth is Christmas is a great time for us to sing praises to God. Christmas carols are a great place to start, and focusing on Jesus' birth and life can bring fresh meaning to our normal worship songs. And wow, what a reason to worship! God came to be one of us. Jesus came to rescue us and restore God's creation. He brought us life. Sing out loud. Sing with all your heart. Christ has come! Worship with all your might.

TRIPLE DOG DARE

- Read or recite your favorite Christmas songs and think about what they mean.

- Write your own song of Christmas praise.

- Close your eyes and sing this year's Christmas songs from your heart.

MISSION ACCOMPLISHED!

What did you do? What did you learn?

TRUTH
Listen and learn from your mistakes.

DO-OVER!

Do-over! It's some guys' favorite rule. They call it after every third strike, missed free throw, or dropped pass. They might try it after math tests, too, but teachers don't buy it. Lots of life doesn't allow do-overs.

The truth is God gives us do-overs, and they're chances for us to listen and learn from our mistakes. He forgives us for our mistakes and sins, but He also lets us experience the consequences of choices we make. Those consequences are usually bad. They hurt and cause us problems. But they help us learn. When the temptation comes again, remember the suffering or pain you felt last time. Make the most of your do-overs.

TRIPLE DOG DARE

- What did you last get punished for? What did you learn from it?

- Where do you need a do-over? Write down the lessons you're having trouble learning, along with one idea each for doing things differently.

- Give a do-over. Forgive a friend or relative you're holding a grudge against.

What did you do? What did you learn?

MISSION ACCOMPLISHED!

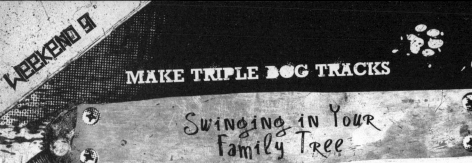

MAKE TRIPLE DOG TRACKS

Swinging in Your Family Tree

The Bible tracks and tells about God's work through many centuries and generations. And that means you can follow God's work through many families. What about your own family? What's your spiritual heritage? Have your ancestors walked with God or rejected His ways? Does your family pass down stories of God's miracles and blessings? Are your problems and temptations the same ones your parents and grandparents wrestled with? Take a look and see how you fit into God's work in your family.

TRIPLE DOG DARE!

Fill in this family tree with the names of each relative.

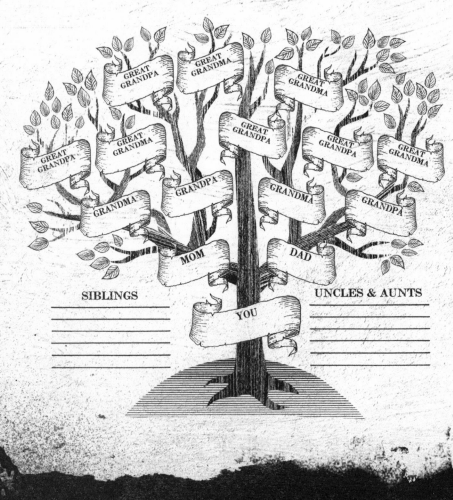

TRIPLE DOG BONUS

Keep going and trace your ancestors even further back. Record your findings here.

YOUR PAGE

A new year is coming—a fresh start!
Write down some dreams for next year.

TRUTH God is always there to guide you.

LOST

The moment you realize you're lost is scary. In a fraction of a second all your surroundings go from fun, friendly, and comfortable to unknown, confusing, and threatening. That's when your stomach dives like the front car over the roller coaster's biggest hill. That's when it feels like an earthquake shook up your world and you're struggling to find something, anything, you recognize.

All you need is one recognizable guide to bring back your bearings. If you're lost in the woods, a compass can point you in the right direction. If you've been swept away by a mob, one friend's voice can be the lifeline back. If you're in an unknown city or country, one sign with a road or landmark you know can make all the difference.

The truth is we always have a life guide in God's voice. He never leaves us. He doesn't throw us out into the wild to die. He doesn't hide from us. He's not trying to hide His will from us, laughing while we make mistakes. His Spirit is with us, directing us in our conscience. His Word gives us guidelines and familiar markers along our life's path. When you feel lost, stop and listen.

TRIPLE DOG DARE

- Pay attention to the navigational system in your family's car. How is it similar to God?

- Read the Bible like your roadmap. Get familiar with God's directions in it.

- Need help making a decision? Ask God and your parents for help.

What did you do? What did you learn?

MISSION ACCOMPLISHED!

TRUTH
God came to earth to be with us!

GOD WITH US

We hear it so much we can get used to it—too used to it. We lose our wonder and amazement. Don't miss the miracle.

The truth is Christmas celebrates a miracle—God came to earth to be with us. To walk and work and suffer and sweat and stink with us so He could bring us so much more! Jesus was God's promise made true. He was and is God's gift, and His story still continues.

Christmas is a busy day, but don't let its power get crowded out. Celebrate. Sing. Share love and presents. Do it all with thankfulness and wonder in your heart because God is with us!

TRIPLE DOG DARE

O Worship God with songs today. Sing your favorite Christmas and all-the-time praise songs. Get your whole family to join in.

O Thank God for each family member and relative you see and talk to today.

O Write thank-you notes for all of your gifts.

MISSION ACCOMPLISHED!

What did you do? What did you learn?

TRUTH
We all need to take time to think about life and how we're living it.

PRESS PAUSE

Your life moves pretty fast: school all day, practice, homework, playing, keeping up with friends, family dinner (if everyone can get coordinated at one time), chores, sleep, start all over. And really, when are you only doing one activity at a time? More often, you're probably multitasking four things at once while listening to music, watching TV, and texting friends.

The truth is we all need to take time to think about life and how we're living it. "Give careful thought to your ways" was God's message to Israel when they were supposed to be rebuilding the temple. The Israelites were caught up in the daily deeds of trying to get by, but they were missing God's big plan.

It's also easy for us to get caught up in all the daily stuff we do, but we need to press Pause and ask important questions. Where is all our activity leading us? Where does God want to lead us? Are we spending our time wisely in God's eyes? Are we distracted and missing His big plans? Is what we're doing now helping us move toward where we want to be in five years?

TRIPLE DOG DARE

- Write answers to the previous questions.

- Look at all your activities on a calendar. What do they say about you?

- Write three things you want to accomplish this week, three things this year, and three more things during your entire life.

What did you do? What did you learn?

MISSION ACCOMPLISHED!

TRUTH
Get strong by looking at God, not your problems.

DON'T LOOK DOWN

Don't look down! You've heard it a million times. But everything inside you pulls your eyes like an anchor. Maybe it's the fear of the unknown. Maybe it's curiosity. Maybe it's the sense of the yawning nothingness below. You glance. Then you stare. The bottom is so far away the cars look like toys and the people are ant-size. Suddenly you're stuck. Your muscles are locked. Your vision starts swimming and your head spins. Dizziness takes over and fear has you frozen.

You've lost your focus on where you're headed. The fear of what *could* happen has squashed your confidence in what *can* happen.

The truth is we get stronger by looking at God instead of our problems. When we stare into our fears, they grow huge and we shrink small. But when we focus on God, we see how ginormously powerful He is. He towers over our puny problems that start shrinking by the minute. And we get filled with His strength.

TRIPLE DOG DARE

- Go to God first. Talk to Him before facing a challenge that makes you nervous.

- Picture God stomping on your problem. List all the ways He can solve it.

- Walk a balance beam or tightrope (tie a strong rope low between two trees). Notice the difference when you look ahead versus looking at the ground.

MISSION ACCOMPLISHED!

What did you do? What did you learn?

TRUTH
Don't get tired of doing the right thing

ENDURANCE

The tortoise beat the hare because he kept on keeping on. You know the story: Slow and steady wins the race. The tortoise was all about consistency. He kept moving even when he was tired. He kept his eyes on his goal.

The truth is God wants us to keep going and not to get tired of doing good. He wants us to endure like the tortoise running an ultramarathon. Even when we're tempted to slack off or quit—and sometimes we all are. Sometimes we feel like breaking a rule just because. Sometimes we get tired of being called a goody-goody.

That's the time to look toward the finish. That's when we need to look to God and dig deep. Take a shot of His energy drink, and get a second wind from His Holy Spirit. Keep choosing right. There's reward ahead, maybe sooner, maybe later. But God won't forget. Keep doing good.

TRIPLE DOG DARE

- Listen to your favorite worship music for a spiritual-energy refresher.

- Go to bed on time every night this week. It's easier to make wise choices when you're well rested.

- Train for endurance. Read the entire Bible next year.

What did you do? What did you learn?

MISSION ACCOMPLISHED!

Finished Strong

Congratulations! You made it. You finished this book. You made it to the end of a year. You are a true Triple Dog Daredevil who's tackled challenges all year long and hopefully seen your relationship with Jesus grow in new ways.

A lot has probably happened to you in the last 365 days. You've made some mistakes for sure; we all have. But you've also taken some new dares and gotten them right. Way to go! That's reason to celebrate and feel satisfied. I'm proud of you, just like your parents are, I'm sure. You can feel proud too.

But it's also just the beginning. Living out God's Triple Dog Dares is a way of life, and you've got lots of life ahead. You've probably built some good new habits this year—keep them going! You've hopefully learned new truths in the Bible—keep learning! You must have put new actions to your faith—keep living them out!

Your life will bring new challenges all the time—keep rising to meet them! Pick yourself up when you get things wrong, and keep going. Above all else, always look to God. He's always with you, ready to help and give you strength. The truth is He'll never give you a Triple Dog Dare without also giving you help to get it done. You can count on that.

Ready for your last Triple Dog Dare from me?

TRIPLE DOG DARE!

Look back through this book and your last year. What was your favorite Triple Dog Dare? Why?

What was your hardest Triple Dog Dare? Why?

Biggest things I learned:

Good habits I formed:

Bad habits I broke:

My goals for next year:

Friends whom I can give a copy of this book to for next year:

THE ULTIMATE TRIPLE DOG DARE

This book is all about mixing your beliefs with action. You've been reading all the way through about how that combo helps you to know God better. But it all begins with you taking the ultimate Triple Dog Dare: giving your life to Jesus and beginning a personal relationship with Him.

How do you do that? It starts with a decision—your decision to give your life to God. He's already sent you an invitation. God loves you so much that He sent His Son Jesus to earth to take the punishment for your sins by dying on a cross. Jesus rose from the dead to defeat sin and death. And He's inviting you to join Him in God's family. He wants to be the best friend you can ever have in life, and He wants you to know God and His love firsthand. You can by doing something with that invitation: accepting it.

Talk to God and tell Him you want His love and His life. Be honest and tell Him if you have questions. Let Him know you believe Jesus is the only true God and that you need Him. Ask Him to forgive all the wrongs you've ever done and ever will do—He will! Tell Him you love Him and want to know Him. And thank Him for His true spiritual life that will last forever, even after you die.

There are no magic words to say. God will listen to your heart. But if you're still unsure about how to talk to Him, you can pray this either out loud or silently:

Dear God, I need You and want to know You personally. Please forgive me for all the wrong I do. I believe Jesus was Your Son who died for my sins so that I can be Your child. I give You control of my life. Please use it and make me into who You created me to be. Thank You!

If you prayed that or something similar, congratulations! You've taken the biggest and best Triple Dog Dare of your life. Tell someone about it, especially your parents or whoever gave you this book. (Talk to them, too, if you're thinking about or have any questions about giving your life to God.)

You might feel a change; you might not. It's a little different for everyone. But you can trust that God has changed you inside. You're His, and He won't ever let go of you. He'll lead you on the greatest adventure of your life. It won't always be easy, but God will always be with you to love you and help you. Enjoy the journey!

Weekend 5: Be These Attitudes

Answers: 1-h or d, 2-e, 3-g, 4-i, 5-a, 6-b, 7-d or h, 8-c, 9-f

Weekend 18: Favorite Fruit

Answers:

ACROSS: 1. goodness, 3. love, 5. self control, 7. peace, 8. faithfulness,

DOWN: 1. gentleness, 2. kindness, 4. joy, 6. patience

Weekend 41: Hall of Faith

Answers: 1-l, 4-i, 8-b, 11-a, 6-d, 2-g, 3-k, 5-c, 12-e, 10-f, 13-h, 7-m, 9-j

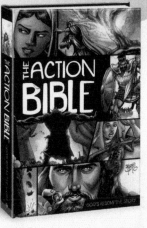

Original ACTION HEROES found here

Introduce Them to God's Story

The 750 pages of full color, comic-style art in *The Action Bible* will capture your child's imagination and heart. The greatest story ever told comes alive through 215 fast-paced stories, meeting kids where they are and helping them fall in love with God's Word.